The Wire

CLASS : CULTURE

SERIES EDITORS
Amy Schrager Lang, Syracuse University, and Bill V. Mullen, Purdue University

*The*Wire

RACE, CLASS, AND GENRE

Liam Kennedy and
Stephen Shapiro

EDITORS

The University of Michigan Press
Ann Arbor

for the family hero, Lynn Shapiro Macy,
and for Nancy

Copyright © by the University of Michigan 2012
All rights reserved

Published in the United States of America by
The University of Michigan Press
Manufactured in the United States of America
⊚ Printed on acid-free paper

2015   2014   2013   2012   4   3   2   1

A CIP catalog record for this book is available from the British Library.

Library of Congress Cataloging-in-Publication Data

The wire : race, class, and genre / Liam Kennedy and Stephen Shapiro, editors.
    p. cm. — (Class: culture)
  Includes index.
   ISBN 978-0-472-07178-4 (cloth : alk. paper) — ISBN 978-0-472-05178-6 (pbk. : alk. paper)
   1. Wire (Television program)   2. Race relations on television.   3. Social classes on television.   I. Kennedy, Liam, 1961–   II. Shapiro, Stephen, 1964–
PN1992.77.W53W53   2012
791.45'6552—dc23   2012012838

Acknowledgments

We thank Mike Davis for early help. Philip Barnard, Anne Schwan, and the WReC collective (Nick Lawrence, Neil Lazarus, Graeme MacDonald, and Pablo Mukherjee), Diane Negra, Paula Gilligan, Barry Shanahan, and Catherine Carey all gave intellectual and emotional support. Our thanks to LeAnn Fields at the University of Michigan Press for her support and patience.

The editors gratefully acknowledge permission to re-publish the following: Marsha Kinder, "Re-Wiring Baltimore: The Emotive Power of Systemics, Seriality, and the City," *Film Quarterly* 62.2, Winter 2008–9, 50–57; John Kraniauskas, "Elasticity of Demand: Reflections on *The Wire*," *Radical Philosophy* 154, 2009, 25–34; Peter Dreier and John Atlas, "*The Wire:* Bush-Era Fable about America's Urban Poor?" *City and Community* 8.3, September 2009, 339–40; Paul Anderson, "'The Game Is the Game': Tautology and Allegory in *The Wire*," *Criticism* 52.3–4, Summer–Fall 2010, 373–98.

The best image to sum up the unconscious is Baltimore in the early morning.

> —Jacques Lacan, "Of Structure as the Inmixing of an Otherness Prerequisite to Any Subject Whatever"

Contents

Part Three: Race, Ethnicity, and Class

Introduction: All the Pieces Matter

Liam Kennedy and Stephen Shapiro

In an early draft outline of his ideas for *The Wire*, the producer David Simon clearly expressed his ambitions for the show:

> *The Wire* is a drama that offers multiple meanings and arguments. It will be, in the strictest sense, a police procedural set in the drug culture of an American rust-belt city, a cops-and-players story that exists within the same vernacular as other television fare.
>
> But as with the best HBO series, *The Wire* will be far more than a cop show, and to the extent that it breaks new ground, it will do so because of larger, universal themes that have more to do with the human condition, the nature of the American city and, indeed, the national culture.[1]

Neither in this early projection nor in later commentaries on the show is Simon modest about stating his aims and achievements in reinventing the police procedural "as a vehicle for making statements about the American city and even the American experiment."[2] Much of the commentary the show has generated—among fans, reviewers, and scholars—would seem to endorse Simon's chutzpah. Since its initial run (HBO, 2002–8) ended and it took on a productive afterlife in DVD sales and Internet piracy, the show has been routinely acclaimed as the best drama television series of the past decade.

There is much to admire in the innovations of *The Wire*. It is an unusual and ambitious urban crime show in the perspectives and layers it brings to characterization and plotting, and in the nuanced portrayal of race conflict, city politics, and the moralities of urban criminality and policing. It references many other urban crime narratives—literary, cinematic, and televisual—yet develops its own distinctive subgenre, the urban procedural, a fabrication of urban spatial relations that intercuts worlds usually unrelated in political and social studies, never mind television cop shows. More consistently than any other crime show of its generation, *The Wire* challenges viewers' perceptions of the racialization of urban space and the media conventions that support these perceptions. It reminds us just how remarkably restricted the grammar of race is on American television and related media, and of the normative codings of race—as identity, as landscape—across urban narratives, from documentary to entertainment media. The typical mise-en-scène, of black kids dealing drugs on ghetto corners, is an everyday snapshot of the structural impoverishment and isolation of an underclass whose hypervisibilty in other media frames (including gaming) is either manifestly exoticized and pathologized or only momentarily made visible through instances of spectacular disaster, like Hurricane Katrina, rather than as a long-standing, structural presence.

While recognizing the originality and progressive features of *The Wire*, this volume of essays also offers a cooler assessment, posing critical questions about its design, message, and appeal. In particular, we set out to examine in what ways and with what effects the show uses the genre of the police procedural to comment on "the nature of the American city" and "the American experiment." That these two concepts are conjoined in Simon's perspective is suggestive of a particular view of the city as a crucible and laboratory of national concerns. It is a view that is laced with contradictory perspectives on the meanings of citizenship, capital-labor relations, and justice, and on the sources and workings of power in the urban order. Simon's ambition to cognitively map the city as a totality promises to illuminate this urban order afresh, but the urge to make it legible—"It's all connected" is a key motif of the show—glosses the limitations of left-liberal critique enveloped in established genres and narrative forms. Like any cultural production, *The Wire* is caught up in the conditions and contradictions of its own powerful social critique.

This more critical framing is not intended to gainsay the remarkable reception the show has received. Few other television dramatic series have received the mixture of academic and media adulation that surrounds *The Wire*. When David Simon won the MacArthur "genius" grant in 2010, he was the first television show creator and executive producer ever to have been laureled with an accolade otherwise given to more traditional-form artists, social policy administrators, or academics. While David Chase's *The Sopranos* (1999–2007) is often seen as breaking ground for academic interest outside of television studies, its skills remained, more or less, safely within the conventions of the organized crime film genre, perhaps allowing for its almost immediate popular and industry award success. *The Wire*, on the other hand, manipulates the urban police procedural form as an instrument to push forward a number of social critiques about race, drug war policing, deindustrialization, and the failure of American civic, educational, and political institutions. Consequently, *The Wire*'s reception history is conspicuous for its lack of industry recognition in the shape of awards, audience numbers, and even initial television journalistic support. Even after its third season, *The Wire* was at risk of being cancelled because of its small audience.[3] Yet after season 4, *The Wire*'s profile swiftly changed, especially among those who would have otherwise spent little energy on a television series. The eminent sociologist William Julius Wilson spoke for many when he explained his appreciation for *The Wire*'s narrative power in giving the lie to official statistics about urban poverty, "the devaluation of labor, the often shady world of urban politics, the troubled urban education system, and the negligence of the mainstream media in coverage of important local issues."[4]

Within the academy, the special status of *The Wire* can be gauged in terms of its impact on established contours of evaluation surrounding television productions. A conspicuous example is the journal *Film Quarterly*, which produced a special section of commentary on the show in 2008, with editor Rob White arguing that *The Wire* "deserves to be called a TV masterpiece and a major work of recent American fiction in any medium."[5] The coverage and accolades were unusual for a prestige academic journal that is known for being the champion of cinema auteurship in contrast to more popular or mass mediums, like television, the existence of which it rarely acknowledged. This was not always so. *Film Quarterly* initially began in 1945 under the title *Hollywood Quarterly*. Robert Shaw explained the journal's mission in a 1946 issue of *Public Opinion Quarterly* as a "fusion of university scholarship and the educational values inherent in mass media workmanship," through a collaboration between the University of California Press and the Hollywood Writers Mobilization Unit. It was to be the "first noncommercial periodical in this country or abroad devoted to the mature and scholarly discussion of the common problems and common objectives of the arts and sciences as related to radio, motion picture and television."[6] This initiative led to some innovative commentary on "arts and communication" in the later 1940s and 1950s but it foundered in the context of Cold War cultural and political pressures. By the later 1950s, when it was renamed *Film Quarterly*, it abandoned television studies. Rather than task the journal for its cultural-form conservatism, we refer to its history of publication to emphasize just how exceptional an achievement *The Wire* was felt to be to merit such a celebration of a "progressive" television show, as if its quality finally allowed the journal to come out against the Cold War self-censorship locked within its history and the return of its pressure within the post-9/11 Bush-era presidency.

The Wire similarly broke other kinds of cultural glass ceilings. Throughout the first decade of the twentieth-first century, television studies shifted as it began to expand commentary to recognize (subscription) television series as themselves involved in engaging with and interrogating social concerns, rather than merely reflecting or containing them.[7] But if *The Sopranos* broke the initial barrier of academic interest in departments beyond the perimeter of media, film, and television studies, *The Wire* exceeded this achievement by being a show that was not only considered a serious interlocutor with contemporary social issues, but increasingly as an informed generator for academic research and teaching, a de facto scholarly contribution in its own right about urban policy, the war on drugs, the transition from a manufacturing economy to one based in services and speculation, and the failures of public education and public sphere journalism.

With its return to an effort to represent a social totality through a panorama of a contemporary city and ethnographic dedication to realism through research, rather than cinema verité camera work, *The Wire*'s success seems based not simply on its ability to immerse viewers in an unfamiliar world and train them in a foreign slang and *Weltanschauung*, but to touch an elective affinity among viewers that the *subject* of their show is also about their own experience, even while the narrative of petit bourgeois ethnic whites and inner-city African Americans is not. The *Wire*'s achievement is not simply within its high-value narrative vision, but its promise to change the viewer's own preexisting perception about urban social ecology within twentieth-first-century America. In this collection, we have arranged essays that look to combine both enthusiasm for and critical evaluation of *The Wire*, the latter being the rarer move in discussions of the series. The essays here attempt to give readers a chance to further develop their critical appreciation of and reflection on *The Wire*. Our aim is not to place the show on a medallion platform, but to see it as an opportunity for discussions that will outlast the short time-span that television commentary often receives.

Despite David Simon's comment that he was "not under the illusion that the show has the rigor of academic work or even the exactitude of journalism," *The Wire* became widely used as a primary text that organized university class offerings in a range of disciplines.[8] As we write, a fast-growing corpus of academic scholarship is reading the show from multiple perspectives, often using it as a mirror for particular theoretical or disciplinary concerns. Academics and other commentators have their own investments in the show's critical energies, of course, and this volume provides a range of perspectives, some clearly in tension with each other, yet all responsive to the challenges *The Wire* poses to what we imagine American urbanism to be today. Throughout this volume, our authors comment on the show in terms of both representation and political economy, covering not only its televisual history and form and its reinvention of police and crime genres, but also examining its treatment of race and ethnicity, and its critique of neoliberal capitalism and its projection of a compelling urban imaginary. The views and approaches to the study of *The Wire* on display in this volume are indicative of the peculiarities of its intellectual appeal and in some part symptomatic of the moment it critiques.

Chapter Synopses

To provide focus for some key themes and help direct readers to these, we have divided the book into three parts, focusing on form and genre, the urban order and capitalism, and class, race, and ethnicity. The sections are porous, of course, and readers will find conversations developing across multiple chapters.

The first part provides commentaries on televisual and other media contexts of *The Wire*'s production, reception, and use of language and genre. Emphasizing the televisual context of the show, Jason Mittell views it as "a historical artifact of a particular moment in the medium's and country's history." After narrating the historical development of HBO shows that created the possibility and context for *The Wire*'s appearance, he reads the much-maligned fifth season about the *Baltimore Sun* as being less a polemic about the damaged state of investigative journalism and more of a self-aware comment on limits to narration within the format of an HBO series. The truism of HBO is that it allows a greater freedom of style, language, scenography, and story-arc pacing. Mittell suggests that HBO, however, has its own limits of possibility, not the least being an inability to break through to a mass-market audience. Frank Kelleter considers how *The Wire* produces self-descriptions that have activated or shaped its reception, particularly among academic readers. Viewing the show as "a serial text that comprises both the television narrative of the same title and the public discourses accompanying it," he asks what transactions and investments are operating in academic readings. With particular attention to (Anglo-)American scholarship, he identifies a range of responses—including duplications, identifications, and dislocations—that signify the relationship of academic study to its object of knowledge. Much of this academic corpus around *The Wire* mimics its retelling of the "American story" as a series of self-identifications.

The two further chapters in this first part explore the ways in which the form and language of the series work to deal with the contradictions and complexity that it consciously and sometimes unwittingly displays. Marsha Kinder looks at the way the serial exploration of the urban system, which works through dysfunction, can be resolved through sentimental bonds. Emotional suture is a kind of viewer's "Stockholm effect" where our generated affect cements us to the characters, rather than an analysis of the structural and systemic factors that the characters bear. In the end, Kinder suggests, viewers are released from the perplexing fatalism of Simon's vision through our emotional identification with the characters and a set of keywords, like "home," that are a magical thinking that waves away the problems screened before us. Paul Anderson takes up the relationship between language and social vision in *The Wire* with a discussion of how linguistic allegory and tautology function as elements of communal interaction, its possibilities and limits. Anderson suggests that even when the characters of *The Wire* do use allegory, the play of insight does little to either better or protect their lives from the damages of the drug trade. Tautologies like "the game is the game" mystify the relations of power; they act as a fetishistic invocation that works to blanket listeners with a noncritical acceptance of the status quo. Yet Anderson also explores the potential for critical tautologies, homilies that have their own combustion to scramble accepted hegemonies and do the kind of work that allegory is otherwise assumed to achieve.

In the second part, authors examine the show's representation of urban policy and neoliberal capitalism. Carlo Rotella sees *The Wire* as dissecting "Kojak liberalism," which has been reluctant to critique "law and order" politics of replacing state welfare programs with policing and penitential ones. He sees *The Wire*'s focus on the telephonic "wire" as renovating the urban police procedural genre and providing an imaginative space for reimaging, if not resurrecting, a new mode of liberalism in the twenty-first century. Televised police procedurals are in dialogue with the changing nature of market forms in the United States. Rotella argues that while viewers might still enjoy the violence of the street chase (1970s) or drama of the interrogation box (1990s), *The Wire* shows them to be increasingly obsolete forms; this is the age where processing information and network efficiency protocols are more important, concerns similar to informatic-dominated capitalism. Contrarily, Peter Dreier and John Atlas see *The Wire*'s urban panorama as still limited by the horizontal constraints of a liberal vision that is uncomfortable with political activism, due to its hewing to a fatalism about social transformation. Viewers of *The Wire* are rarely presented either with the encouragement that change is possible or a sense that contemporaneous with the show's run there *were* and *are* activist organizations laboring to change the lived conditions of Baltimore's lower classes. Dreier and Atlas outline these groups as a history that remains untold and often implicitly ignored by *The Wire*. The show's erasure of these presences, perhaps due to its creators' knowledge of the city as coming from time spent mainly with the police, rather than community groups, means that viewers are abandoned on the streets after having been guided to the corner of moral outrage.

The chapters by Liam Kennedy and Stephen Shapiro and John Kraniauskas share a close focus on the workings of capitalism in *The Wire*. Kennedy and Shapiro are centrally concerned with how neoliberalism has shaped the institutional and social matrices of American urbanism. They illuminate the show's critique of key aspects of neoliberal urbanism, in particular its promotion of speculative capitalism, its devaluation of "obsolete" social formations and landscapes, and its strategies of urban governance. Yet they also illustrate how *The Wire* produces confused messages about this mode of capitalism, and evinces a romantic sense of loss in relation to earlier modes of capital-labor relations. John Kraniauskas considers *The Wire*'s "accumulative compositional strategy" of adding and overlaying plot in the effort to convey a sense of the entire city-world. He relates this to other accumulation strategies that promote fictitious or speculative capital, cleansed of human traces of consumption and distribution. *The Wire*'s larger theme is the inability of the police and perhaps even the urban procedural to make the leap from tracking commodities, the drug trade, to following the money, as Lester Freamon desires. The elasticity of capital's flows, beyond the limits of Baltimore and its police jurisdiction, means that even as we watch its detectives hitting the limits of their power and deductive skill, we, too, sense a frustration at inhabiting a representative genre that, similarly, cannot expand to change its form to pursue the expansion of money.

The third part foregrounds issues of race, ethnicity, and class to consider how these identity formations are mediated by *The Wire*'s narratives and characters. Gary Phillips asks if *The Wire* is "à la Van Vechten, whites getting a thrill exploring the black exotic? A twenty-first-century pimping of African American pathologies by hipster whites?" His answer is yes in part, but not overall, since this terrain was declaimed throughout the twentieth century by African American authors. As he reveals the long history of similar narratives, many of which are barely known, let alone recovered within academic canons, *The Wire* was not unique or first in telling a tale about the drug war and African American criminality as a social response to inequality. Knowing this cultural history may pose the question of placement: why does an Anglo (white) product receive the material resources, distribution, and acclaim, when similar African American products barely register on the cultural barometer? Ruth Barton delves into a different cultural history to illuminate white ethnic codes at work in the show. In particular, she explores the function of Irishness in *The Wire* as a national imaginary for the non-Irish, a cultural receptacle in which concerns about eroding work and gender identities can be placed to both protect and constrain larger cultural critique. Stereotypes drawn from dramatic and lens media history allow for the "stage Irishman" to be drunkenly sprawled throughout the series, whether on the hangover bed or the pooltable's funereal velvet. McNulty's Irishness captures a "structure of feeling . . . of anger and loss but also anarchic and celebratory," but its limitations are also represented through one of the most frequent set pieces in *The Wire*: Irish alcoholism as compensation for male occupational and professional sense of decreased worth in the contemporary world. While viewers are never invited to identify with the pleasures of heroin and crack cocaine use, and the African American gang ethos is similarly to absent from using the products of sale, we are repeatedly invited to go "drinking with McNulty."

The last two chapters share a focus on class and memory. Sherry Linkon, Alexander Russo, and John Russo see the series as a long meditation on the broad effects of deindustrialization and trace this shift through the concept of "communities of memory," the transgenerational sharing and mentor training through models of emulation and storytelling. Memory construction is repeatedly emphasized by *The Wire*'s characters as both one of the first casualties and and as a bulwark against the loss of urban productive labor; when manual construction, be it in policing or the shipyard, disappears in favor of virtualized flows (such as policing by statistics), then memory construction becomes more important and contested, especially since it will be in these story-exchanges where the ideal of "good work" will be defined in both nostalgic and frustrated tones. The ambivalent relation of work to memory in a time of economic restructuring may be one reason why *The Wire*'s generic form, as urban procedural, focused on the pleasures of ratiocinative detection, has had considerable resonance. Hamilton Carroll expands on the relations among work, identity, and memory by focusing on the uncertain deployment of whiteness in *The Wire*. With close attention to season 2, with its lament for the vanishing world of white-dominated working-class jobs, Carroll explains the racial performances of both presumed black and white identities from the 1970s, as the moment before labor's structural decline, as a response to the onset of globalized neoliberalism. *The Wire*'s elegiac lament for the lost world of blue-collar work and its ligatures of tribalized families displays a realm where the characters not only strive to act like white ethnics, as

Barton details, but also try to embody the loss of identity by assuming African American stylistics. In neither case, white or black, does the retrospective hyperbolic citation of racialized styles succeed as a means of either deeply uncovering the logistic of globalized capital or successfully protecting those who bear its costs down in the yards.

Notes

1. David Simon, "The Wire: A One-Hour Drama for HBO," September 6, 2000, http://kottke.org.s3.amazonaws.com/the-wire/The_Wire_-_Bible.pdf, 2.

2. Simon, "The Wire," 2.

3. *Washington Post*, December 15, 2004.

4. Anmol Chaddha and William Julius Wilson, "Why We're Teaching 'The Wire' at Harvard," *Washington Post*, September 12, 2010.

5. Rob White, "Make-Believe, Memory Failure," *Film Quarterly* 62.2 (2008): 4.

6. Robert Shaw, "New Horizons in Hollywood," *Public Opinion Quarterly* 10.1 (1946): 71–77.

7. Initial instances would be David R. Simon, *Tony Soprano's America* (Boulder: Westview Press, 2002); Regina Barreca, ed., *A Sitdown with the Sopranos: Watching Italian American Culture on TV's Most Talked-About Series* (New York: Palgrave Macmillan, 2002); and David Lavery, ed., *This Thing of Ours: Investigating the Sopranos* (New York: Columbia University Press, 2002).

8. "HBO's *The Wire*: Racial Inequality and Urban Reality," JFK Forum, Institute of Politics, John F. Kennedy School of Government, April 4, 2008, http://dubois.fas.harvard.edu/video/hbos-wire-racial-inequality-and-urban-reality-william-julius-wilson. University courses included David Brody's Examining Urban Crime: Policing, Politics, and Delinquency through *The Wire* (Washington State University, Spokane, 2008); Todd Solano's Inside HBO's America: A Case Study of *The Wire* (Syracuse University, 2008); this collection's Jason Mittell's Urban America and Serial Television: Watching *The Wire* (Middlebury College, 2009); Linda Williams's What's So Great about *The Wire* (University of California, Berkeley, 2009); Boyd Blundell's Social Justice and *The Wire* (Loyola University, New Orleans, 2009); Anne-Maria Makhulu's *The Wire* (Duke University, 2010); William Julius Wilson's HBO's *The Wire* and Its Contribution to Understanding Urban Inequality (Harvard University, 2010); Charles Ogletree's Race and Justice: *The Wire* (Harvard University, 2011); and York University sociology class, *The Wire* as Social Science-Fiction (2010). In addition to academic symposia such as the panels at Harvard Law School in 2008 and University of Michigan's "Heart of the City: Black Urban Life on *The Wire*" (University of

Michigan Black Humanities Collective and the Center for Afroamerican and African Studies, January 2009), there have been a series of academic essay collections and special journal issues. Essay collections include Tiffany Potter and C. W. Marshall, eds., *The Wire: Urban Decay and American Television* (New York: Continuum, 2009) and the special issues of *Film Quarterly* 62.2 (Winter 2008), *Criticism* 52.34 (2010); *darkmatter* 4, http://www.darkmatter101.org/site/category/journal/issues/4-the-wire/; *City* 14.5 and14.6 (2010); and *Critical Inquiry* 38.1 (Autumn 2011). There is also a monograph partially dedicated to the show, Jason P. Vest, *"The Wire," "Deadwood," "Homicide," and "NYPD Blue"* (Santa Barbara, Calif.: Praeger, 2011). "Educated" fan-oriented books are Rafael Alvarez, *The Wire: Truth Be Told* (New York: Grove Press, 2009) and Steve Busfield and Paul Owen, eds., *The Wire Re-Up* (London: Guardian Books, 2009).

PART ONE

Form and Genre

1

The Wire in the Context of American Television

Jason Mittell

I think you need a lot of context to seriously examine anything.
  —Gus Haynes, "Unconfirmed Reports"

It is tempting to regard *The Wire* as a work that transcends its medium. The show is certainly regarded by most critics as one of the greatest, if not the ultimate, works of television fiction, but its accolades usually exceed the bounds of the television medium. Hailed by many for its novelistic scope and tone, the show has also been named on lists of the top films of the 2000s, and is often framed as an updated Greek tragic drama by way of Zola and Dickens. It has been embraced by academics across the disciplines as an object of analysis both in scholarship and in pedagogy, with courses dedicated to the series in diverse disciplines such as sociology, anthropology, urban studies, and criminology, as well as the more obvious realm of media studies. It would be fair to say that no work of television is seen as more legitimate and important across the academy than *The Wire*, but through this process of legitimation, scholars frequently ignore or downplay its context as grounded within the structures and systems of American television.

If *The Wire* teaches us anything, it is the importance of context. The individual stories of characters ranging from Bubbles to Bunk are less the tales of individuals than narratives of pieces within a larger whole. As one of the series's promotional taglines argues, "all the pieces matter." We can only understand the individual elements of the series, whether it's the portrayal of urban geography or arguments about the decline of the manufacturing and labor economy, as parts of a whole televisual portrait of a city that shapes what is said and how it is received. First and foremost, *The Wire* is a work of television, and only by framing it in the context of twenty-first-century American television can we hope to understand its origins, its cultural achievements, and its representational strategies. Thus even in a book such as this one, focused on what *The Wire* tells us about the social world it represents on screen, we need to step back and remember how it got to the screen in the first place, and how that context of television impacts its representational strategies.

This is a core argument that I make in my own course about the series—we focus on the show's hot-button social issues like crime and urban decay, but always keep one eye on the *The Wire*'s context as a work of televised fiction. Media studies as a discipline is similarly devoted to the importance of context, and thus as a teacher and scholar of the show, I always emphasize that its portrayals and politics must be viewed within the particular opportunities and possibilities of the television medium. This essay emerges directly from that course, and was written originally for my students as an opening crash course in American television as it pertains to *The Wire* and its unique place within the medium's history. Thus instead of offering a critical argument about the show's content or form, I offer a more descriptive outline of the specific industrial, technological, aesthetic, and genre contexts of television that helped shape *The Wire*, and enabled it to make it to commercial television in the first place. I dodge specificities of plot so as to make it appropriate for a new viewer looking to avoid spoilers. Hopefully, the essay can serve as a useful overview for the show's viewers and students as it becomes less a piece of contemporary culture and more of a historical artifact of a particular moment in the medium's and country's history.

Television Industry

The Wire emerged at a particular moment in the history of television that was uniquely situated to allow such an original series to flourish. The American television industry has traditionally been a closed market dominated by a small number of commercial national networks, making it quite difficult for innovative programming to find its way to the air. The 1980s and 1990s saw the rise of the multichannel era, with dozens of cable channels entering the marketplace and providing alternatives to traditional broadcast networks. Even though most of these channels were initially owned or later purchased by the same corporate conglomerates that owned the networks, an effect of the multichannel era was to create alternative options for producers looking to place programs. Until the late 1990s, few cable programs directly matched the standard fictional fare of networks, with high-budget comedies and dramas clustered on networks while cable focused on cheaper nonfiction genres, like news, sports, how-to, and talk shows, alongside a back catalog of reruns and films. The lower production costs for such programming meant that cable channels could turn a profit with lower ratings and less advertising revenue than networks, setting the standard that a cable "hit" had a far lower threshold of popularity than traditional television shows.[1]

Home Box Office (HBO) was an early cable channel starting in the 1970s that followed a different business model than most of its cable counterparts. HBO defines itself as a premium channel, charging an additional subscription fee beyond the standard monthly cable or satellite bill; in exchange, HBO features no advertising (aside from its own internal promotions) and can include greater degrees of nudity, violence, profanity, and controversial content than on network and basic cable programs. The effect of HBO's business model is that it is not driven by getting high ratings to sell slots to advertisers, but instead looks for programming that is sufficiently desirable to convince viewers to spend an extra ten to fifteen dollars a month for the service.[2]

At first, HBO primarily programmed unedited feature films, making it a desirable way to see movies at home before VCRs were widespread across America. HBO's earliest original programming featured sports programming, especially boxing, stand-up comedy shows full of raunchy profanity, and titillating "documentaries" like *America Undercover* (1983–present) and *Real Sex* (1992–present). Such programming made HBO a popular option for many cable subscribers, but established its reputation as a fairly lowbrow channel catering to prurient interests, not the highbrow purveyor of quality television it's known as today. From early in the channel's history, HBO appealed to a comparatively large African American subscriber base, in large part due to its sports programming and inclusion of black comics in its stand-up specials.[3]

The mid-1990s saw a shift in HBO's strategy—the channel started offering fictional series comparable to the genres of network television, but with an edgy approach to stand out from more conventional net-work shows. Earlier attempts at programming more mainstream televi-sion genres, like sitcoms *1st and Ten* (1984–90) and *Dream On* (1990–96), were most notable for their use of profanity and nudity to spice up otherwise conventional programs. *The Larry Sanders Show* (1992–98) was never a huge hit, but its critically acclaimed satirical take on late-night talk shows did appeal to a group of upscale viewers that could afford the channel's premium cost and helped build HBO's reputation for quality. Subsequent sketch comedies like *Mr. Show with Bob and David* (1995–98) and *Tracy Takes On . . .* (1996–99), along with edgy talk shows *Dennis Miller Live* (1994–2002) and *The Chris Rock Show* (1997–2000), helped improve HBO's reputation as a sophisticated chan-nel that could appeal to hipper and more affluent adult audiences.

Three programs from the late 1990s paved the way for *The Wire*. HBO's first dramatic series, *Oz* (1997–2003), established that the chan-nel would push boundaries of controversial content and portray a world never seen on television before. Set in a maximum-security prison ward with a diverse cast portraying hardened criminals and corrupt prison guards, *Oz* took advantage of HBO's loose content restrictions by featur-ing sex, violence, profanity, and extreme representations of homosexual rape, drug use, and interethnic gang wars. While never a hit, the show's dour and grim tone demonstrated HBO's ability to create a series that aimed less to entertain through comforting formulas than to shock and challenge viewers' sensibilities and expectations. The series also helped establish HBO's reputation as a creator-centered channel, as the show's head writer and producer Tom Fontana was able to push boundaries and pursue his vision in ways that would never be allowed on broadcast networks.

With *Oz* HBO launched a notable slogan that effectively encapsu-lated its strategy: "It's Not TV. It's HBO." HBO's first real hit fictional series followed this slogan by taking advantage of the channel's loose content regulations and boundary-pushing attitude. *Sex and the City* (1998–2004) featured an overt sexual tone, frequent nudity and profanity, and an explicit attitude matching its female-centered vision of upscale New York as a consumerist utopia. The series straddled the line between comedy and drama more than HBO's previous efforts, creating a genre mixture that typified the channel's willingness to avoid formula and con-vention. While little in *Sex and the City* resembles *The Wire*'s take on urban America in content or form, the show demonstrated the viability of HBO creating high-profile buzz-worthy original programs that broke television conventions as a strategy to attract and retain subscribers.

The show that truly established the HBO brand as "not TV" and set the stage for *The Wire* was *The Sopranos* (1999–2007). The groundbreaking series took a film genre rarely seen on television, the gangster story, and offered a highly serialized tale of a mafia family in contemporary America. The series was hailed as one of the masterworks of the television medium, winning numerous awards and firmly cementing HBO's reputation as a highbrow channel with sophisticated original programming. It demonstrated the possibilities of HBO creating programming that not only justified its subscription fees, but also expanded the aesthetic and creative possibilities of the television medium. *The Sopranos* quickly became the most critically praised and highest rated show in HBO's history, creating a template for groundbreaking original drama that pushes boundaries of content and form.[4]

The Sopranos solidified a key difference between HBO and other channels: its focus on being "creator-centered." In typical American commercial television, programs are dependent on network approval and high ratings to remain on the airwaves, which leads creators to yield to network pressures and suggestions, often in reaction to market research and "testing" with focus groups. This system often results in "least objectionable programming," where producers and networks strip away any controversial or challenging content to avoid alienating audiences or advertisers. The history of commercial network television is littered with examples of programs that get watered down and re-shaped by network pressure, with innovations often becoming huge hits when networks are least involved in providing notes and suggestions, such as *The Simpsons* (1990–present) and *All in the Family* (1971–79).

Because HBO is not worried about pleasing sponsors, they are less concerned with week-to-week ratings and avoiding controversy; instead it established itself in the late 1990s as a channel where creators were free to experiment and take risks. After the success of *The Sopranos*, the channel became known as a place for innovative writers to pursue unique projects that did not fit the mold of conventional networks, and where executives would provide the opportunity for risk-taking and creative vision more than is typical for television. *The Sopranos* pointed to the possibilities of serialized television as a complex storytelling medium in ways that had rarely been seen before, and HBO was known as the innovative laboratory for ambitious creators. Additionally, it signaled that HBO would tackle content that could not possibly survive the scrutiny of commercial sponsors on broadcast networks, as the advertising system privileges programming about aspirational lifestyles, sympathetic characters, and nonobjectionable content—all edicts that *The Sopranos* and later *The Wire* would flout. Additionally, the channel's popularity with African American viewers enabled it to include more racially diverse programs that the ratings-conscious networks would dare to—*Oz* was a notable precedent in featuring a range of roles for African American actors, a tradition furthered by *The Wire* with a diverse cast unprecedented within network programming.

In the wake of *The Sopranos'* success, the early 2000s were a boom time for risk-taking unconventional programming on HBO, including the cringe-inducing comedy *Curb Your Enthusiasm* (2000–present), the family drama set in a funeral home, *Six Feet Under* (2001–5), the twisted circus fantasy *Carnivàle* (2003–5), the revisionist Western *Deadwood* (2004–6), the male-bonding Hollywood comedy *Entourage* (2004–11), the racy historical epic *Rome* (2005–7), the polygamist family drama *Big Love* (2006–11)—and, of course, *The Wire*. HBO's success led to similar edgy and risky programming emerging on other cable channels, including both premium competitor Showtime with *Queer as Folk* (2000–2005), *The L Word* (2004–9), *Weeds* (2005–present), and *Dexter* (2006–present), and basic cable channels like FX (*The Shield* (2002–8), *Nip/Tuck* (2003–10), and *Rescue Me* (2004–11) and AMC (*Mad Men* (2007–present) and *Breaking Bad* (2008–present). All of these series could be considered successful, despite rarely getting ratings that would be considered passable on broadcast networks. The alternative programming model pioneered by HBO in the late 1990s emphasized shorter seasons, more complex serialization, and programs that appealed to a smaller niche audience to thrive in the multichannel television era.

The Wire came to HBO through the precedent of another facet of its unconventional programming strategy: the miniseries. While miniseries of three to eight episodes had been quite popular in American network television in the 1970s and 1980s, they had fallen from popularity by the 1990s, as they proved to be too risky to gamble on with advertising dollars. While HBO programmed them infrequently, it has been willing to explore miniseries as a midway point between stand-alone made-for-TV movies and ongoing series, resulting in such acclaimed projects as *Tanner '88* (1988), *From the Earth to the Moon* (1998), and *Band of Brothers* (2001). HBO first worked with *Wire* creator David Simon on the 2000 miniseries *The Corner*, based on his nonfiction book cowritten with Ed Burns chronicling a year in the life of the inhabitants of a drug corner in Baltimore. *The Corner* was a critical success for HBO, garnering the Emmy for Outstanding Miniseries and a Peabody Award for excellence in broadcasting. The miniseries brought together the key production team that would later run *The Wire*, including Simon, Burns, executive producer Robert Colesberry, and producer Nina Kostroff Noble, established a precedent for on-location shooting in Baltimore, and built an effective working relationship with HBO executives, thus paving the way for creating *The Wire*.

One key way that *The Wire* differed from other prestigious cable channel programs is the background of the creators. Most fictional television programs, whether on network or cable, are created and produced by experienced television writers. Other HBO shows were run by well-established television writers, such as *Oz*'s Tom Fontana (previous experience on *St. Elsewhere* and *Homicide*), *Curb Your Enthusiasm*'s Larry David (*Seinfeld*), *Sopranos*' David Chase (*The Rockford Files* and *Northern Exposure*), *Deadwood*'s David Milch (*NYPD Blue*), or *Sex and the City*'s Darren Star (*Melrose Place*). The writers of *The Wire* come from diverse backgrounds mostly outside of television, with creator David Simon known primarily as a journalist and nonfiction writer with a short writing stint on *Homicide* (1993–99) (which was based on his nonfiction book), and executive producer Ed Burns drawing from his experience as a Baltimore police officer and schoolteacher. Other writers include crime novelists George Pelecanos, Richard Price, and Dennis Lehane and journalists Rafael Alvarez and Bill Zorzi. The only staff writer on the show beside Simon who had significant background in television was David Mills, a journalist friend of Simon's who had broken into the industry in the early 1990s on *Homicide* and worked regularly on crime dramas throughout the decade, but Mills only came to *The Wire* in its later seasons. Virtually no other American fictional television series has a writing staff full of television outsiders, marking *The Wire*'s strong connection to HBO's motto, "it's not TV, it's HBO."

However, we should not overstate the degree to which HBO's slogan separates *The Wire* from its medium of television. While it is less driven

Wire production staff draw upon diverse real-life backgrounds and blur with on-screen persona. From left: *Wire* writer Bill Zorzi is a real-life political reporter-editor for the *Baltimore Sun* and plays a fictionalized reporter Bill Zorzi in season 5; creator David Simon drew upon his background as a *Sun* reporter; and actor Clark Johnson plays fictional *Sun* editor Gus Haynes as well as directing four episodes of the series.

by ratings, commercial constraints, and network interference, HBO still is ruled by many of the norms of production and episodic structure that typify television. Episodes of *The Wire* were produced following the factory-style division of duties common to virtually all film and television, and required significant budgets that mandated a potential for return revenue on HBO's investment. Even though its economic model differs from advertising-supported broadcasting, HBO is still a commercial enterprise owned by the multinational corporation Time Warner, not a public service broadcaster on the model of the BBC or American public television, and thus we must always consider the industrial and institutional motivations behind the series.

Television Technology

Certainly *The Wire* could have only emerged out of the world of premium cable, with its acceptance of controversy and profanity and tolerance for a small but devoted audience. The show was also dependent on the particular context of television technology in the 2000s, making certain modes of viewership and fan engagement possible.

Traditionally television has been a schedule-driven medium, with networks programming series with prescribed time-slots. Decades of research within the American television industry has suggested that most viewers typically only watch around one-third of the episodes of a favored series, and that even ardent fans could not be guaranteed to see more than half of a series during its first run. Thus producers realized they could not assume that a viewer had seen previous episodes or were watching a series in sequential order, leading to a mode of storytelling favoring self-contained episodes that could be consumed in any order, and built-in redundant exposition, a form that also served the highly profitable rerun market. Even heavily serialized programs like daytime soap operas include a great deal of redundancy to fill in gaps of missed episodes or distracted viewers.

The rise of home video helped change this limitation. VCRs became more widespread in the 1980s, although the difficulty of programming timers to record a show made it relatively uncommon for viewers to use the technology to "time-shift" favorite programs. The rise of DVRs in the 2000s made time-shifting a much more common practice, with viewers automatically recording their favorite series and watching at their convenience—even though DVRs are still only found in a minority of households, they helped change the television industry's assumption that viewers could not be expected to watch a series regularly and in sequence.[5]

For HBO, scheduling has always been more flexible than networks, as it regularly shows the same program numerous times throughout the week; with the rise of digital cable, HBO multiplied into a number of subchannels (like HBO2, HBO Comedy, and HBO Family), allowing a series to air dozens of times throughout the week and viewers to catch up at their convenience. *The Wire* also took advantage of video-on-demand technology, with HBO making the later seasons available on demand in advance of the regular schedule, as well as allowing viewers to binge in the archives of the show at their convenience. This flexible schedule and on-demand viewing allows HBO to support programming like *The Wire* that refuses episodic closure and demands in-sequence viewing.

HBO has also been a leader in the TV-on-DVD trend. Since many of its original series receive much more publicity and buzz than actual viewership, HBO sells DVD sets of most of its series, allowing nonsubscribers to purchase or rent a series (thus augmenting the channel's revenue). *The Wire*'s DVD sales certainly exceeded expectations given its overall low ratings on HBO, and the availability in the bound volumes of DVD box sets enabled the series to develop into a cult phenomenon, passed along among friends. DVD viewing allows more flexible viewing, compiling a series aired over months or years into a more compressed time-frame, comparable to the collected publication of nineteenth-century serial novels of Dickens or Tolstoy. DVD publishing also allows a series to be collected like literature and cinema, raising the cultural status of television programs.[6]

Illicit technologies also allow the program to spread beyond the limits of HBO subscribers. File-sharing software like BitTorrent and illegal streaming sites are filled with illegally shared copies of HBO series, enabling the shows to be watched without cost via computers. *The Wire* has another robust realm of illicit distribution—pirate DVDs of the series circulate in the urban underground economy. Watching the show via these pirate copies has reportedly made the series a favorite among the African American urban underclass who are portrayed on screen. Many of these viewers lack the residential stability or spare income to subscribe to HBO, but embrace the informal distribution of black-market DVDs as part of the underground economy portrayed on the show.

Digital technologies also helped create a dedicated fanbase around *The Wire*. While the show did not get the mainstream press coverage of *The Sopranos* or *Deadwood*, a number of dedicated fans used blogs to promote the show and convene fan discussions, such as popular blogger Jason Kottke and online magazine *Slate*.[7] Additionally, television critics have moved into blogging, with group critic blogs like The House Next Door and individual critics like Alan Sepinwall and Tim Goodman emerging as important online advocates for the series.[8] These distribution and consumption technologies have enabled *The Wire* to reach a broader audience than HBO's ratings might suggest, and fostered a dedicated viewership for the series that developed over time and continues long after the finale aired.

Television Aesthetics

Shifts in the television industry and technology since the 1990s have enabled the creative possibilities of television to expand in interesting new ways that would have been unthinkable in earlier eras. *The Wire* fits into many of these trends, while also establishing its own norms and style.

One key development is in a mode of storytelling that critics have labeled "narrative complexity." Breaking down the boundary between highly serialized daytime soap operas and strictly self-contained episodic series in primetime, the 1980s saw the growth of more serialized primetime programs, like *Hill Street Blues* (1981–87), *St. Elsewhere* (1982–88), and *Cheers* (1982–93). While such programs did incorporate more long-term story arcs, they primarily used serial formats to narrate relationship dramas of romance or character development; such shows typically avoided complex plot structures that required viewers to watch every episode in sequence to follow the story.[9]

The 1990s saw more serialization emerge in action and mystery plots—*Twin Peaks* (1990–91) focused on a murder mystery over the course of two seasons, *The X-Files* (1993–2002) weaved a complex conspiracy narrative for years, and *Buffy the Vampire Slayer* (1997–2003) featured season-long battles between the heroes and a "big bad" villain. While such shows were cult rather than mainstream hits, they opened the door for a series to focus its efforts on telling longer stories across a range of genres, as comedies like *Seinfeld* (1989–98) and dramedies like *Northern Exposure* (1990–95) played with long-form storytelling.

The rise of original cable programming contributed to this growth in narrative complexity, as *The Sopranos* married a serialized format with experiments blurring fantasy and reality, subjective narration, and purposefully ambiguous storytelling techniques more typical of art cinema than television. The 2000s saw a proliferation of narrative complexity, among hit shows like *Lost* (2006–10), *Desperate Housewives* (2004–present), and *24* (2001–10), cult series like *Alias* (2001–6), *Arrested Development* (2003–6), and *Battlestar Galactica* (2004–9), and short-lived experiments like *Boomtown* (2002–3), *Jack & Bobby* (2004–5), and *Day Break* (2006). For prestigious premium cable programs, complex storytelling became the norm, a reward for elite audiences willing to pay for more sophisticated entertainment and eventually collect series on DVD.

In many ways, *The Wire* is part of this trend of narrative complexity. The show is highly serialized, with each episode serving as a chapter in a much larger volume. No episode stands alone, and it is virtually inconceivable to watch the series out of order with any coherence. The story being told is quite complex, portraying a wide array of characters and asking viewers to follow along with complicated procedures and systems without their being spelled out. Plotlines dangle for years, re-emerging without notice or explicit exposition. Certainly a show like *The Wire* depended on the trails blazed in the 1990s that allowed its mode of long-form storytelling.

In other ways, *The Wire* is much more conventional in its aesthetics than other contemporary serialized programs. Unlike *The Sopranos* and *Six Feet Under*, *The Wire* uses objective narration, unfiltered by individual characters—we never get dream sequences, internal monologue, or restricted perspectives. *The Wire* draws its presentational mode more from traditional workplace dramas like medical or cop shows, than its more experimental predecessors on HBO. *The Wire* avoids the temporal play of other complex series, like *Lost* and *24*, and refuses self-conscious techniques like flashbacks, voice-overs, and reflexive captions common on other contemporary programs—the only flashback is a brief cutaway of D'Angelo recognizing William Gant in the pilot episode, a moment that Simon still regrets, citing it as mandated by HBO to ensure viewer comprehension. The visual and storytelling style of *The Wire* is more naturalistic, drawing upon the conventions of documentary and social realism to match Simon's own background in nonfiction journalism.

One of the show's chief strategies might be called "productive confusion." While traditionally commercial television has demanded redundancy and clarity at all costs, to allow for new or erratic viewers, Simon and the writers have always assumed that viewers should have to work to understand their fictional portrait of Baltimore. They refuse to dumb down the worlds they portray, or offer expository dialogue to explain terms, procedures, or motivations; instead, they want viewers to feel disoriented and confused, with the accompanying satisfaction when a narrative element becomes clear weeks or even years later. Even more than its narrative techniques, *The Wire*'s internal storyworld is arguably the most complex ever to appear on American television, providing a rich experience that encourages—or even demands—multiple viewings.[10]

While the show's aesthetics certainly build on a multitude of influences that offer options to both the creators and the industry, virtually no programs that have followed *The Wire* seem to have embraced its innovations, aside from Simon's follow-up HBO series *Treme* (2010–present). *The Wire* remains the most densely packed and populated world ever seen on American television, and demands more of its audience to understand its narrative than virtually any other show. Whether the show will prove to yield a new branch of possibilities for television creativity, or be remembered as a truly unique exception to the norms of the medium, there is no doubt that *The Wire* stands as an exceptional peak within the terrain of fictional television.

Television Genres

American television tends to rigidly adhere to genre categories, structuring the names of individual channels, like Cartoon Network or Game Show Network, and defining scheduling blocks, like daytime soap operas and late-night talk shows. In the mixed realm of network primetime, the norm still assumes clear delineation between genres, with sitcoms, medical dramas, family melodramas, news magazines, and reality programs all occupying their own particular slots in the schedule. Cop shows are possibly the most prevalent genre in prime time, filling network schedules in the 2000s with successful multishow franchises *Law & Order* (1990–present), *CSI* (2000–present), and *NCIS* (2003–present), as well as stand-alone series such as *Without a Trace* (2002–9), *Cold Case* (2003–10), and *Criminal Minds* (2005–present).[11]

The Wire emerged within this context of a heavily saturated television environment full of crime dramas and police procedurals that mostly followed a set of distinct formulas and conventions, many of which were established by the first hit crime show, *Dragnet* (1951–70). In a standard cop show, each episode focuses primarily on a single case that is wrapped up by the end of the episode, typically resolved with a sense of closure, if not with justice being served. The only continuing characters in such shows tend to be the police themselves, as criminals rarely repeat beyond a single episode and the crime narratives are told nearly exclusively from the perspective of the police. The personal lives and relationships among police are ignored completely or marginalized as background stories with little connection to the primary cases. Each series focuses on one police unit within an urban police department, often with little connection to other aspects of city government and other institutions. Additionally, crimes themselves are rarely explored as a facet of larger social ills or systemic problems, but rather are treated as the acts of psychotic or corrupt individuals.

When David Simon pitched his series, he made it quite clear that he would not be offering a conventional cop show. In his letter to HBO accompanying the pilot script, Simon highlights how HBO had established its reputation by "creating drama in worlds largely inaccessible to network television, worlds in which dark themes, including sex and violence, can be utilized in more meaningful and realistic ways than in standard network fare," referencing series like *Sopranos*, *Oz*, and *Six Feet Under.*[12] In pitching *The Wire*, he argues that HBO could take a similar approach to deeper and more realistic storytelling by tackling and revising the network staple of the cop show:

> But it would, I will argue, be a more profound victory for HBO to take the essence of network fare and smartly turn it on its head, so that no one who sees HBO's take on the culture of crime and crime fighting can watch anything like *CSI*, or *NYPD Blue*, or *Law & Order* again without knowing that every punch was pulled on those shows. For HBO to step toe-to-toe with NBC or ABC and create a cop show that seizes the highest qualitative ground through realism, good writing, and a more honest and more brutal assessment of police, police work, and the drug culture—this may not be the beginning of the end for network dramas as industry standard, but it is certainly the end of the beginning for HBO. The numbers would still be there for *CSI* and such; the relevance would not. We would be stepping up to the network ideal, pronouncing it a cheap lie, and offering instead a view of the world that is every bit as provocative as *The Sopranos* or *The Corner*. But because that world of cops and robbers is so central to the American TV experience, *The Wire* would stand as even more of a threat to the established order.[13]

Clearly in Simon's own pitch, if not actual creative vision, the conventions of the cop drama are a central target to be debunked and reconceived, and thus we need to situate the series within that context to understand its meanings and impacts.

The Wire's most evident revision to the cop show is its rebalancing of the relationship between cops and criminals. Throughout the first season, the narrative focuses with relative equal time on the Barksdale criminal operation and the police unit investigating them. Given the single-case scope of the entire season, the effect of this structure is to refocus the narrative away from the genre norm of protagonist cops chasing relatively anonymous criminals, and toward an in-depth portrait of two competing organizations that refuse clear heroes and villains amid the moral complexities of urban life. Via this rebalancing, *The Wire* merges the police procedural with the more immersive vision of criminal life pioneered by HBO on *The Sopranos* and *Oz*.

The procedural elements of cop shows, pioneered by *Dragnet* and sustained throughout decades of popular programs, are quite vital to *The Wire*, although they are revised in two crucial ways. Typically, a police procedural highlights the practices and tactics used by cops to crack a case, providing viewers with an immersive look into the mechanics of crime fighting over the course of an episode. On *The Wire*, the focus on procedure is drawn out across episodes, as the major crimes investigated each take at least a season and often leave elements dangling unresolved for the next season. Thus while network procedurals are typically viewed as the most episodic form of drama, *The Wire* creates the hybrid of the "serial procedural" to highlight the long-term, messy, and often frustrating elements of police work.[14]

The second way that *The Wire* reframes television's cop show conventions is by extending the procedural attention to detailed practices beyond the police precinct. In the first season, we learn the procedural details of the Barksdale crew, such as their telephone codes, division of labor, and system of distribution. Subsequent seasons broaden the scope even further by incorporating a range of institutions that surpass the typical terrain of the cop show, with the shipping docks, City Hall, school classroom, and newsroom all serving as the site of procedural drama to document how various systems function as part of urban life. The narrative approach to people doing their jobs and navigating the politics of hierarchical systems remains consistent across the different sites, but by broadening the storytelling scope beyond the cops and criminals of the first season, *The Wire* transforms from a revisionist cop show into a multifaceted urban procedural drama.

In the end, *The Wire* refuses the generic identity it was originally pitched as, turning into an urban drama unique to the history of the medium. Cop shows nearly always focus on cities, but only portray one facet of urban life rather than highlighting the intersections between multiple institutions and sites. They rarely portray the social reasons or conditions for crime, treating each case as an isolated incident to be solved within forty-five minutes of screen time, not as symptomatic of larger issues or contexts. *The Wire* treats Baltimore as a multifaceted city of interlocking institutions, portraying the citizens of the city as beholden to the forces created by the microprocedures of bureaucracies, politics, and individual players. Even though nearly every character has a robust, distinct personality, they are all secondary to the systems they both serve. While many crime dramas boast that their specific cities function as a character in the narrative, in *The Wire* Baltimore is the lead character with dozens of supporting players.

While *The Wire*'s focus remains fixed on Baltimore throughout its run, the fifth season returns to some of the themes Simon raised about crime dramas in his pitch letter. In season 5, the new institution added to the urban panorama is the *Baltimore Sun*, the city's venerable newspaper and Simon's former employer. A main function of the newspaper plotline is to highlight how the news media misses the vital stories of urban life, relegating characters whom we know to be major players in the underground economy and street life to marginal mentions or unreported stories. While the press around the fifth season focused on how the story line was merely a vehicle for Simon's ranting retributions toward his former employers or his misdiagnoses of the state of twenty-first-century journalism, I believe the more important issue was what *The Sun* plot has to say about the limits of television storytelling.

In many ways, *The Sun* stands in for the media as a whole, including both nonfiction journalism and fictional television. Every debate in the newsroom over the importance of context, being true to memorable characters regardless of their power or economic status, and the priorities between realism and sensationalism mirrors the very issues Simon's pitch letter raises between his vision of *The Wire* and the conventional cop show. In the episode "Unconfirmed Reports," the debate in the newsroom over how best to tell the story about Baltimore's failing schools is a thinly veneered comment on how *The Wire* approaches the same story in season 4. The managing editors want an easy-to-digest, self-contained series that will resonate with awards committees, while Gus argues for a broader contextual look at the urban system—which Whiting mocks as "an amorphous series detailing society's ills," a dismissive critique that might equally apply to *The Wire* itself. Instead, season 5 plays with a sensationalist, faked story of a serial killer that stands in for the type of crime drama that Simon held in opposition to *The Wire*'s goals of realist detail and social complexity. The Pulitzer awards that the *Sun* strives for might as well be the Emmys, the television insider recognition that *The Wire* never received despite universal critical acclaim.

We cannot forget to place *The Wire* in the context of television because the show itself reminds us that it both belongs to and departs from its medium. The cynical read of season 5 is that the *Sun,* like other media forms, fails to make a difference by falling short of informing and engaging its audience about what is truly important in the contemporary city. But *The Wire* itself serves as an example of what television can do to inform, engage, move, and inspire viewers through an innovative form of urban drama. We can examine, praise, and critique the ways that the series represents Baltimore as a stand-in for the postindustrial city, but just as the final season reminds us that the way the story of the city is told helps shape the urban condition, we need to remember that the way *The Wire* tells its story through its televisual context is vital to understanding its meanings. By telling the stories that neither other fiction nor most nonfiction covers, *The Wire* highlights the power and possibilities of television, emerging out of its medium's context and, instead of transcending it, pointing television in new directions.

Notes

1. See Jason Mittell, *Television and American Culture* (New York: Oxford University Press, 2010) and Megan Mullen, *Television in the Multichannel Age: A Brief History of Cable Television* (Malden, Mass.: Blackwell, 2008).

2. For more on the history of HBO, see Gary R. Edgerton and Jeffrey P. Jones, eds., *The Essential HBO Reader* (Lexington: University Press of Kentucky, 2008).

3. Jennifer Fuller, "Branding Blackness on US Cable Television," *Media, Culture & Society* 32.2 (2010): 285–305.

4. See Deborah L. Jaramillo, "The Family Racket: AOL Time Warner, HBO, *The Sopranos,* and the Construction of a Quality Brand," *Journal of Communication Inquiry* 26.1 (2002): 59–75.

5. Amanda D. Lotz, *The Television Will Be Revolutionized* (New York: New York University Press, 2007).

6. Derek Kompare, "Publishing Flow: DVD Box Sets and the Reconception of Television," *Television and New Media* 7.4 (2006): 335–60.

7. See http://www.kottke.org/tag/thewire, and http://www.slate.com/

default.aspx?search_input=the+wire&x=0&y=0&search_loc=on&qt=the+wire&id=3944.

8. See http://thehousenextdooronline.com/search/label/TheWire%22%5 Ct%22_blank, http://sepinwall.blogspot.com/search/label/TheWire%22%5Ct%22_blank, and http://sfgate.com/cgi-bin/blogs/sfgate/category?blogid=24&cat=932%22&5Ct%22_blank.

9. Jason Mittell, "Narrative Complexity in Contemporary American Television," *The Velvet Light Trap* 58 (2006): 29–40.

10. For more on the show's narrative strategies, see Jason Mittell, "All in the Game: *The Wire*, Serial Storytelling and Procedural Logic," in *Third Person: Authoring and Exploring Vast Narratives*, ed. Pat Harrigan and Noah Wardrip-Fruin (Cambridge: MIT Press, 2009), 429–38, and Tiffany Potter and C. W. Marshall, *The Wire: Urban Decay and American Television* (New York: Continuum, 2009).

11. See Jason Mittell, *Genre and Television: From Cop Shows to Cartoons in American Culture* (New York: Routledge, 2004).

12. Rafael Alvarez, *The Wire: Truth Be Told*, 2d ed. (New York: Grove Press, 2010), 35.

13. Ibid., 37.

14. See Mittell, "All in the Game."

2

The Wire and Its Readers

Frank Kelleter

What is *The Wire* to American culture? What work does it perform? Which actions, which actors, does it set into motion? Which discourses and practices are channeled, challenged, or stabilized by this television series?

Such questions, though hardly esoteric, were rarely asked in early analyses of *The Wire*. Instead, the importance of this text—the importance of its arrival on American screens and the importance of its aesthetic innovations—was taken for granted by most writers. Early commentators on *The Wire* treated such questions as if they were already answered or their answers only in need of exemplifying confirmation. Much was certain before the various "studies" set out to do their work of explication, even as the show was still running. *The Wire*, one could read, revolutionizes American television with dense storytelling. It paints an uncompromising image of the institutional, economic, and racial dimensions of inner-city decline. In painstaking detail and epic breadth, it brings to light what the American media have so far kept in the dark. It formulates a sophisticated indictment of postindustrial capitalism. It critiques the state of a nation that thinks it can afford to ignore these harsh realities. In a word, *The Wire* is "the best television show ever."

How did everyone know?

By watching *The Wire*, no doubt. But what does that mean? When Jacob Weisberg, in his influential *Slate* article on September 13, 2006, called *The Wire* "surely the best TV show ever broadcast in America," he (and other commentators making similar assessments at the time) did not, properly speaking, initiate this topos.[1] True, a look at the first published reactions to *The Wire* reveals that journalism and the blogosphere were influential in setting the tone and agenda of many subsequent academic discussions (probably indicating the growing alignment of both spheres, not least in the shrinking time available in either for written reactions).[2] But before any so-called external observer ever offered an interpretation of the series, the series did so itself—and not only in the sense of providing an occasion for exegetic follow-up, simply by being itself, but in the more active sense of producing self-descriptions that have steered its cultural work and activated narrative practices outside its textual boundaries.

The following chapter is part of a longer essay that discusses (1) the ways in which *The Wire* has been reading itself, (2) the ways in which Anglo-American scholars have been reading *The Wire*, and (3) the ways in which serial self-descriptions and critical practices have been interacting within the larger system of American (popular) culture. The present volume reproduces the second section of this larger work. Altogether, I argue that *The Wire*'s aesthetics and its academic reception fulfill mutually dependent functions within an overarching sphere of national auto-reference. A brief summary of the first section ("Serial Self-Descriptions") serves to explain why I refer to *The Wire* as a serial text that comprises both the television narrative of the same title and the public discourses accompanying it.

Serial Self-Descriptions

Can a text read itself? Can a text read anything? Not like an intentional person, for sure, but then the question can be turned around: How many texts, how many readings, are present in a person's intentions? And is their presence not an active one—one that produces further dealings and motions? Who is acting when a writer "follows" an aesthetic decision she has made? Effective in that decision, as in its consequences, are always other agencies, some far removed from the person acting, some not known to her, some not even human.

I am, of course, advocating a concept of agency as developed and employed in actor-network theory.[3] With regard to a television series—inevitably multiauthored, produced and consumed in many-layered systems of responsibility and performance, always dependent on the material demands of its technological medium—it seems particularly appropriate to think of agency (and certainly authorship) as something dispersed in a network of people, institutions, technologies, objects, and forms.

So, yes, a text can read itself, especially if it is a serial text. Personal vision and intentional choices are no doubt of consequence in serial storytelling, as are copyrights and proper names, but a television series is never authored by any *one* writer, producer, or even company. There are many reasons for this, among them the fact that serial publication by definition overlaps with serial reception. A series, unlike a finished oeuvre, can observe its own effects on audiences as long as the narrative is running. Moreover, it can react to these observations, making adjustments in form and content, just as audiences can become active in a narrative's development if the narrative is still unfolding—if it is a serial narrative, that is. The commercial framework of such transactions further complicates our established distinctions between production and reception, authors and readers, intentions and objects.[4]

Thus, instead of proceeding from the assumption that *The Wire* is "David Simon's *The Wire*" or "HBO's *The Wire*," we can ask how the show came to be perceived this way—and what the practical (that is, action-bound) consequences of such perceptions are in terms of its relation to itself, to its viewers, and ultimately to the larger cultural system from which it draws and to which it contributes. As befits a work-net of agencies—and as befits a commercial series—*The Wire* is busy describing itself at different levels of public discourse, setting in motion different actors and deploying different textual modes.[5] For one thing, paratextual commentaries by producers (of whatever status), in interviews or on DVD special features, suggest how the series wants to be read. Moreover, *The Wire* already interprets itself in its narrative and the very act of telling a story. In fact, any popular series is forced to keep creating identities in reaction to understandings and ascriptions brought forth by its continued existence. To the extent that a long run keeps involving ever more actors in the narrative—or keeps enlisting ever more involved actors—the boundaries between text and paratext are in need of constant revision if a series wants to maintain control of its public actions.[6]

The larger work from which this chapter is taken delineates three identities constructed by *The Wire* for itself: its institutional identity (as an HBO Original Series), its artistic identity (as journalistic fiction),

An image from the opening credit sequence of *The Wire*

and its narrative identity (as a complex serial). A few points on these issues:

1. *The Wire*'s identity as an HBO Original Series is characteristically conflicted. The series takes care to distance itself visually, atmospherically, and by other means from shows such as *The Sopranos* or *Deadwood*, even as it profits from institutional and artistic associations with these "complex" series.[7] Thus, in text and paratext *The Wire* repeatedly claims that it does not compete with other quality productions on American television, including HBO's own, but rather transcends the medium of commercial television altogether. To underline this point, the show resolutely foregrounds its economically counterintuitive decision to tell a story largely centered on the black underclass of a city as unglamorous as Baltimore. The implicit contention that this is "not TV" (while other HBO shows supposedly are, despite their channel's slogan) is not entirely wrong; many people working on the series are re-

ally from Baltimore and many are really television outsiders. But what does that mean? I suggest we approach *The Wire*'s claim of maverick authenticity, not as a matter of fact nor as a false pretense that hides other motives, but as an action tied into other actions. Just as the conspicuous display of local knowledge by David Simon and other personnel lends credibility to the show's aesthetic operations, so the show's credibility and aesthetics give incentive and guidance to the ways Simon and others can present and understand themselves as Baltimoreans. This circuit of actions is not restricted to industrial producers; it continues in public and academic responses to *The Wire*, where the local credentials of those who speak—that is, the questions: where are you from? what do you know? what have you seen? and so on—gain significance and channel further doings.[8]

2. The show's widespread description of itself as, in essence, a piece of literature is equally ambiguous. On the one hand, *The Wire* pays tribute to novelistic forebears and profits from their prestige and aesthetics. The model in question is not so much the social realism of Dickens and Balzac—notwithstanding public declarations to the contrary—but literary naturalism of the late nineteenth and early twentieth centuries.[9] Many ruling assumptions of the series, such as its appreciation of scope and precision in representation, its fascination with the lower classes, and above all its belief in the priority of environment over character, derive from (American) naturalism's philosophical investment in scientism, antigentility, and determinism. On the other hand, *The Wire* confronts the naturalistic novel as a contestant, trying not only to live up to its example but to supplant it. Thus, the show repeatedly claims that it *uses* fiction in the service of factual reportage.[10] *The Wire* is deeply confident that privileged access and sustained attention to the underside of urban life guarantees accuracy of coverage. This is a reporter's confidence in the transparency of social reality; the aspiration is to capture unfamiliar life by sheer force of local knowledge. Such an ethos strongly tends to identify reality with what is hidden away from view, while viewers are offered the gratification of feeling like insiders themselves: to join the few who have seen the show, or seen it first, or shared its knowledge, or shared it most knowingly.

3. A pervasive topos in descriptions of *The Wire* holds that everything that happens in the narrative is somehow "connected" and "remembered," suggesting that all events follow the rules of a complicated

but coherent plot or "game." Of course, memory is a mechanism of retrospective selection, so it is quite challenging to imagine a narrative in which all happenings were actually remembered. And true, like any series, *The Wire* creates many of its effects of unity retroactively, by taking up and explaining clues introduced earlier. This is not to minimize the range and sophistication of unity-building devices in *The Wire*. But we can view the show's interest in enacting the identity of a complex "serial" (rather than a sprawling "series") as conflict-ridden. Even in its self-contained, crypto-novelistic structures—most notably in its canon-bound materialization as a closed DVD set, complete with modes of storytelling that count on exactly such a type of distribution and reception—*The Wire* generates evolving structures with a vested interest in reproduction: a "series" playing a "serial" (in the industry definition of these terms). Continuation is the name of the game, not just organization. Or put differently: The show's investment in the organization of complexity is inevitably bound up with the complications of serial proliferation.[11] While aiming for the status and the practices of a unified oeuvre, the series thus remains structurally geared toward its own return and multiplication. Bringing to the flow of television the concentration and slowdown of self-contained works—and this with notable success—*The Wire* cannot help but engage in incessant movements forward and outward.

If one privileges *The Wire*'s journalistic idea of itself, all of this can be explained as strategy; that is, as the necessary practice of fiction enhancing the effectiveness of sociological reportage. I propose, however, that seriality is a major force in the cultural work of *The Wire*. To understand what this show is *doing*—to understand what it contributes to the culture it draws from—and to understand why it has become the darling of contemporary American (media) studies, its momentous serial agency needs to be taken into account. In more abstract terms: the performance of complexity in (and by) *The Wire* amounts to paradoxically repeated attempts at narrative totalization. Not only in its uneasy (initial) identity as a police procedural, the show hopes to render uniform a dense and multilayered structure in which "all the pieces matter."[12] As a series, too, it provides comforting reductions of the narrative complexities it has produced, and produced for the explicit purpose of organizing and reducing them.[13] Finally, in terms of subject matter, *The Wire* is busy organizing the intricacies and entanglements of the neoliberal city at the beginning of the twenty-first century into recognizable patterns—patterns that can be serially reproduced in follow-up narratives, stories within and without the serial text, political convictions, ideological positions, rallying cries of identification. *The Wire* makes followers.

Hetero-descriptions

Serial stories, with their feedback loops of production and reception, are force fields of connection. They activate practices and mobilize practitioners far beyond their textual bounds. Thus, in turning now to academic discussions of *The Wire*, my point is not that scholarship merely repeats the show's images of itself but that it continues the conflicts present in these images into national arenas of self-identification.

Of course, to read public readings of *The Wire* as active within the narrative's own cultural work complicates many of the certainties put forward by the series and its observers. This, however, is not meant as a way of "exposing" scholarship's "complicity" in this or that ideological hazard of *The Wire*. Rather, I wish to track how American (media) studies participate in the activities of their objects—or, more ambitiously put: how American (media) studies and American (media) practices act as interdependent forces of a larger cultural system called American culture.

Why this stress on America? It is a fact well known but worth repeating that scholars of contemporary texts are always doing more than simply analyzing those texts, especially when they operate within and on the same environment as their texts—which is the case when Americanists from the United States produce knowledge about America. Whatever else their goals and results, these types of study are always also acts of cultural self-description—and they can be analyzed as such, to trace dependencies between a culture's knowledge and performance of itself, ideally from a perspective not directly contributing to such self-identifications.[14]

The question, then, is not simply why *The Wire* has generated so much admiration among academic commentators, but which shapes this admiration takes, which transactions it stimulates, which debates and assurances it enables. Needless to say, few of the positions identified in the following can be attributed unambiguously to single contributions that would contain no other dispositions. But there are some pervasive trades between *The Wire* and its readings in the United States and other English-speaking countries. (The divergences between U.S. and non-U.S. analyses will be discussed at the end of this chapter.) I distinguish the following moves: competitive duplication, downward identification, activist concern, upward recognition, and analytical dislocation.

Duplication

In its thematic selections and interpretive interests, English-language scholarship on *The Wire* is to a large degree dependent on prior discussions in the press and on the Internet. These journalistic discussions, in turn, exhibit a pronounced tendency to duplicate isolated self-descriptions of the show, relying on David Simon's interviews, HBO public relations material, and other journalistic pieces. Such circularity certainly reflects the time pressures of daily text production. But self-reinforcing as these communications are, they do not simply repeat the show's interests. Rather, they *speed up* its cultural activities. By condensing discordant aesthetic identities into easily reproducible meanings and quick formulas (such as "televised novel," "complexity," "authenticity"), they may decrease their object's aesthetic density, but what *The Wire* loses in terms of experiential wealth it gains in terms of public effectiveness. Commonplaces culled from the show's repertoire of identifications give currency to its text, turning it into a versatile object of public exchange.

At first glance, it would seem inappropriate for scholarship to engage in this kind of reductionism. It would seem more fitting to trace the show's simultaneous buildup and diminution of complexity rather than to perpetuate auto-references with regard to only one side of the equation. But then, studies of popular culture are by definition confronted with a confusing array of daily growing material. They are continually challenged to bring informational order to such proliferation. Often working as archivists of the present, scholars of commercial culture are under an obligation to document "what is out there"—which can result in analyses that read like consumer reports with a cultural studies vocabulary.

Even so, when academic publications (under which category I include everything published with an affiliation to institutions of higher learning) duplicate statements from the show's paratexts, they often transform them into statements of fact or treat them as if they were results of analysis. Sometimes quoting David Simon verbatim, without always acknowledging or realizing they are doing so, contributions maintain that "In *The Wire* there is no such thing as good and evil as clear-cut moral categories," "The structure of the programme itself is that of an epic novel," "[*The Wire* is] a modernized and American version of Greek Tragedy," and "Simon was writing a televised novel, and a big one."[15] In particular, statements about the complexity of *The Wire* have taken on a mantra-like quality, paradoxically draining the term "complexity" of complexity.[16]

Such reductive duplications help to assimilate *The Wire* in a more or less fixed manner to public and scholarly convictions, many of them perpetuating the show's own narratives and attachments. In this way, competing (political, epistemological, even theological) positions can deploy *The Wire* as an exemplification of their own assumptions and beliefs. The serial text is turned into an intermediary for public contest, a stable currency for dissimilar purchases: *The Wire*, we read, "illuminates," "embodies," "reveals," "harmonizes with" ideas of critical pedagogy, urban development theory, "theoretical conceptions of black masculinity," libertarian conservatism, "Marx's critical engagement with primitive accumulation," "Catholic teaching in the 20th century [and] readings from church documents," Paul Tillich's "structure of hope," human resource management, and "the roles and behaviours of managers in the UK's National Health Service."[17]

Sociological and ethnographic approaches in particular have absorbed the series' claims to realism, attempting sociological or ethnographic analyses less than they are using *The Wire* to illustrate their own methods and results. In fact, the majority of examples quoted above are taken from the collection *The Wire: Urban Decay and American Television* and the conference "*The Wire* as Social Science Fiction?" organized by the Leeds Centre for Research on Socio-Cultural Change in the UK. Both ventures declare that they are interested in the connections of *The Wire* to the social sciences, especially urban sociology. However, with a few telling exceptions, contributors understand such connections not in terms of mutual dealings between the series and urban sociology (texts contextualizing each other) but in terms of the show's use-value *for* urban sociology. The ruling assumption is that there exists a sociohistorical background of facts that is represented—reported, in fact—in the show's surface narrative. Hence, *The Wire* can be employed as a convenient shortcut to observing social life in action: "a useful visual tool for . . . criminologists," "the best ethnographic text on the US today," or even "an illustrative example of the kind of non-fictional case study that social scientists might ideally aspire to."[18]

This last description is interesting for the chiasmus it performs. If I understand the argument correctly, it likens *The Wire* to a veritable case study of social life, while the show's narrative power is held up as a model for sociological writing. Unwittingly, such acceptance of *The Wire*'s documentary pretenses highlights the fictional base of many social science accounts—especially in the United States, it should be added, where these accounts are in intense competition for public attention and political relevance. The actual exchanges between sociology and *The Wire*, which are visible in such publications, invite investigation into the narrative dimension of sociological knowledge production itself.

For the actors involved, however, such mutuality mostly serves as a source of embarrassment, judged by the compulsive way in which they return to the fiction/fact dynamics and try to collapse one term into the other. When William J. Wilson and Anmol Chaddha taught *The Wire* in a sociology class at Harvard—a move guaranteed to draw some public attention—they explained their motivation as follows: "[Teaching about] urban inequality . . . we get some help from Bodie, Stringer Bell, Bubbles, and others. . . . [*The Wire*] shows ordinary people making sense of their world."[19] Such sociological interest in the show's realism conflicts with the show's identity as a television series in at least two ways: Stringer Bell and Omar are hardly "ordinary," nor are they "people." To be able to treat them like people, that is, to use television series as "new fictional sources," sociologists and ethnographers have to explain the text's practice of storytelling as insignificant for their research interests.[20] Strategies to do so include talking about fiction not as a set of multiauthored social acts but as a finished, onetime *translation* of reality into a textual medium;[21] conceding that *The Wire* is fiction, but then proceeding as if it were not (summarizing plotlines as evidence of what is wrong with municipal politics, talking about Carcetti as if he was the real mayor of a real city, and so on);[22] taking up David Simon's suggestion that narrative is a *tactic* in the service of social reportage;[23] claiming that the show is reflexively "blurring the boundaries" between fact and fiction, but concluding that in doing so it establishes some kind of "superior story" that weds the emotive force of narrative to the authenticity of documentation.[24]

These uses of *The Wire* single out specific self-descriptions at the expense of others, mostly drawing on the show's journalistic identity as promoted by Simon. On the one hand, this attests to the text's cultural force, its ability to contribute to ongoing social debates. On the other hand, the activities of the series are limited to those that can be easily assimilated to the reader's own chosen sphere of action. In principle, there is nothing wrong with that; one can always legitimize such limitation as a matter of research interest and focus. But the text's other activities will not be put to rest. What is more, they carry on *within* the exclusions of such allegorical readings, opening them in turn for (self-) investigation and ultimately challenging the scientific range of methods unable or unwilling to engage in such investigation. A sociologist who excludes the agency of fiction from her understanding of American society—or an Americanist who regards TV narratives as illustrative mirrors rather than influential makers of American culture—will almost certainly produce insufficient knowledge, and unnecessarily so. In the end, to duplicate *The Wire*'s claims to realism serves to confirm what a discipline already knows about reality. Such duplications invite questions about the culture-making force of fiction itself: questions about where the prior knowledge that guides these observations actually comes from.

Downward Identification

If some of the readings quoted above appear more plausible than others, this is because they stay close to what is already known about the series. Transforming auto-references into external observations, they exhibit a strong tendency towards self-confirmation, both concerning an observer's explicitly held convictions and the veracity of public knowledge in general. Have local witnesses repeat often enough that *The Wire* looks exactly like Baltimore and this will become a matter of experiential fact even for people who have never visited the city or lived in it.

However, stories mobilize not only knowledge but also sentiments.

They are forces of conviction and identification alike, able to substantiate what is already held but also to bring near what is emotively distant (or to configure what they bring near as new feelings). In this regard, one of the main achievements of *The Wire* is how it inverts entrenched routines of racial representation on American television. Featuring a majority of African American characters (rather than the token ethnic representative typical of American ensemble casts), arranging them over a wide social spectrum of shifting moral properties (rather than focusing on one class and affirming middle-class values even in depictions of the urban poor), and portraying members of the black underclass as individualized subjects of ambiguous actions (rather than objects of police work or sentimental victims), the show is engaged in a "de-centering of whiteness" unusual in contemporary popular entertainment.[25]

Some critical discussions are content to register this politics of representation and to approve its motives. More accept the show's invitation to identify with its underclass characters and continue the emotive work of *The Wire* into scholarship. Only a few contributions raise questions about this type of identification, and when they do, it is usually to stress their own privileged association with the social world presented or to distance themselves from what they perceive as illegitimate appropriations.

In all these cases, the affiliation of academic scholars with inner-city characters exhibits strong traits of downward identification, no matter the ethnic or social origin of the writer in question. In fact, most scholars are acutely aware of their present remoteness from the world shown in *The Wire* and, significantly, perceive it as a deficit to be explained, excused, or neutralized. This puts them under constant pressure to state their own relations to a (representation of) social reality explicitly removed from their own.

Alignment between reader and characters can be achieved in a number of ways. One rare example, published in the *Journal of Speculative Philosophy*, selects a particular figure (Omar) and sets him up as a model that can be emulated in situations socially distant but ideally close to the daily struggles of middle- and upper-class biographies: "we Omar wannabes" can draw on this "free spirit . . . who live[s] unconcerned with what others expect" in order to fight our own "unending battle with the *status quo*."[26] At the other end of the spectrum are descriptions that turn characters more or less openly into *objects of desire,* as in a gay reading that applauds the show's "eroticization of the hood."[27]

To understand why the series is able to push the boundaries of narrative into ever wider fields of public practice, it is important to see how its emotive offerings encourage readers to write themselves into the story and to publicly behave like characters of the show. Not a few scholars simulate closeness to their favorite fictional gangsters and junkies by reproducing their slang in the middle of critical analysis, freely quoting from their sayings, or referring to them like old acquaintances—which for all practical purposes, as serial characters, they are. Another, more powerful, strategy is to establish one's autobiographical credentials as an African American, Baltimorean, former member of the proletariat, minority speaker, or other identity , all the while reproducing the show's insistence that privileged access yields authentic knowledge (not "where you're at" counts but "where you're from").[28]

Accordingly, at the 2009 conference in Leeds, the participants from Baltimore were scheduled early in the program. Similarly, the collection *The Wire: Urban Decay and American Television,* after gently cautioning against the "documentary fallacy" in the volume's introduction, offers as its first contribution the memoir of a former inhabitant of Baltimore's Eastside, now a published poet and holder of an endowed chair of English, who reminisces about the people that inspired leading gangland characters in *The Wire.* He creatively refers to them by their fictional names: "[Proposition] Joe and I were attending junior high school at the same time. We might have known each other . . . When Omar was a young teenager in the mid-1980s . . . I was a blue-collar worker in the city before going off to Brown University's creative writing program."[29] Carrying on the serial narrative into his recollections of the city, the writer thus includes himself in the fictional story-world ("Proposition Joe and I")—a move that draws attention both to the lived relevance of *The Wire*'s urban representations and to the operations of fiction in any sort of temporal self-identification.

According to the same logic, self-consciously white writers can name themselves as such, admitting that their attitude to the show is guided by a need for "sharing" and calling this need "white" (but then quoting "my friend Winston," presumably an African American, to authenticate the speaker's position).[30] In another turn, self-consciousness about self-consciousness can yield irony, as in Christian Lander's—not exactly scholarly but obliquely critical—inclusion of *The Wire* in *Stuff White People Like,* a compendium of taste more revealing about class-bound and national embarrassments than ethnic ones.[31] This confessional mode is not restricted to American writers who identify as members of larger groups in order to tap into—or mock—the show's group-intensive gratifications; it easily crosses national borders, at least into other English-speaking countries.[32]

Evidently, all these identifications are dependent on the assumption that *The Wire* paints an accurate picture of race and class in Baltimore and, by extension, America. The series itself stresses its documentary credentials by reminding viewers again and again that single events are based on "true stories" "heard by" Simon (the truth of the story residing exactly in the fact that it was heard by, and most probably told to, a reporter).[33] Casting policy, too, provides much-publicized proof of credibility. Not only are approximately 65 percent of the cast black, but many characters are actually played by amateurs from Baltimore, some of them real-life inspirations for other parts, some of them "real gangsters," in that revealing conjunction of reality and outlaw existence popular in American storytelling.[34] The two most famous correlations between Baltimore people and serial figures are convicted murderer Felicia "Snoop" Pearson playing the character of Snoop, and the marriage of Don Andrews (reportedly a model for Omar) and Fran Boyd (a former junkie and informant for Simon's *The Corner*), described in one academic article as "a real-life fulfillment of the promise the series at times presents to the viewer."[35] In striking contrast, three leading characters, McNulty, Stringer Bell, and Tommy Carcetti, are played by English and Irish actors who first had to learn how to speak with a Baltimore accent.

These eye-catching "blurrings" of the fact/fiction divide are frequently read as reflexive gestures, in which the series "raises some issues surrounding the notions of performance, authenticity, and 'otherness.'"[36] However, in terms of their foreignness to Baltimore, there is little self-reflection in Dominic West's performance of McNulty and none in Idris Elba's of Stringer Bell or Aidan Gillen's of Carcetti. On the contrary, the naturalistic styles of these actors significantly reinforce the show's feel of realism. More interesting than their nationality, then, is the reason why they were selected in the first place. Simon says he switched to British players for the parts of McNulty and Stringer Bell because all Americans who auditioned for the roles had watched too many American cop shows and copied them in their performances.[37]

This is a revealing statement and it rhymes with *The Wire*'s media philosophy. To a large degree, the show's effect of authenticity depends on canceling the presence of American television from its representational identity. To make a convincing case for realism, *The Wire* has to subtract its own (medium's) activities from the social world it depicts. In this sense, to have a gangster played by an actor unspoiled by American television corresponds with the decision to represent Baltimore's social reality as one in which television plays no part. *The Wire* treats its viewers to a world in which cops and criminals are blissfully ignorant of, and thoroughly uninfluenced by, the ways cops and criminals behave on TV—a supposition actually shared with most conventional television drama: realism at the expense of realistic (self-)representation.[38]

Unlike many of its HBO competitors, then, *The Wire* has remarkably little to say about television. Apart from a few inside jokes that serve to underline its distance from both traditional series and other quality programs (when a gangster prefers network fare to *Deadwood* or when another points to the self-referential absurdity of *Dexter*), watching television does not feature as a social practice in the series. When the media finally do play a role in season 5, the question is typically one of representation versus misrepresentation; the final season suggests that the decline of journalism is epitomized by reporters making things up. The underlying assumption is that the media convey reality, either correctly or incorrectly. Since *The Wire*'s own claims to realism are strongly tied to the notion of accurate translation, the show has no interest in treating the media, and hence itself, as actively shaping the things they represent.[39]

It is interesting to note that such discrepancies have led one sociologist to invite "real thugs" to watch the show with him—and write about it in a nine-part article series for the Freakonomics blog linked on the *New York Times* website. Sudhir Venkatesh's experiment and its rhetoric deserve an analytical essay of their own. I shall restrict my remarks to saying that the gangsters' engagement with *The Wire*, as filtered through Venkatesh (a former student of William J. Wilson), points at once to the idealized nature of the series' narrative and to the ways in which this narrative mobilizes emotionally charged self-performances among those reportedly represented.[40] The self-described "rogue sociologist" looks on to report dangerous knowledge gleaned from the show and "a group of gangland acquaintances," now operating as if in unison as a collective actor. Noting that *The Wire* "accorded with my own fieldwork in Chicago and New York," Venkatesh claims that watching it with "a few respected street figures" is the best way "to ensure quality control." Confirming the results of fieldwork through fieldwork on his informants' reactions to what he takes to be an illustrative version of these results, Venkatesh winds up suspended between amused monitoring and representations of toughness that surpass even *The Wire*'s claims to brutal authenticity. Dutifully reminding his informants that it is only a TV show (when one of their favorite characters is killed) does not get him out of this tautological round—perhaps the problem is in the word "only"—but further into it: "I was thrown a "f—k you" stare that only men with deep knowledge of hand-to-hand combat could give."[41] Deep knowledge about a rough existence: Venkatesh's rhetoric marks downward identification as a dead serious matter.

Activist Concern

Among academic readings of *The Wire*, there is one small group that deviates from the generally admiring tone of scholarship. These contributions largely share the show's interest in reportage but question its correctness and effects. Assessing the series against the background of its own critique of capitalism, they hold that *The Wire* does little to mend or counteract the social conditions it so forcefully condemns.

The first sustained—and, to date, most nuanced—formulation of this argument appeared not in a scholarly article but in a 2008 essay published by Michael Bowden in *The Atlantic*. Bowden quotes Yale sociologist Elijah Anderson, author of studies such as *Code of the Streets*, *Streetwise*, and *A Place on the Corner*, who called the series "an exaggeration. I get frustrated watching it." Bowden concurs: "[Simon's] political passions ultimately trump his commitment to accuracy or evenhandedness." Taking up Anderson's diagnosis of "a bottom-line cynicism" in *The Wire*, he describes the series as "relentlessly . . . bleak."[42]

Remarkably, this critique, too, draws on one of the show's auto-referential topoi, if disapprovingly so. The term "bleak," habitually reproduced after Bowden's article to mark the series' more disillusioned aspects, calls to mind—and was probably inspired by—Charles Dickens's *Bleak House,* one of the major references for the show's literary ambitions. Similarly, some scholars complain about the "fatalism" of social vision in *The Wire,* acknowledging the text's self-definition as Greek tragedy updated for postmodern times.[43] Almost all these readings accept David Simon as the authoritative source of textual meaning (in the case of Bowden explaining central features of the narrative as results of the author's mental conflicts). Altogether, they function like special cases of the sociological duplications described above, singling out separate images of the series, accelerating them in public discourse, but this time not to ally themselves with them but to formulate distinct counternarratives.

Counternarratives have a way of illuminating deep-seated contradictions of the stories they are written against. In this, they can be sharp tools of analysis.[44] At the same time, to tell a story with the explicit purpose of proving another story wrong usually presupposes commitments of a more systematic kind than expressed even by the term "conviction." Such dedicated critiques are often spoken from the position of exceptionally strong and extensive obligations, like a religious faith or a formalized political ideology: supernarratives that confront other texts not only with an impulse of integrating them but as direct rivals in world-explanation. Thus, to complain that the society presented in *The Wire* is "irredeemable"—a key term among concerned activists—means to hold a vision, and probably a plan, of social redemption.[45] In its more pragmatic form, focused on concrete troubles in concrete localities, this type of critique combines praise for *The Wire*'s ability to "raise awareness" with indictment of its failure "to offer any understanding that the problems facing cities and the urban poor are *solvable.*"[46]

It is a normative project, both in its doctrinaire and its reformist shape. These readings would want to *change* the text. "What is needed," one critic writes, is to take up "the moral appeal of [Simon's] tragic argument" but employ it for "additional engagements" and "affirmative articulations of political and social problems capable of transforming the tragic conditions of the city."[47] Ultimately, this amounts to blaming the series for what it is, advocating not just different or more critical readings but hoping for different narratives to replace it. Again, there is nothing wrong with that; it is an incentive to cultural production. But as scholarship, these readings sometimes show little interest in investigating the real work done by a real narrative. At their most extreme, they reduce actions to an agenda. Their continuation of the series is instrumental, often attempting to discontinue what they see as its harmful effects.

Small wonder, then, that activist accounts approach textual structures in a decidedly selective manner. They note, correctly, that the final episode shows social roles reproducing themselves "fatalistically" through new agents (Michael takes Omar's position, Dukie becomes a second Bubbles, Sydnor replaces McNulty) but ignore that McNulty and Bubbles "go home" in the end, and how this has prompted many a commentator to describe the finale as highly satisfying and life affirming. One viewer's bleakness is another viewer's hope. But it is possible to ask how such discrepancies can exist at all, how the narrative enables these dissimilar effects, and what the co-presence of closure and continuation tells us about the serial text, its cultural doings, and the culture it helps sustain.

While activist readings challenge the accuracy of *The Wire*—an "exaggeration," says Anderson; no community activists, no black working class in this fictional Baltimore, say others[48]—they accord with the case-study approach of Williams and Venkatesh in excluding the productivity of mass-media storytelling from their notion of social reality. Consider that the inversion of racial and hetero-normative stereotypes in and by *The Wire* already has an activist dimension. Designing an openly homosexual outlaw character like Omar may not be a feat of social realism, but it is a forceful intervention in the representational customs of American television.[49] This is true for many characterizations and constellations in *The Wire*: they work on existing social practices. To ignore this means to regard these practices not as practices at all but as handy symbols of social realities to which they are true or not.

In turn, concerns about the activist value of *The Wire* have affected the show's self-understanding, probably even before they were first voiced by external observers. The makers of *The Wire* are, by necessity, highly sensitive to charges of social irresponsibility, because the uniqueness of their product rests to a large extent on its claims of political dissent. For Simon, something even more personal is at stake, as season 5's thinly veiled attacks on Bill Marimow and John Carroll, senior editors of the *Baltimore Sun*, have backfired into a debate about different types of journalism. At heart, this debate is about effective and ineffective forms of social commitment. The *Columbia Journalism Review*, interviewing both sides, pointedly concludes that there is indeed a difference "between Simon's broad sociological approach and the rifle-shot approach taken by Carroll and Marimow, and rewarded all over the country by the Pulitzer board: the latter approach demonstrably affects—possibly even saves—individual lives."[50]

Perhaps the tenacity with which *The Wire*, despite its proclaimed boredom with moral dichotomies, takes sides against bad institutions, bad corporations, bad superiors, bad elites, and bad Emmy committees, compensates for a feeling of comparative futility. As if hoping for a purpose that would channel the diffuse serial proceedings of their creation into more targeted kinds of action, six writers for *The Wire* issued a statement on March 5, 2008 (over Time/CNN no less) in which they declared "War on the Drug War" by the following means: "If asked to serve on a jury deliberating a violation of state or federal drug laws, we will vote to acquit, regardless of the evidence presented." Associating the "American dissent" of "jury nullification" with Thomas Paine's somewhat inaccurately summarized spirit of "civil disobedience against monarchy," they brought out heavy artillery for an unlikely fight.[51] I suggest we read this resolution, explicitly connected to *The Wire* in its title and marketing, as the reentry of activist concerns into serial self-observation. Serial producers, too, have an interest in keeping their product handy and controlling unpredictable ideological sprawl.

Upward Recognition

In addition to the readings discussed so far, *The Wire* has attracted, as all cultural artifacts seem destined to do, interpretations inspired by large explanatory systems commonly classified as Theory. I am talking about model-type academic discourses with ambitions of virtually unlimited applicability. Sometimes correlated with formalized beliefs or explicit political convictions, they are not necessarily determined by a social agenda nor bound by disciplinary methods (as is the case-study definition of *The Wire* described above). Instead, Theory aspires to an essentially philosophical project of truth, even when it claims to have left behind such notions, typically justifying its performative contradictions by declaring that any transcendence requires repetition of the thing to be transcended. Highly dependent on the charisma of individual master-thinkers, Theory offers to the time-pressed humanities an attractive repertoire of argumentative shortcuts both prestigious (because of their performed depth and difficulty) and efficient (because of their secure reproducibility, once mastered). In scholarship on *The Wire*, the writings of Michel Foucault, Gilles Deleuze, and to a lesser degree Jean Baudrillard and Guy Debord are the most active such models. A typical proposition reads:

> [*The Wire* is] the most Foucauldian show on television, the show which reveals the most about the technologies and techniques of contemporary discipline and punishment. We can map Foucault's theories about institutions fairly directly onto the Baltimore presented in *The Wire*, demonstrating how his ideas about power and discipline remain vitally important for social theory.[52]

The logic of this passage, representative of much critical practice in this vein, is tautological: The reader deploys Foucault to make sense of the narrative, then finds the narrative to mirror Foucault's "ideas" (this is not only a Foucauldian reading but the series itself is Foucauldian), and finally concludes that such agreement indicates the accuracy of these ideas. While the phrase "the Baltimore presented in *The Wire*" suggests that the object is, in fact, a media artifact, the distinction between artifact and exegetic tool is collapsed again in the concluding "demonstration" that Foucault's ideas are important for social theory *because* they are present in a television series. The question is: important in which ways? To understand what is happening here, consider that this passage is not interested in asking how and why Foucauldian notions of power have entered American commercial narratives. Rather, their presence there proves these notions to be correct.

On the one hand, this is another approach that takes for granted that *The Wire* "offers a comprehensive, faithful portrait of contemporary urban life, an essential case study for any theory of social organization."[53] On the other hand, Theory readings, judged by their argumentative economy, are less interested in illuminating the conditions of inner-city life with the help of televisual illustrations than they are in proclaiming that "the truth of [Foucault]" is "nowhere else in contemporary culture . . . so apparent as in *The Wire*."[54] The rhetorical thrust is clear, repeatedly juxtaposing scenes from the show with authoritative quotations from the master texts: "In *Discipline and Punish*, Foucault describes how . . . ," "*The Wire* confirms another of Foucault's maxims . . . ," "law enforcement as depicted in *The Wire*" exemplifies and ultimately proves "[a]n axiom of Foucault's theory of discipline," so that the series "merely illustrates with surprising accuracy his argument."[55] These recognitions establish the narrative as a powerful allegory, connecting it upward to nothing less than axiomatic truth.

So far, I have found no readings that would trace the actual trades between this truth's content and the self-descriptions of *The Wire*. However, given the ease with which Foucault's texts can be applied to the series' social vision, it seems likely that the plausibility of such applications rests on more than just their philosophical aura. McMillan points to the narrative's "affinity with the social theory of Michel Foucault," but then refrains from investigating the terms and conditions of this affinity by declaring that "in [a] general sense, the concerns of Foucault and *The Wire* are identical."[56] What is meant is that Foucault's concerns include, like a framework, the concerns of the series. This reading essentially distinguishes between two *types* of texts, one offering a complex reconstruction of philosophical truth, the other playing out the philosophy's maxims as story.

It is the second type of text, the narrative, that is seen as doing something, but its doings are serviceable to the conceptual showings of the first type. All of this is quite in accordance with philosophical models of textuality that regard a text's practices (its rhetoric, its local involvements, its historical dealings) as part of its ephemeral nature, necessarily inferior to the universal (limitless) propositions of thought. To deprive Foucault's writings in this manner of their cultural occupations—their rhetorical business connections—means to privilege them as unmoved movers behind the busy exchanges of storytelling. This works even with philosophies that speak up for dissemination and currency, such as those of Derrida or Deleuze. Conversely, a television series associated with such metanarratives can participate in the prestige of timeless writing: *The Wire* is "not simply great television, but *great art*," we read, because it does more than mimic social reality: it dramatizes its essence.[57]

If the narrative deviates too conspicuously from the axioms of the framework, there are a number of possibilities to account for this: One can proclaim a countertruth of fiction that is said to "resist" such theoretical reduction (a position not yet established in the literature, as far as I can see). Alternatively, one can limit descriptions to those elements that harmonize with the master-theory. For example, McMillan grounds his notion of victorious institutions and failed heroism in a quite partial—"Platonic"—concept of heroism, disregarding the presence of existential modes of heroic perseverance in *The Wire* (well documented in audience reactions that privilege the theme of individualism).

In addition, one can describe the narrative as differentiating, modifying, or extending the theoretical framework (preferably extending it onto other master theories). Thus, McMillan enhances his Foucauldian reading by saying that *The Wire* redefines the modern totality of surveillance for the more fluent conditions of postmodern society. He explains that the show depicts individuals subverting the "panopticum," but in doing so they are creating their own networks of surveillance. Thus, the postindustrial weakening of central institutions is reintegrated, via Deleuze and Guattari's concept of machinic "assemblages," into a Foucauldian allegory of all-powerful institutions.[58]

Similarly, and finally, one can align the narrative with the doctrines of another master thinker and have it engage in a truth struggle by proxy. The dialogic nature of this strategy invites examinations more dynamic than those offered by an integrative single-truth model. Thus, a suggestive reading of the show sets Foucault's motif of the panopticum in critical exchange with Debord's concept of the spectacle. Correctly noting that surveillance in *The Wire* is a messy and often futile affair, Joseph Schaub finds the show to be about "the failure of disciplinary surveillance" because it privileges the "low-tech gaze" of patient observation over the power of high-tech control. Possibly helped by the comparative informality of Debord's concept, Schaub can utilize this insight for descriptions that are relatively uncommitted to framework axioms but sensitive to the particularities of media (and other) effects. Thus, the spectacle's affinity to "narcissism" allows investigation into *The Wire*'s relations to contemporary docudramas and reality TV—and, theoretically, to itself and its audiences.[59]

The productivity of Theory-inspired readings in literary, media, and cultural studies is immense. With the help of their framework model of textuality, even secondary insights can be granted master-theoretical status, for example when the constructive role of institutions in identity formation is presented as "Foucault's truth" or when an approach is called Foucauldian merely for maintaining that relations of power are important in social life. *The Wire* actually shares many of these insights, but it may have arrived at them by other routes, some of them possibly intersecting with the activities and translations of Foucault's texts. Ultimately, this raises the question of how these intersections are being traveled and by whom, which narratives and assumptions are shared or developed, and which transactions between *The Wire*, American sociology, and other truth agencies are actually taking place.[60]

To enable such descriptions, it seems useful to accord to one's objects and tools alike the status of culturally effective interactors. Narratives exist not as phenomena in need of model explanations, but explanatory models are implicated in our narrative worlds, and both are probably better served by lateral association than upward recognition. However, to make such associations requires a degree of self-awareness, not to mention breadth of contextualization, usually not available to individual writers but accessible only in the collective effects of mutual observation. A less costly and time-consuming method is enacted by a fourth class of approaches.

Analytical Dislocation

Analysis—understood as attention being paid to the ways in which interrelated parts construct or simulate a whole—can dislocate an object from the knowledge it holds and distributes about itself. Through this, analysis can disarticulate commonplaces in favor of critical redescriptions, breaking habits of meaning-making by making them explicit. Readings of *The Wire* that put such concerns at the center of their efforts are obviously close to the approach chosen by this essay. This makes it more difficult for the present writer to bring to bear an analytical perspective on them, but a few patterns can be discerned.

In general, analytical redescription is always more likely to challenge than to accept *The Wire*'s depictions of itself, regardless of their adequacy. Often this leads to suspicion about ulterior motives. Thus, many critical readings understand "critique" as an uncovering of hidden purposes or latent determinations, frequently in conjunction with philosophical framework theories such as those discussed above. Dan Rowe and Marti Collins, for instance, conduct a rigorous content analysis (of the first season) that questions the show's alliance with Foucauldian concepts of governmentality but not the empirical veracity nor the superior epistemological status of these concepts.[61] In this manner, analytical dislocations can be relocated within prior assessments—and *The Wire* can be judged ("critically") by its secret deviation from axiomatic norms of dissidence. A ruling figure of thought in this regard describes the show as "complicit" in the very acts of power it condemns. Thus, the series' own practice of social critique, heavily invested in the notion of disembodied authorities working behind the scenes, is applied against itself and surpassed by the explanations of an even more critical observer. Not rarely, this observer concludes that such complicity proves power to be so total that it always incorporates its own critique—a conclusion that actually parallels *The Wire's* own simultaneous indictment of and aspiration to total vision.

It should be noted that such critical readings, despite their reliance on philosophical text models, prove highly perceptive when it comes to identifying the recursive doings of *The Wire*. They also have an interest in tracing connections between self-descriptions and hetero-descriptions. Sara Taylor looks at HBO's distribution policies, the role of fandom, and "parafilmic material" to disclose "the presence of both reflexivity and compliance to the principles of neoliberalism in *The Wire*."[62] This perspective, whatever its partisan commitments (particularly to Lisa Duggan's understanding of neoliberalism), enables Taylor to link the show's narrative complexity to its commodity operations: full appreciation of the story requires the purchase of a complete DVD set.

Similarly, a Foucauldian frame allows Ryan Brooks to illustrate how *The Wire*, despite its insistence on being no cop show, works to produce a powerful notion of "good police" that contrasts the skillful and intuitive labor of individuals with the damage done by judicial checks and balances. In fact, the show's visual and narrative structures establish a "hierarchy of information" that ensures that the viewers usually know *more* than the gang members and *less* than the police. In other words, a self-propelling series: "there is always more delinquency to uncover." Brooks draws a conclusion that relates the show's inward affiliations (with itself) to its outward affiliations (with its audience):

> *The Wire* dramatizes the effects of power while simultaneously denying its own power, as a literary entity, to regulate the behavior of its viewers. . . . [T]he show also disavows its own rhetorical strategies by con-

trasting this rigid discipline with its own authentic knowledge or truth. . . . [T]hese treatments should be understood as part of the narrative power game of *The Wire*, which is an attempt to train viewers to critically question these hierarchies and which, like a police surveillance unit, must remain hidden in order to have its coercive effect.[63]

Other formal analyses are less devoted to detecting "coercive effects." This is not to say that they are disinterested—or should (or even could) be. In fact, they are frequently carried out by television scholars with a keen interest in defining and defending their field of studies. Much argumentative energy is spent on issues of disciplinary identity. In this context, discussions of *The Wire* in terms of its novelistic or literary qualities are likely to be seen as including "a demeaning attitude towards television."[64] A deep investment in the quality of television combined with a necessarily ambivalent attitude toward the concept of Quality TV (when it associates the medium with more esteemed precursors) imparts to these studies a pronounced sense of disciplinary competitiveness. In this manner, their pervasive concern with televisual complexity and medial self-reflexivity parallels the ambiguous strategies of identification and distinction employed by many contemporary television series themselves. Media studies of this type even participate in the same processes of competition and one-upmanship so characteristic of their objects, for example by pointing to the material superiority of television over literature or cinema when it comes to telling extensive stories.[65] In fact, of all agents of continuation, American television studies are most directly involved in the formalization, acceleration, and dissemination of *The Wire*'s cultural work.

In terms of analytical intelligence, such proximity can be advantageous. Media scholars and Americanists bring to bear an elaborate historical and formal knowledge on their understanding of *The Wire*—knowledge that is particularly suited, if not indispensable, for exploring the cultural movements of an American television series. Whatever their motivations and judgments in terms of disciplinary (and other) identities, these accounts almost inevitably shed light on the narrative's interaction with other narratives, media, and players. For example, *The Wire*'s claims of innovation can be recontextualized—and made explicit as time-bound ambitions—on a wide field of actors, as in Marsha Kinder's consideration of the show's engagement with movies such as

Francesco Rosi's *Salvatore Guiliano*, Sidney Lumet's *Serpico*, Stanley Kubrick's *Paths of Glory* (cited by Simon), Jean-Luc Godard's *Weekend*, and, especially, Elia Kazan's *On the Waterfront*, whose divergent representation of dock workers hints at "the rivalries between movies and television for hyper-realistic representation and systemic analysis, as if the narrative format of cinema is now insufficiently expansive for covering the complex networked society."[66]

Similarly, Jane Gibb and Roger Sabin ask "how new is 'new'?" and suggest "ways in which *The Wire* may be part of a genre tradition" that spans from *Kojak* through *Hill Street Blues*, *Miami Vice*, and *NYPD Blue* all the way to *Homicide*. Unexciting as this claim may seem at first glance, its analytical argument manages to historicize the show's antigeneric self-image and with it the ideas of timeless textuality and reportorial authenticity that play such a central role in scholarship: "[I]n ten, twenty years time," the authors argue, "*The Wire* will look as creaky as those shows appear today." It bears mention that *Dragnet*, the mother of all police procedurals, which appears now like a caricature of television noir, was heralded in the 1950s as the pinnacle of television realism, actually beginning each episode with the line, "Ladies and gentlemen, the story you're about to see is true," followed by a montage of urban locales—an iconographic network—over which the narrator intoned the sentence: "This is the city." Mindful of such transactions, Gibb and Sabin suggest a descriptive approach that is richer in detail and more attuned to the cultural dynamics of its object than sociological duplication, downward identification, activist concern, or upward recognition: "*The Wire* remains the latest in a succession of crime shows that have had a dialogue with each other, as well as with their broader sociological context, and in so doing have allowed America to talk to itself."[67]

Another example of interactional analysis can be found in Jason Mittell's groundbreaking article on *The Wire*'s connection to computer games. Skeptical of Simon's literary comparisons—and hoping instead "to celebrate" *The Wire* "on its own medium's terms"—Mittell phrases his argument in a cautious manner, almost like a thought experiment, but even in such guarded terms it transcends the concerns of disciplinary identity with which it starts. Reminding his readers that "there were many key televised precedents for long-form gradual storytelling for [Simon] to draw upon," Mittell expands this backwards perspective onto present times and charts *The Wire*'s exchanges with its immediate media environment. In so doing, he identifies a crucial arena for contemporary American reality production: "a spectatorial game, being played on-screen for the benefit of an audience."[68]

Thus, the series' creative usage of serial memory—its simultaneous increase and reduction of complexity, in the parlance of this essay—becomes visible as a matter of "ludic joy" and "replayability," that is, as procedural training that actively involves viewers in the storytelling (and, by implication, in reality construction) even as it seeks to foreclose popular interference.[69] "The show demands audiences . . . invest in their diegetic memories by rewarding detailed consumption with narrative payoffs," writes Mittell, and as with any productive account, there are a number of ways to proceed from here. Say, by investigating television's commerce with the connectivity of digital competitors or thinking about what it means for cultures when their storytelling media converge around a paradigm of interrelated procedures and short-timed tasks for long-timed continuations. In either case, analytical dislocation enables perspectives that are particularly responsive to the historical agility of serial narratives.

Examples of this kind of approach are rare.[70] What is more, based on my corpus it seems evident that British, Irish, and Australian scholars are more likely than American scholars to challenge the self-images of *The Wire* or set them in dialogue with the series' other involvements.[71] American contributions that do so often subordinate their acts of redescription to an ultimate confirmation of the show's social vision or to proclaiming its status as a masterpiece of television.

So far, only non-American contributions have begun to ask how American writings about *The Wire* relate to the series' cultural activities and conditions. Even so, this is by no means a common question—an indication, perhaps, of the influence of American rehearsals of American studies over practices in other countries. At the 2009 Economic and Social Research Council conference, according to the paper abstracts, only three presentations (out of fifty) were dedicated to such questions, one of them evidently caught up in a national agenda of its own: David Hesmondhalgh (from the University of Leeds) analyzed how the critical reception of *The Wire* in the United Kingdom "has been marked by a reverence of US production" that is said to go hand in hand with disrespect for British television. Natasha Whiteman (from the University of Leicester) examined how critics and academics "mark their af-filiation to the series" through configurations of its quality, comparing such receptions to "modes of identification with media texts evident within online fan communities." Finally and most remarkably, Rebecca Bramall (from the University of Brighton) and Ben Pitcher (from Oxford Brookes University) concluded that *The Wire*'s "appeal to left-wing aca-demics working in the fields of sociology, cultural studies and cognate disciplines" derives from the show's "beguiling projection of sociologi-cal desire, providing a totalizing vision of and orientation to the social, a fantasy of the intelligibility of contemporary urban life." According to this reading, *The Wire* resonates with the self-perception of academic practice, defined by its belief in the social value of detailed observation, methodological commitment, and systematic explanation. The show encourages identification among scholars by echoing back to them an "idealized representation" of what they think about themselves.[72]

The fact that the dominant discourses in the United States differ, sometimes dramatically, from such accounts is not a sign of their defi-ciency or negligence. Rather, it expresses their participation in the cul-tural doings of the series, that is, their status as American self-studies. As such, they are open to an American studies analysis. It can be asked: What are *The Wire* and its readers doing in and for American culture? How do *The Wire* and its contestations contribute to a larger cultural system that calls itself, not entirely correctly, America? For this geo-graphically vast, socially incongruous but in no way continentally comprehensive formation to achieve and maintain a sense of its reality, mass-produced commercial narratives are crucial agents of continuity. Their performances create unlikely coherence on a daily basis. Starting from these observations, it becomes possible to read *The Wire* as a se-rial narrative and a junction of narratives whose cultural work—a work on needs and conflicts of self-definition—makes (and has) a national home.[73]

Notes

For suggestions and critique, I wish to thank Jared Gardner, Christy Hosefelder, Andreas Jahn-Sudmann, Kathleen Loock, Alexander Starre, and Daniel Stein.

1. Jacob Weisberg, "The Wire on Fire: Analyzing the Best Show on Televi-sion," *Slate*, September 13, 2003, http://www.slate.com/id/2149566 (accessed

August 19, 2010). Almost simultaneously, Brian Lowry wrote in *Variety*: "When television history is written, little else will rival *The Wire*, a series of such extraordinary depth and ambition that it is, perhaps inevitably, savored only by an appreciative few" ("The Wire," *Variety*, September 2006, http://www.variety. com/awardcentral_review/VE1117931487.html?nav=reviews07&categoryid=23 52&cs=1&p=0 [accessed June 1, 2010]).

2. How often do we advise a colleague or are told by one: "You should publish this before someone else does"? The implications for academic knowledge production are interesting. For the present essay, I have surveyed a sample of approximately 200 publications from newspapers, Internet sources, and academic venues, compiled with the help of Anne Clausen, to whom I wish to express my gratitude. The bulk of these contributions appeared between 2006 and 2010, with a significant academic reception starting in 2008. The contributions published in the present volume are not part of my corpus.

3. See Bruno Latour, *Reassembling the Social: An Introduction to Actor-Network-Theory* (Oxford: Oxford University Press, 2005), especially 43–50, 213–18.

4. See Frank Kelleter, "'Toto, I Think We're in Oz Again (and Again and Again)': Why Popular Culture Loves Repetition," in *Remake | Remodel*, ed. Kathleen Loock and Constantine Verevis (forthcoming). Many of the themes discussed in the following have been developed in the six-project research unit "Popular Seriality—Aesthetics and Practice" at Göttingen University, http://popularseriality.uni-goettingen.de. For serial authorship in particular, see the project "Authorization Practices of Serial Narration: The Generic Development of Batman and Spider-Man Comics," directed by Daniel Stein and myself.

5. For the coinage "work-net," see Latour, *Reassembling*, 132. My interest in self-description is obviously indebted to Niklas Luhmann's understanding of the term, although this essay treats self-descriptions not under systemic but pragmatic considerations; see Niklas Luhmann, *Die Gesellschaft der Gesellschaft* (Frankfurt am Main: Suhrkamp, 1999), 879–93.

6. This is especially true for long-running series that may be older than their contemporary human actors (the term "actor" referring here to any force involved in a series' continuation). New writers have to perform their authorship against the limiting background of established roles and rules within the narrative (for example, what are a hero's superpowers, which character traits are possible, and so on) and often in competition with established ownership claims outside the narrative (see Bob Kane's jealous guardianship of the original Batman character); long-term readers can challenge innovations with an authoritative appeal to "continuity" (notice the effect of the *Comic Book Price Guide*, first published in 1970, on superhero storytelling). For these and additional examples, see again the project "Authorization Practices of Serial Narration" by Stein and myself. *The Wire* does not follow the format of the open-ended series frequent

in comics, but the disruption of text/paratext distinctions is no less visible in so-called serials that work with progressing story-arcs. In general it can be said that the difference between a "series" and a "serial," well established in Anglo-American media studies since Raymond Williams's *Television: Technology and Cultural Form* (London: Fontana, 1974) is less clear-cut than even suggested by the usual heuristic disclaimers. In the following, I will use the adjective "serial" as a general term for all types of commercial seriality, not just narratives extending story arcs over many episodes. In fact, my own distinction between series and oeuvres makes such "serials" into a subtype of the first category (whereas so-called miniseries—preestablished structures with a limited number of episodes usually produced en bloc prior to their initial reception—fall under the category of oeuvre or work).

7. The best discussion of narrative complexity in contemporary American television is one of the first: Jason Mittell, "Narrative Complexity and American Television," *Velvet Light Trap* 58 (2006): 29–40.

8. It is worth mentioning that *The Wire*'s wish to distance itself from other HBO competitors felicitously feeds back into HBO's business model. In fact, this feedback plays a decisive part in the show's sustained success—a success that cannot be measured in ratings or Emmys won, but might well depend on the fact, often emphasized, that the show won no Emmys and had remarkably low ratings. (Things might look different for DVD sales.) In the subscription model of television, prestige can translate directly into money.

9. On the influence of naturalism on *The Wire*, see also J. M. Tyree, "*The Wire*: The Complete Fourth Season," *Film Quarterly* 61.3 (2008): 36; and Ryan Aiello, "*The Wire*: Politics, Postmodernism and the Rebirth of American Naturalism," M.A. thesis, California State University, Chico, 2010.

10. Hence *The Wire*'s conspicuous aversion to the idea of inventing things. When, in the fifth season, the hierarchy of fact and fiction is inverted, as if by way of experiment, the results are perverse representations. A bad reporter, Templeton, makes up imaginary informants and a serial killer to advance his career. Significantly, *The Wire* associates this wickedness with realist *fiction*: The man is in search of "the whole Dickensian aspect" when he spends a night with the homeless to get the feel of the street. ("The Dickensian Aspect" is the title of episode 56; the newspaper's executive editor tells Templeton that this is what he expects from him.)

11. Altogether, *The Wire*'s acclaimed multiperspectivity is not fundamentally different from the pliability of conventional serial ensemble casts. Characterization in *The Wire* puts a premium on charisma and physical beauty (Stringer Bell, McNulty, Kima); contrastive couplings are common (McNulty and Bunk, Stringer and Barksdale, etc.); free agents (Omar, Cutty) are positioned in heroic counterpoint to the constraints of institutional systems; "framing" figures map the show's moral universe (the Greek, Marlo, and the newspaper

editors as "the natural endpoint[s]," respectively, "for corner culture," global-ized capitalism, and media corruption). Omar, the desperado, is clearly modeled on legendary Western characters, down to his shotgun, duster, and personal code without specification to what it entails. Omar's initial quirks—buying Honey Nut Cheerios in his pajamas—are considerably toned down in later seasons in favor of mythological resonances immediately comprehensible to a media-savvy audience.

12. See detective Lester Freamon in *The Wire:* "We're building something here . . . and all the pieces matter." This sentence, spoken within the diegesis, at the same time lets the viewers know how the series wants to be seen (or watched)—and quite successfully so, judged by the frequency with which it is repeated in analytical articles. For the term "narrative totalization," compare John Kraniauskas, "Elasticity of Demand: Reflections on *The Wire*," *Radical Philosophy* 154 (2009): 27, published in this volume.

13. Compare Andreas Jahn-Sudmann: "An essential function of any series consists in reducing self-generated complexities or organizing them in such a manner that they are narratively clear and comprehensible" ("Serienzeit und serielle Zeitlichkeit," *Zeitschrift für Medienwissenschaft*, March 2011, http://www.zfmedienwissenschaft.de/index.php?TID=54 [accessed May 20, 2011], my translation).

14. It is a question of a different order, although important, how discourses of American TV reverberate in other countries. This question can be ignored in the present context because scholarly activities in non-English-speaking coun-tries are largely irrelevant for research practices within the United States. In the United States, the field of American studies is only rarely compelled to imagine itself open to competent outside descriptions, especially if they are phrased in foreign languages. The field tends to conceive of American studies outside the United States, not as offering the possibility of epistemologically advantaged redescriptions, but, if at all, as part of its own transnational diversity (see Kel-leter, "Transnationalism: The American Challenge," *Review of International American Studies* 2.3 [2007]: 29–33).

15. Angela Anderson, "No Such Thing as Good and Evil: *The Wire* and the Humanization of the Object of Risk in the Age of Biopolitics," *darkmatter* 4 (2009), http://www.darkmatter101.org/site/2009/05/29/no-such-thing-as-good-and-evil-thewire-and-the-humanization-of-the-object-of-risk-in-the-age-of-bio-politics/ (accessed October 7, 2010); Blake D. Ethridge, "Baltimore on *The Wire:* The Tragic Moralism of David Simon," in *It's Not TV: Watching HBO in the Post-television Era*, ed. Marc Leverette, Brian L. Ott, and Cara Louise Buckley (New York: Routledge, 2008), 155 (Ethridge makes direct reference to Simon); Lawrence Lanahan, "Secrets of the City: What *The Wire* Reveals about Urban Journalism," *Columbia Journalism Review*, January–February 2008, 24.

16. For example, "*The Wire* presents a complex and nuanced portrait of

American urban culture that transcends cynicism with a faith in the complexity of people and circumstances." Ralph Beliveau and Laura Bolf-Beliveau, "Posing Problems and Picking Fights: Critical Pedagogy and the Corner Boys," in *The Wire: Urban Decay and American Television*, ed. Tiffany Potter and C. W. Marshall (New York: Continuum, 2009), 102.

17. Beliveau and Bolf-Beliveau, "Posing," 102; Peter Clandfield, "'We Ain't Got No Yard': Crime, Development, and Urban Environment," in Potter and Marshall, *The Wire*, 37–49; James Braxton Peterson, "Corner-Boy Masculinity: Intersections of Inner-City Manhood," in Potter and Marshall, *The Wire*, 107–21; Peter Suderman, "Tension City," *National Review*, April 21, 2008, 59–60; Jason Read, "Stringer Bell's Lament: Violence and Legitimacy in Contemporary Capitalism," in Potter and Marshall, *The Wire*, 124; Boyd Blundell, "Social Justice and the Wire," Department of Religious Studies, Loyola University, first-year seminar syllabus, n.d., http://img.slate.com/media/8/WireSyllabus.pdf (accessed July 8, 2010); "ESRC Conference: *The Wire* as Social Science Fiction?" November 26–27, 2009, Leeds Town Hall, ESRC Centre for Research on Socio-Cultural Change, n.d., http://www.cresc.ac.uk/events/Wireconference.html and www.cresc.ac.uk/events/wire_programme.html (accessed October 15, 2010). Papers from this conference were published in the journal *City*, 14.5 and 14.6 (2010). The show can also disprove positions: Dawinder Sidhu uses it as "an element of practical reality" that "challenges" the constitutional theories of Charles Posner ("Wartime America and *The Wire*: A Response to Posner's Post-9/11 Constitutional Framework," *George Mason University Civil Rights Law Journal* 20.1 [2009], http://papers.ssrn.com/sol3/papers.cfm?abstract_id=1414006#%23 [accessed August 28, 2010]).

18. "ESRC Conference." At its broadest and least concrete, this argument underlines the didactic value of *The Wire* "as a conversation starter about crises of the human condition" (with all the troubling implications this phrase holds for an auto-utilitarian notion of didacticism). At least one contribution to the ESRC conference feels it has to stress that *The Wire*, despite its utility for the classroom, "should not be regarded as a replacement for qualitative ethnographic research."

19. William J. Wilson and Anmol Chaddha, "Why We're Teaching 'The Wire' at Harvard," *Washington Post*, September 12, 2010, http://www.hks.harvard.edu/newsevents/news/commentary/teaching-the-wire-at-harvard (accessed October 12, 2010). Wilson's participation is interesting because his sociological work has criticized popular media for covering urban poverty chiefly as a problem of individual lifestyles ("culture of poverty"), with little room left for narratives and images that stress systemic conditions or larger economic frameworks (see Wilson, *When Work Disappears: The World of the New Urban Poor* [New York: Knopf, 1996]). Thus, Wilson is very much aware of fiction's power to shape

social attitudes, and he is in a good position to recognize—and applaud—*The Wire*'s achievements in challenging representational conventions of race and class. (Walter Benn Michaels's endorsement of the series follows similar insights; see "Going Boom," *Bookforum*, February–March 2009, http:www.book forum.com/inprint/015_05/3274 [accessed October 7, 2010].) All the more striking is Wilson's and other critics' readiness to downplay the fabricated character of a commercial story-world that is an active player in the very society they are describing.

20. "ESRC Conference."

21. The ESRC conference describes the television series as a "popular culture laboratory," where "ethnographic research on the city" is "translated" into fiction. Thus, *The Wire*'s representation of Baltimore's educational system is described as "one of the ideal frames where the fictional side of the show turns into reality" ("ESRC Conference").

22. See David Alff reading *The Wire* as "a televisual annotation of regional history." David Alff, "Yesterday's Tomorrow Today: Baltimore and the Promises of Reform," in Potter and Marshall, *The Wire*, 26.

23. Compare Simon: "The story is labeled as fiction, which is to say we took liberties in a way that journalism cannot and should not do." David Simon, introduction to *The Wire: Truth Be Told*, ed. Rafael Alvarez (Edinburgh: Canongate, 2009), 1–31, 29. Compare the definition of *The Wire* as an "obsodrama": a documentary that has been fictionalized to remove legal constraints ("ESRC Conference"). See also Clandfield about the show's "constructive use of fictional license" and "legitimate tactical response to the misrepresentation of inner cities" ("We Ain't Got," 44).

24. "ESRC Conference."

25. See Jane Gibb and Roger Sabin, "Who Loves Ya, David Simon?" *darkmatter* 4 (2009), http://www.darkmatter101.org/site/2009/05/29/who-loves-ya-david-simon (accessed October 7, 2010). Even the representation of sex is driven by an attempt at inverting stereotypes: Sexual relations between white characters are marked by a passionate loss of control, whereas sexual relations between black characters are largely depicted as caring and sensuous affairs. (I am indebted to Markus Engelhardt for this observation.)

26. Harvey Cormier, "Bringing Omar Back to Life." *Journal of Speculative Philosophy* 22.3 (2008): 205–13.

27. James Williams, "The Lost Boys of Baltimore: Beauty and Desire in the Hood," *Film Quarterly* 62.2 (2008): 58. Williams continues: "[*The Wire*] evokes at times the imagery of black homo-thug gay porn websites." Gangster hunks and dashing officers "in their heightened availability and vulnerability [constitute] one of the great unavowed pleasures of *The Wire*. What is one person's urban nightmare is another man's fantasy" (59).

28. Daniel McNeil, "White Negroes and *The Wire*," *darkmatter* 4 (2009), http://www.darkmatter101.org/site/2009/05/29/white-negroes-and-the-wire/ (accessed October 7, 2010).

29. Afaa M. Weaver, "Baltimore before *The Wire*," in Potter and Marshall, *The Wire*, 16–18. For "documentary fallacy," see Courtney Marshall and Tiffany Potter, "'I Am the American Dream': Modern Urban Tragedy and the Borders of Fiction," in Potter and Marshall, *The Wire*, 9.

30. Judd Franklin, "Common Ground: The Political Economy of *The Wire*," *darkmatter* 4 (2009), http://www.darkmatter101.org/site/2009/05/29/common-ground-thepolitical-economy-of-the-wire/ (accessed October 15, 2010).

31. Christian Lander, *Stuff White People Like: The Definitive Guide to the Unique Taste of Millions* (New York: Random House, 2008), 108–10.

32. "We, *The Wire* Discussion Group at the University of Leeds" takes collective hold of the drama of marginalization, declaring that "the series also came to symbolise our own problematic relationship with an academic institution in which we all play, at best, marginal roles" ("ESRC Conference").

33. Marshall and Potter, "I Am," 13.

34. Lisa W. Kelly, "Casting *The Wire*: Complicating Notions of Performance, Authenticity, and "Otherness,'" *darkmatter* 4 (2009), http://www.darkmatter101.org/site/2009/05/29/casting-the-wire-complicating-notionsof-performance-authenticity-and-otherness/ (accessed June 7, 2010).

35. Marshall and Potter, "I Am," 12. The *New York Times* called the wedding "a street version of Cinderella and Prince Charming" (Ian Urbina, "From Two Broken Lives to One Beginning," *New York Times*, August 9, 2007, http://www.nytimes.com/2007/08/09/us/09baltimore.html?pagewanted=all [accessed September 30, 2010]). Simon himself pitched the story to the *Times*, insisting that there would be not only an article but also a "Vows" piece (see Margaret Talbot, "Stealing Life: The Crusader behind "The Wire,'" *New Yorker*, October 22, 2007, http://www.www.newyorker.com/reporting/2007/10/22/071022fa_fact_talbot [accessed July 9, 2010]).

36. Kelly, "Casting *The Wire*." See also Marshall and Potter, "I Am," 10.

37. Marsha Kinder, "Re-writing Baltimore: The Emotive Power of Systemics, Seriality, and the City," *Film Quarterly* 62.2 (2008): 54. See also Kelly, "Casting *The Wire*."

38. See Kelleter, "Serienhelden sehen dich an," *Psychologie Heute* 38.4 (2011): 70–75; similarly Ash Sharma, "'All the Pieces Matter': Introductory Notes on *The Wire*," *darkmatter* 4 (2009), http://www.darkmatter101.org/site/2009/05/29/editorial-all-thepieces-matter-introductory-notes-on-the-wire/ (accessed October 7, 2010).

39. In a similar manner, the final season's wrap-up ending—"an almost absurdly exhaustive festival of closure"—reinforces *The Wire*'s ambitions toward narrative totality (Adam Sternbergh, "Sternbergh on 'The Wire' Finale: The

Anti-'Sopranos'," *New York Magazine,* March 10, 2008, http://nymag.com/daily/entertainment/2008/03/sternbergh_on_the_wire_finale.html [accessed August 19, 2010]). The deceits of the fictional *Baltimore Sun* that are told about *in* the final season ultimately emphasize the veracity *of* the show's own naturalistic reportage.

40. Venkatesh's gangsters would like to see more winners and losers in the story, not everyone defeated (which they take to be typical for a narrative authored by a white writer), more sex, especially between black and white characters, more dominant female characters in the ghetto, less concession to the serial demands of suspense and revenge plots ("In the ghetto, you never have this kind of thing last so long. People kill each other right away, or not at all"), and less stress on the complexity of business transactions ("The one thing I don't like about this show is you never make plans when you're hustling. Not for more than a few days anyway"); see Sudhir Venkatesh, "What Do Real Thugs Think of *The Wire?* Part Seven," *Freakonomics,* February 22, 2008, http://freakonomics.blogs.nytimes.com/2008/02/22/what-do-real-thugs-think-of-thewire/ (accessed October 20, 2010).

41. Venkatesh, *Gang Leader for a Day: A Rogue Sociologist Takes to the Streets* (New York: Penguin, 2008); Venkatesh, "What Do Real Thugs Think of *The Wire?*" *Freakonomics,* January 9, 2008, http://freakonomics.blogs.nytimes.com/2008/01/09/what-do-real-thugsthink-of-the-wire/ (accessed October 20, 2010); "What Do Real Thugs Think of *The Wire?* Part Three," *Freakonomics,* January 25, 2008, http://freakonomics.blogs.nytimes.com/2008/01/25/what-do-real-thugs-think-of-thewire/ (accessed October 20, 2010).

42. Mark Bowden, "The Angriest Man in Television," *Atlantic,* January 2008, http://www.theatlantic.com/magazine/archive/2008/01/the-angriest-man-in-television/6581 (accessed October 7, 2010).

43. See Simon: "I enjoy Shakespeare but *The Wire* is definitely not influenced by the good-evil continuum that seems to begin with Shakespearean drama. It's more about fate and systematic predestination, with the Olympian gods supplanted by postmodern institutional authority" (Talbot, "Stealing Life"). For academic reproductions of the Greek drama connection, see Ethridge, "Baltimore on *The Wire.*" Reihan Salam holds that the show's fatalism "transcends ideology: it strengthens the hand of paternalists of the left and determinists of the right. In that regard, the show is frankly destructive" ("The Bleakness of *The Wire,*" *American Scene,* January 1, 2008, http://theamericanscene.com/2008/01/01/the-bleakness-of-the-wire [accessed October 29, 2010]). Erika Johnson-Lewis, oddly to me, sees a contradiction between *The Wire*'s interest in institutional structures (its fatalism) and the supposedly detrimental effects of extended serial storytelling on activist empathy: "it wallows far too long in the decay and dejection of contemporary urban life" ("The More Things Change, the More They Stay the Same: Serial Narrative on *The Wire,*" *darkmatter* 4 [2009], http://

www.darkmatter101.org/site/2009/05/29/the-more-things-change-the-more-theystay-the-same-serial-narrative-on-the-wire/ [accessed October 7, 2010]).

44. See Salam: "I'm struck by how many of my friends believe they have more refined moral sensibilities because they watch and swear by *The Wire,* as though it gives them a richer appreciation of the *real* struggles of inner-city life, despite the fact that they are exactly as insulated as they were before" ("Bleakness"). Similarly, Johnson-Lewis argues that the show "leave[s] the viewer to feel secure in his or her moral superiority for watching the gritty realism of *The Wire*" ("The More Things Change").

45. For "irredeemable," see Johnson-Lewis, "The More Things Change."

46. Peter Dreier and John Atlas, "Bush-Era Fable about America's Urban Poor?" *City & Community* 8.3 (2009): 332 (published in this collection). The authors see *The Wire* as "similar to much of American sociology" in this regard, "which, despite its reform impulse, is better at describing the various forms of inequality and injustice in society than at identifying the political opportunities that make mobilization and reform possible" (331).

47. Ethridge, "Baltimore on *The Wire*," 163–64.

48. Bowden, "Angriest Man in Television"; Dreier and Atlas, "Bush-Era," 332–33.

49. The record may be less impressive for female characters. For Omar as "a kind of *agent provocateur,*" see Kathleen LeBesco, "'Gots to Get Got': Social Justice and Audience Response to Omar Little," in Potter and Marshall, *The Wire,* 217.

50. Lanahan, "Secrets of the City," 29.

51. Ed Burns, Dennis Lehane, George Pelecanos, Richard Price, and David Simon, "*The Wire*'s War on the Drug War," *Time,* March 5, 2008, http://www.time.com/time/nation/article/0,8599,1719872,00.html (accessed October 7, 2010).

52. Alasdair McMillan, "Dramatizing Individuation: Institutions, Assemblages, and *The Wire*," *Cinephile* 4 (2008), http://cinephile.ca/archives/volume-4-post-genre/dramatizing-individuation-institutions-assemblages-and-the-wire (accessed June 10, 2010).

53. Ibid.

54. Alasdair McMillan, "Heroism, Institutions, and the Police Procedural," in Potter and Marshall, *The Wire,* 53.

55. Sophie Fuggle, "Short Circuiting the Power Grid: *The Wire* as Critique of Institutional Power," *darkmatter* 4 (2009), http://www.darkmatter101.org/site/2009/05/29/shortcircuiting-the-power-grid-the-wire-as-critique-of-institutional-power/ (accessed October 7, 2010); McMillan, "Dramatizing"; McMillan, "Heroism," 54; William Rodney Herring, "'There's Never Been a Paper Bag for Drugs. Until Now.' Or, What Is 'Real Police Work'?" February 18, 2008, http://locus.cwrl.utexas.edu/herring/node/111 (accessed June 24, 2010).

56. McMillan, "Heroism," 51.

57. "[It] doesn't simply reproduce or 'comment' upon social reality, but sets out instead to unravel the twisted fabric of social assemblages" (McMillan, "Dramatizing").

58. Ibid. Also see Herring about *The Wire*'s potential "to resist discipline" ("There's Never Been"). Compare also Sharma, "All the Pieces Matter."

59. Joseph Schaub, "*The Wire:* Big Brother Is Not Watching You in Bodymore, Murdaland," *Journal of Popular Film and Television* 38.3 (2010): 126. Schaub writes: "The fact that *The Wire* uses the banner of 'fiction' to tell stories premised on reality should hardly come as a surprise in an era when the banner of 'reality' is so often used to market shows with an obviously fictitious premise" (130). Schaub does not address *The Wire*'s own narcissistic promptings within and without its narrative. Instead, he accepts season 5's self-characterization as media-critical "watchdog for democracy" (130).

60. See section 3 of the larger essay from which this essay is drawn (to be published separately).

61. See Dan Rowe and Marti Cecilia Collins: "our study found that *The Wire* was not entirely successful at avoiding clichés and stereotypes that are entrenched in most procedural crime dramas." At the same time, the study describes Foucault's concept of governmentality as "one of the most useful . . . explanations of power" because it demonstrates "that Western liberal democracies have systematically found ways to assert control over virtually every aspect of life" ("Power Wire: Understanding the Depiction of Power in TV Drama," *Journal of the Institute of Justice & International Studies* 9 [2009]: 182).

62. Sara Taylor, "*The Wire:* Investigating the Use of a Neoliberal Institutional Apparatus and a 'New Humanist' Philosophical Apparatus," *darkmatter* 4 (2009), http://www.darkmatter101.org/site/2009/05/29/the-wire-investigating-the-use-of-aneoliberal-institutional-apparatus-and-a-new-humanist-philosophical-apparatus/ (accessed October 7, 2010).

63. Ryan Brooks, "The Narrative Production of 'Real Police,'" in Potter and Marshall, *The Wire,* 73. The following quote is on pp. 64–66.

64. Ted Nannicelli, "It's All Connected: Televisual Narrative Complexity," in Potter and Marshall, *The Wire,* 190.

65. See Nannicelli declaring that *The Wire* is less conventional than the cinematic "network narratives" analyzed by David Bordwell and Kristen Thompson (ibid., 195). On the tendency of serial narratives to surpass or outbid each other, see the project "The Dynamics of Serial Outbidding *(Überbietung):* Contemporary American Television and the Concept of Quality TV," directed by Andreas Jahn-Sudmann and myself as part of the research unit "Popular Seriality" (n. 4 above).

66. Kinder, "Re-writing Baltimore," 54.

67. Gibb and Sabin, "Who Love's Ya." For *Dragnet,* see Jason Mittell, "All in

the Game: *The Wire*, Serial Storytelling, and Procedural Logic," in *Third Person: Authoring and Exploring Vast Narratives*, ed. Pat Harrigan and Noah Wardrip-Fruin (Cambridge: MIT Press, 2008), 434; *Television and American Culture* (New York: Oxford University Press, 2010), 181; and especially *Genre and Television: From Cop Shows to Cartoons in American Culture* (New York: Routledge, 2004), 121–52.

68. Mittell, "All in the Game," 429, 434, 431. Quotations in the following paragraph are from pp. 433, 432, 435.

69. Compare Simon: "We are cautious about allowing any feedback to induce us to appease or please viewers . . . [V]iewers generally don't know what is good for them as an audience, or for *The Wire*. . . . So I'm afraid we are not at all open to suggestion or petition when it comes to character or story" (Jim King, "Exclusive David Simon Q & A: Personal Interview," *Borderline Productions*, August 16, 2006, http://www.Borderline-productions.com/TheWireHBO/exclusive-1. html [accessed June 7, 2010]).

70. In addition to the contributions mentioned in this chapter, there are only a few attempts to discuss *The Wire* in such terms, mostly focused on generic configurations. Linda Williams, for example, taught the series at UC Berkeley with regard to its melodramatic aspects (see Drake Bennett, "This Will Be on Midterm. You Feel Me?" *Slate*, March 24, 2010, http://www.slate.com/id/2245788/ [accessed July 8, 2010]). Amanda Ann Klein examines the show's adherence to and deviation from conventions of melodrama and sentimentality ("'The Dickensian Aspect': Melodrama, Viewer Engagement, and the Socially Conscious Text," in Potter and Marshall, *The Wire*, 177–89).

71. Let me be clear that "more likely" does not mean "generally predisposed." Celebratory readings prevail in non-American settings as well, including my own academic culture in Germany.

72. "ESRC Conference."

73. These issues are taken up in a third section ("Habits") of the longer essay from which this chapter is derived. Like almost all stories America has told about itself, *The Wire* stages and engages basic issues of national existence: What, in America, constitutes reality? What constitutes society? What constitutes identity? Consistent with the approach followed so far, the answers offered by *The Wire* to these questions should be regarded, not as the series' actual meanings, but perhaps its most lively ones: effective commonplaces of cultural reproduction.

3

Rewiring Baltimore: The Emotive Power of Systemics, Seriality, and the City

Marsha Kinder

Among the most striking things about *The Wire* are the breadth and depth of its systemic analysis of urban corruption in Baltimore and the emotional power it elicits. I will argue that these dynamics are made possible by leveraging the full narrative potential of television, particularly the expansive narrative space provided by seriality and ensemble casting, which accommodates the city as the primary unit of analysis.

The Networked City as Intertext

Through its network of intertextual allusions (to TV, cinema, literature, theater, and journalism), which continues growing through the final episode (with its pointed references to Shakespeare, Kafka, and H. L. Mencken), *The Wire* explicitly mentions both precursors and foils, with which it should be compared, training us how to remix or resist what we previously have been encouraged to admire. In season 5, metro editor Gus Haynes (Clark Johnson) tells his staff of writers at the *Baltimore Sun* (the paper where series creator David Simon was a crime reporter for twelve years): "There are a million stories in this naked city, but you mooks only have to bring in two or three." When Simon came to visit TV critic Howard Rosenberg's class at USC on March 3, 2008, he acknowledged *Naked City* as an important influence on *The Wire*. (Unless otherwise noted, quotations from Simon in this essay are taken from this visit.) Running from 1958 to 1963 on ABC, this classic TV cop series broke new ground with its gritty realism and its narrative focus on New York City. Yet an urban focus doesn't guarantee systemic analysis, as demonstrated not only by *Naked City* but also by one of *The Wire*'s primary foils, *CSI: Crime Scene Investigation*, the most popular crime series currently on TV. In the final season of *The Wire*, a glib psychologist offers his services as a criminal profiler, citing his previous work for CSI, and is summarily rejected. Set in glamorous Las Vegas, the city where no one is held accountable for their actions and where chance rules supreme, *CSI* uses its location as ironic backdrop for its optimistic depiction of infallible scientific police work, which spares no expense. But *CSI* never illuminates its urban context—either its actual setting of Las Vegas or the city of Los Angeles, whose race-based trials of O. J. Simpson and the cops who battered Rodney King and their disturbing outcomes help explain the popular appeal of this escapist procedural series. As strategic sites for its formulaic spin-offs, *CSI* chose Miami and New York, cities associated thematically with international drug wars and the terrorist disaster of 9/11, and commercially with popular precursors like *Miami Vice*, *NYPD Blue*, and *New York Undercover*.

In contrast, *The Wire* is committed to a systemic analysis of Baltimore, combining narrative strategies from two earlier TV Baltimore crime series with which Simon was personally connected. *Homicide: Life on the Street* (1993–99), a realistic TV police series based on Simon's nonfiction book, *Homicide: A Year on the Killing Streets*, focused primarily on cops rather than criminals who changed from week to week; and Simon's own 2000 HBO miniseries, *The Corner*, based on a nonfiction book he cowrote with Ed Burns (*The Corner: A Year in the Life of an Inner-City Neighborhood*), had a narrower narrative field (one year in the life, on one corner, in one season comprised of six episodes). This series was better suited to the family as the basic unit of analysis, for it lacked the broad canvas of *The Wire*, whose first season combined cops from homicide with drug dealers on the corner. (The casting of Clark Johnson, one of the cops from *Homicide*, in *The Wire* emphasizes the connection between the two series.) Simon says when he first proposed *The Wire* series to HBO, he mentioned only the drug war—not his goal of building a city and performing a systemic analysis that would dramatize the dire need for policy reform.

Yet this narrative focus on the city distinguishes both *The Wire* and *Naked City* from other successful serial crime fiction structured around the family—like the HBO series *The Sopranos* (1999–2007) and Francis

Ford Coppola's cinematic *Godfather* trilogy (1972, 1974, and 1990), neither of whose systemic analyses rivals the breadth of that found in *The Wire*. Instead, their focus on the multigenerational crime family brings a strong dimension of melodrama into the gangster genre. The Corleones may stand in for America, but it is the family's ups and downs and internecine betrayals that raise the story to tragedy, and Coppola's casting of Robert De Niro, Marlon Brando, and Al Pacino that keeps us sutured into who's in charge. *The Sopranos* (which ran for six seasons) used its enlarged canvas to go into greater emotional depth for its array of complex characters. But, despite the breadth and high-quality acting of its ensemble cast, there was never any doubt over who was the protagonist: it was Tony Soprano's family that was being investigated, and his memories, phobias, and dreams that were being subjected to depth analysis.

Systemic Suture

While *The Wire* is not the first work of crime fiction to perform such a systemic analysis of corruption, it may be the most successful in making it emotionally compelling; for systemics usually demand a critical distance that is incompatible with most forms of character identification. I am arguing that the uniqueness of the series depends on this combination, whose most interesting precedents (both precursors and foils) come from cinema rather than television. As foils, I'm thinking of the emotional distance in political films like Francesco Rosi's *Salvatore Giuliano* (1960), a dialectic reconstruction of the famous bandit's relationship to political and economic power, or in most of Jean-Luc Godard's reflexive works from the late 1960s and early 1970s, including *Weekend* and *Two or Three Things I Know About Her* (both 1967), which reject realism and emotional suture altogether. Significantly, Simon cites Stanley Kubrick's *Paths of Glory* (1957) as his primary cinematic model and "the most important political film in history," a war film that succeeds in combining systemic analysis with more traditional forms of realism and emotional identification. Yet one can also find this combination in other cinematic precursors within the crime film genre, like Fritz Lang's *M* (1931) and John Mackenzie's *The Long Good Friday* (1980). In moving their focus from a fascinating individual criminal to a broader analysis of the culture that creates and destroys him, they design narrative strategies that are expanded in *The Wire*.

M moves from the compulsive pedophile (played by Peter Lorre) to the police and criminals pursuing him, who increasingly become mirror images of each other. This reflective relationship (like the one between drug dealers and cops in *The Wire*'s first season) proves more terrifying than the irrational acts of the child-killer (however heinous his uncontrollable urges and crimes). The relationship becomes central to the film's systemic analysis of Germany, which prefigured the rise of the Third Reich. This kind of reflective relationship between both sides of the law can also be found in later serial crime fiction like the *Godfather* trilogy, but nowhere is it developed more expansively than in *The Wire*.

The Long Good Friday focuses on an ambitious London gangster, Harold Shand (Bob Hoskins), who, like *The Wire*'s equally charismatic drug dealer Stringer Bell (Idris Elba), tries to go legit by investing in his city's docklands as a future site for the Olympics. Describing himself as "not a politician, but a businessman with an historical sense and global perspective," he fails to understand how the emergent power of the IRA challenges his old-fashioned conception of empire. His political naivety prevents him from seeing beyond the gangster paradigm. In the final close-up when Harold is about to be whacked, he finally realizes his opponents are international terrorists rather than local mobsters, that this movie is a European political thriller rather than an Anglicized Hollywood gangster film, and that he has misunderstood the power dynamics both of the genre and of globalism. If we can't read this close-up, then we misunderstand the movie and its prophetic analysis of Thatcherism in the 1980s. Similarly, despite Stringer's intelligence and driving ambitions, he is still too naive to understand the power dynamics that drive the so-called legitimate worlds of business, law, and politics (dynamics that his young successor Mario Stanfield [Jamie Hector] will also have to fathom). In both crime narratives, this last-minute gain in systemic understanding helps reconcile these gangsters to their premature death, as if it's a fitting tragic payoff for their respective transformations.

Despite the deep pessimism of *The Wire*'s systemic analysis of our crumbling cities and pervasive corruption, unlike these precursors it achieves a delicate emotional balance, for it is not merely one charismatic outlaw who must be transcended, but several promising yet vulnerable characters who generate a series of transformative moments season after season. As actor Jamie Hector put it in an article titled "*Wire* Leaves a Legacy of Hope," which appeared in the *Los Angeles*

Times on the night the final episode was aired, "I believe he [David Simon] is saying there is hope through the people in the institutions."[1] Not restricted to any single family, race, class, gender, sexual persuasion, or generation (though the youngsters from season 4 are the most poignant), these promising characters keep emerging on both sides of the law. The emotional power of the series depends on this dynamic tension between, on the one hand, having so many vibrant characters with enormous potential and, on the other hand, seeing how the culture is wired to destroy them. What results is serial tragedy with a systemic form of suture, which inspires awe and pity week after week and makes it difficult for viewers to turn away.

Although Simon claims that *The Wire* is more about class rather than race ("I just happened to be doing a series about a city that's 65% black . . . *Homicide* already covered race"), the fact that most of these complex characters are African American and most of them brilliantly played by actors we've never previously seen—these facts alone create a sense of hope. As actress Sonja Sohn, who plays Kima Greggs, puts it in the same *Los Angeles Times* feature: "This cast might not be here if there was no hope in the ghetto."[2] *The Wire*'s emphasis on black characters marks an important departure from successful serial crime precursors like the *Godfather* trilogy and *The Sopranos*, whose more traditional Italian American characters share middle America's racism against African Americans, a dimension that might regrettably make it easier for white viewers to identify with them. Aware that this emphasis on race might reduce the size of his audience but determined to pursue it as part of his systemic analysis, Simon acknowledges: "We have more working black actors in key roles than pretty much all the other shows on the air. And yet you still hear people claim they can't find good African-American actors." It is this "richness of the black community," as actor Lance Reddick (who plays Cedric Daniels) calls it, that makes the series "so different from anything that's been on television."[3]

Yet we also are aware that every character in the ensemble cast (whether black or white, and no matter how seemingly central) can be killed off at any moment, as in real life, without threatening the systemic level of the series. Nowhere is this awareness more painful than in the murder of the courageous black homosexual assassin Omar Little (brilliantly played by Michael K. Williams), one of the most powerful characters in the series. This chilling event catches us off guard as

Bubbles in the rehab center

much as it does Omar, for he is gunned down not by Mario's "muscle," Chris (Gbenga Akinnagbe) and Snoop (Felicia Pearson), who are doggedly hunting him down, but by the vicious little street-corner kid Kenard (Thuliso Dingwall). In Rosenberg's class, Simon reminded us that midway through season 3, there's a shot of Kenard playing in the street with other kids and picking up a stick and shouting, "It's my turn to play Omar." *The Wire* presents three generations of street killers (Kenard, Mario, and Omar) as victims of the city, whose failed institutions waste their potential. That's why the *Baltimore Sun*'s failure to cover Omar's death, and the dysfunctional police lab's misidentification of his corpse, are almost as chilling as his murder. As Simon says, the series is all about subtext (what's omitted) and the need to change policy. Yet we care deeply about these issues because of our emotional engagement with these characters who emerge from the ensemble cast.

Seriality and the Ensemble Cast

As a miniseries spread over five seasons, *The Wire* has been structured to take full advantage of television's expanded narrative field. It doesn't merely track the longitudinal history of a police investigation or repeat formulaic situations. Each season *The Wire* shifts the focus to a different segment of society: the drug wars, the docks, city politics, education, and the media. It thereby avoids the endgame of the ordinary TV series, as described by Janet Murray in *Hamlet on the Holodeck: The Future of Narrative in Cyberspace:* "When every variation of the situation has been played out, as in the final season of a long-running series, the underlying fantasy comes to the surface. . . . We can look at it directly, with less anxiety, but we also find it less compelling."[4]

Despite its hyperrealism and its array of black characters, the first season is the most conventional segment, for the drug war is a typical topic for crime fiction. Though the series transforms the genre, it first hooks us with the traditional lures of what is being transformed. Like the *Godfather* trilogy, *The Wire* begins with a compelling narrative segment (season 1) that is firmly positioned within the genre, and lets the second segment perform the dramatic rupture. Titled "The Port," season 2 focuses on the loss of blue-collar jobs at the docks, the weakening of unions, and the rise of global capitalism—a dramatic shift that felt like it was introducing an entirely new series. Not only is a new set of characters introduced, but their networked crimes go global. The mysterious bad guy (played by Bill Raymond) is called "the Greek," though his "muscle" is Ukrainian and Israeli, and the new crime family is East European, as are the prostitutes being illegally imported and victimized. This move evokes another cinematic precursor about dock workers (made by a Greek)—Elia Kazan's Oscar-winning *On the Waterfront* (1954). The evocation encourages us to compare what has happened in the interim not only to the unions but also to the rivalries between movies and television for hyperrealistic representation and systemic analysis, as if the narrative format of cinema is now insufficiently expansive for covering the complex networked society. The tragic ending of season 2 was even bleaker than that of its cinematic precursor, with two generations of the Sobotka family totally wiped out and with the only survivors being the cops, the female love interest Beadie Russell (Amy Ryan), who hooks up with Jimmy McNulty (Dominic West) in season 3, and the mysterious Greeks. This allusion also underscores Simon's claim that his primary dramatic model is Greek tragedy, where characters with potential are doomed by larger forces (in this case failing institutions rather than fickle gods). This is the season that feels most unified and self-contained. According to Simon, they got it right and had nothing more to say on this subject. This season performed its function of raising the series to a systemic level of tragedy.

The Conflict between Systemic Analysis and Emotional Suture

In season 2 we also begin to experience a conflict between this systemic analysis of Baltimore and our emotional engagement with the characters with whom we choose to identify. Although in season 1 it's the combination of these two dimensions that defines the uniqueness of *The Wire*, over the arc of the series the conflict between them keeps building until it reaches a climax in season 5, with the storyline of the fake serial killer. Significantly, this scheme is concocted by McNulty as a "creative" way of getting the funding Homicide needs to take down the reigning drug lord, Mario Stanfield. But by the end of the series, viewers are forced to choose between their commitment to a sympathetic character like McNulty and to the truth, which, as in tragedy, is made to seem an absolute value, only because characters are willing to sacrifice anything for it.

Despite the emphasis on black characters, from the very first episode *The Wire* tempts us into thinking that Jimmy McNulty might be the protagonist of the series. Not only is he one of the cops who provide continuity across all five seasons, but he gets the first credit in the opening titles and his face was prominently featured on the posters and on the cover of season 1's DVD. Although Simon claims he cast British actor Dominic West because all the American actors who read for the part had seen too many American cop series and were unable to go beyond the stereotypes, McNulty evokes Al Pacino's Serpico (who is mentioned in one of the episodes), a self-destructive, white antihero who has trouble with authority and whom many female characters find appealing. The fact that he fits this stereotype becomes ironic in season 5 when an FBI psychologist profiling the alleged serial killer comes up with a description that perfectly evokes McNulty. The show continues to monitor McNulty's ups and downs (on the job, on and off the wagon, and in and out of relationships with women), perhaps because, like the black, gay drug addict Bubbles (one of the most likable characters in the series, played by Andre Royo), he is willing to accept blame for his own actions and their impact on other underdogs.

Since no single individual can solve all of the systemic problems raised in the series, we soon realize that it's the relations that count. From the beginning we are led to compare McNulty with at least three other sets of characters. First, he is compared with his former black partners in the Homicide Division: Bunk Moreland (Wendell Pierce), who is more reliable and less flashy, and his subsequent partner, Kima Greggs, a lesbian who shares domestic problems with her partner that are similar to those McNulty experiences with his ex-wife. Despite McNulty's close emotional ties to both, they harshly condemn his "fake serial killer" plot. Second, McNulty is compared to two brainy black cops who share his antagonism toward authority and his passion for inventing creative ways of fighting crime. Yet their schemes (unlike McNulty's) are not based on lies. Lester Freamon (Clarke Peters) designs the original plan for wiretapping the Barksdale gang, and thus is willing to use resources from the fake serial killer plot to revive his own scheme. Bunny Colvin (Robert Wisdom) sets up an unauthorized buffer zone called "Hamsterdam" where dealers and addicts are not arrested, a scheme (like McNulty's) that enables cops to focus on other more important crimes. Although this plan brings down Baltimore's crime rate, Bunny is forced to retire. The schemes of all three characters prove successful, yet once the authorities discover them, the outcomes are reversed, which demonstrates there's something terribly wrong with public policy. All three schemes demonstrate that individuals can make a difference, even if they can't single-handedly solve all of Baltimore's systemic problems.

McNulty is also compared with two deceptive white men from other sectors, who at first seem to have enormous potential. In season 3, Thomas Carcetti (Aiden Gillen) wins the electoral race for mayor as "the great white hope," but by the end of the season proves to be just as corrupt as the black politicians he replaced. Carcetti's connection to McNulty is strengthened by their boyish good looks and their sexual involvement with the same powerful woman (Carcetti's abrasive campaign manager, Theresa D'Agostino, played by Brandy Burre). In season 5, McNulty's compared to the ambitious journalist Scott Templeton (Tom McCarthy), who also fabricates stories. Early in the season, McNulty says, "I wonder what it feels like to work in a real fucking police department," a line later echoed by Scott: "I wonder what it's like to work at a real newspaper." Although it's easy to condemn both Carcetti and Templeton as self-centered careerists with their eyes on the prize (the governor's mansion or a Pulitzer), it's harder to condemn a self-destructive figure like McNulty, whose motives are rarely self-serving. He plays Huck Finn to their Tom Sawyers, yet all three schemers become (as McNulty puts it in the final episode) "trapped in the same lie." The plot of the fake serial killer violates the commitment to truth and realism that *The Wire* demands throughout the series. In the final season we are forced to choose between our commitment to a truthful systemic analysis and our emotional engagement with McNulty, a painful choice already made by his former partners—by Russell (who was ready to leave him), Bunk (who continually condemns him), and Greggs (who exposes the plot to Commissioner Daniels, played by Lance Reddick).

Without betraying McNulty, Bunk chooses the truth, which is hardly surprising. In the first episode of the final season, one of Bunk's lines of dialogue is chosen as an epigraph: "The bigger the lie, the more they believe." Though Bunk was referring to standard interrogation methods found on most conventional cop series, *The Wire* makes us read it (like the other epigraphs) systemically—emphasizing its resonance across the entire series. Like Bunk, the series ultimately chooses truth over emotion, a priority that distinguishes *The Wire* from other TV crime series, yet it acknowledges that many of its careerist characters still stick with the lie. When his fake plot is exposed and he's still not arrested, McNulty rewrites Bunk's line: "The lie's so big, people can't live with it."

That's why *The Wire* ends with the media and focuses on the city newspaper, an institution whose mission is to discover and disseminate the truth. Yet city newspapers across America are rapidly disappearing. Forced to compete with the Internet as a primary source of news, they can no longer afford to retain expensive international bureaus (which are supposed to gather rather than merely remix the news). And their local coverage is forced to compete with the entertainment model of television journalism. According to Simon, in some ways papers like the *Baltimore Sun* may deserve to disappear because they have failed to cover the most important stories in their city, a journalistic task that has been taken over by his own fictional TV series. *The Wire* clearly blames these failed institutions more than the individual criminals they create and destroy. As Snoop puts it, just before she is whacked, "Deserve got nothin' to do with it."

Before the first episode of this final season had been broadcast, some critics were already claiming that its analysis of the media would be less complex and more Manichaean than that found in earlier seasons, perhaps anticipating the usual endgame for a series. Or maybe it was because the final season was focusing on Simon's former home base, the *Baltimore Sun*, where he had worked several years as a crime reporter (and might have personal scores to settle). But no matter how thorough the show's indictment against the media might be, *The Wire* itself is still a powerful counterexample even though it attracted a relatively small audience (around four million viewers per episode, less than half of what *The Sopranos* normally drew). Despite all the critical praise (for its innovative structure, hyperrealism, and brilliant array of black characters), *The Wire* never won an Emmy (whereas *The Sopranos* won twenty-two). Maybe its cast was too black and its analysis too systemic for middle America. Yet *The Wire* still stands out as a subversive alternative—one that maintains the delicate balance between hope and desperation and makes Snoop's dying words reflexive: "Deserve got nothin' to do with it."

The Final Episode: Systemic Closure

The final ninety-minute episode leverages a number of *The Wire*'s earlier strategies to deliver narrative closure while still maintaining systemic suture. The system of rewards and punishments remains consistent with Snoop's realistic analysis. Corrupt careerists like Templeton, Carcetti, Commissioner Bill Rawls (John Doman), and double-dealing Here Hauk (Domenisk Lombardozzi) are rewarded for their dishonesty with big prizes or promotions. In contrast, those with integrity who tried to improve the system—Daniels, McNulty, Freamon, and honest reporter Alma Gutierrez (Michelle Paress)—are shut out of their institutions, where their commitment could (or should) have made a difference. Yet the systemic analysis also enables us to perceive a generational pattern of replacements that might leave us with a glimmer of hope. Michael (Tristan Wilds) steps up to replace Omar; Mario is forced to follow the path pioneered by Stringer; and (if he's lucky and honest) Dukie (Jermaine Crawford), whose parents were junkies, begins the painful cycle of addiction and recovery that was earlier pursued by Bubbles. As the only character in the series who deserves the modest reward he receives, Bubbles is the one exception to this corrupt system of injustice: for he is finally welcomed upstairs and allowed to dine with his sister and nephew. Unlike the others, he can go home again. As

McNulty looks across Baltimore at end of the last episode of *The Wire*

actress Sonja Sohn puts it, "Bubbles is the only character on the whole show that represents hope, and hope that has succeeded at the end of the series."[5]

Yet McNulty also reaps both rewards and punishments. Once his fake serial killer plot is exposed by his former partner Greggs, he has to relinquish his job as detective, which has been the center of his life. Like Freamon, Alma, and Mario, he can't go home again. Yet his refusal to blame all the fake murders on the copycat killer helps him regain other positions that easily could have been lost. He is allowed to stay at home in the relationship with Russell; he is paired with Freamon as "partners in crime"; he is eulogized by Sergeant Jay Landsman (Delaney Williams) in his "fake wake" as "the black sheep" who is "natural police"); and, perhaps most important, he reemerges as potential protagonist. In the process, our emotional engagement with him is restored. Besides being the center of attention at the wake, McNulty is singled out from the ensemble cast in several long takes. These singular moments with McNulty are followed by montage sequences either of Baltimore's cityscape, the fates of other characters, or the city's ordinary citizens, sequences that use the ensemble to reaffirm systemic analysis. Thus the combination of emotional engagement and systemic analysis is restored, and we are left having it both ways: the protagonist is both McNulty and the city of Baltimore, both the individual and the ensemble.

The interplay between individuals and ensemble is also emphasized by a series of key words and phrases that recur throughout the episode like a musical refrain. Some of the phrases express fear ("keep my name out of it"); other words are more hopeful—like the recuperation of "clean" (as in Gus's "I remember clean" and Daniels's insistence on "clean stats"), and the reaffirmation of "home" (which reasserts *The Wire*'s commitment to Baltimore). In this final episode, although several characters refer to the many meanings of home, it is McNulty who gets the last word. As he stands at the side of the freeway, looking at the cityscape, he turns to the homeless man he has brought back to Baltimore, and says: "Let's go home."

Notes

1. Jamie Hector, "*Wire* Leaves a Legacy of Hope," *Los Angeles Times*, March 9, 2008, E1.

2. Ibid., E22.

3. Ibid.

4. Janet Murray, in *Hamlet on the Holodeck: The Future of Narrative in Cyberspace* (Free Press, 1997), 169–70.

5. Hector, "*Wire* Leaves Legacy," E22.

4

"The Game Is the Game": Tautology and Allegory in *The Wire*

Paul Allen Anderson

Omar Little (Michael K. Williams) is waiting to testify for the state at a gang-related murder trial. A sheriff guards him while working on a crossword puzzle. The Greek god of war has the sheriff stumped. His best four-letter guess—Mars—doesn't fit. "Ares," Omar volunteers breezily. "Greeks called him Ares. Same dude, different name is all." Surprised at the cultural literacy of a black hoodlum from Baltimore's West Side, the white sheriff tries out the word and thanks Omar. "It's all good," the witness purrs. "See, back in middle school and all, I used to love the myths. Stuff was deep. Truly" (2: 6).[1] Omar is fearless and open about all his loves. Viewers following *The Wire* already know that Omar is fearless like the Malcolm who shares his surname, but his comment on Greek and Roman mythology further hints at an unusually high awareness of alternative models for behavior in battle. The gods of classical mythology toyed with mortals, while the latter flailed against fate's mysteries and constrictions. According to series creator David Simon, *The Wire* "is a Greek tragedy in which the postmodern institutions are the Olympian forces."[2] A long parade of battered idealists and would-be heroes endure the fateful logics defining the works and days of urban politics, public education, law enforcement, the underground drug economy, organized labor, and the local media in Baltimore. The work of the series' five seasons is to make all the pieces matter, to thread the institutional layers together into a single fabric of ambition and wreckage.

Omar, a hero of the series, sometimes announces "it's all in the game" with a chuckle after he robs the holders of a drug stash at gun-point. The taunt reminds his victims that even he—an openly gay thug unaligned with any gang or network—must count as a player in the drug economy. Players who question the working rules of "the game," especially low-level gang members, suffer grim consequences. Only a lucky few escape alive. Late in the series, we find one such lucky refugee. Malik "Poot" Carr, formerly with the Barksdale crew, is seen working at a nearby Sports Locker store. He wears a referee's jersey and his work uniform figuratively announces his neutrality as he stands on the sidelines outfitting current players of the drug game in the latest apparel.[3] While the game of drug trafficking is central to *The Wire*, many other figurative and literal games make appearances. Alongside the abundance of literal competitive sports and games on display (from boxing to dogfighting to dice), understanding, and often protesting, the explicit and implicit rules of workplace games is a major concern for characters throughout the series.

Early in the first season, D'Angelo Barksdale teaches several members of his crew a lesson about the drug game by talking about an allegorical game—chess. His chess allegory gestures toward an expanded perspective on their precarious lives. If the silent Olympian gods are playing games with mortals trapped in the urban institutions of *The Wire*, it is worthwhile to consider how a few of the series' characters use figurative game-language to enunciate and negotiate their own working lives. Characters with high power like D'Angelo's uncle, Avon Barksdale, work hard to stay ahead in the unpredictable drug business. Their efforts at control include asserting interpretive authority over the game. As part of that discursive effort Avon returns again and again to a signature tautological proverb—*The game is the game*. He means the phrase to reinforce his authority. These two examples, D'Angelo's chess allegory and Avon's signature proverb, reveal how alternating moments of allegorical and tautological interpretation are put to work in *The Wire*. They exemplify the everyday tools of critical analysis immanent to that world but also point to that which is beyond the characters' horizons of understanding.

Tautological phrases like Avon's *The game is the game* function as conservative proverbs or shorthand renderings of an epic worldview defined by necessity and institutional consistency rather than turbulent change and randomness. Allegorical thinking like D'Angelo's, by contrast, promises the beginning of an alternative perspective. Looking beyond the tautological confines of a fate-bound world identical to itself makes possible a vision at once imaginative and historical where *what is* also includes the thought of that *which is not*—and even that *which should be*. That said, the rhetorical alternatives of tautology and allegory are not necessarily antithetical. Allegorical understanding within the drama can provide moments of insight and even a semblance of critical distance, but it cannot overcome the force of constrained agency amid institutional practices and broader structural determinations. An enlightening allegory about chess offers D'Angelo and his young crew members only a distant and ultimately disillusioning glimmer of hope beyond the tautologies ruling their lives. Even Omar cannot imagine rising above the game while he dances around it and revises its rules. Instead of finding liberation from existing institutional games, disillusioned characters must find other ways to manage their position, or, like the gifted detective and builder of dollhouse miniatures Lester Freamon, they must retire to games of the imagination that rest on far more private terms.

The Pawns of Allegory

The traditional notion of allegory is a narrative with two distinct levels of signification. The manifest or exoteric narrative references and runs parallel to an implied prior narrative. An allegorical narrative, in other words, *is what it is* and also *what it is not*. Since the latter narrative remains latent, understanding the relationship between the two levels may require esoteric knowledge or hermeneutic excavation.[4] Some characters of *The Wire*, like the series' writers and critics, warm to the opportunities of allegorical interpretation. The allegorical imagination offers a kind of environmental adaptation through which low-power characters map and interpret their relative powerlessness amid the institutions towering over their lives.[5] Moreover, members of disenfranchised groups and other social outsiders develop interpretive habits and strategies for reading the dominant culture and its ideological supplements skeptically. Such skepticism can fuel bleak humor, as with Richard Pryor's observation about African American men and the criminal justice system: "They give niggers time like it's lunch, down there. You go down there looking for justice; that's what you find: just us."[6]

Pryor's comment differentiates official and street-level social narratives at the site of homophonous pronunciation ("just us" and "justice") to set an observation about widespread bias in penal sentencing ("giving time") alongside an official ideological narrative of justice's color blindness and impartiality. Pryor as a critical allegorist looks beneath the manifest local narrative of justice to uncover latent narratives of racial domination. *The Wire* similarly scratches at narratives meant to legitimate official institutional authority and uncovers a latent reality of corruption, cynicism, and social failure in a postindustrial urban world. Such revelations may not yield blueprints for social transformation, but they can reinforce tactics for personal and small-network survival and negotiation.

As previously noted, allegory and figurative thinking appear early in *The Wire* when the young boss of the low-rises near Franklin Terrace introduces the game of chess to two of his crew members. D'Angelo Barksdale (Larry Gilliard Jr.) finds Bodie Broadus (J. D. Williams) and Wallace (Michael B. Jordan) playing a game of checkers with chess pieces. He urges that they learn chess: "Chess is a better game, yo." The formal simplicity of checkers makes it less challenging and less true to adult life: checkers evokes a social fantasy about the nongendered equality of opportunity as an achieved original position from which all players on the board begin their working lives. By contrast, an explicit division of labor defines the game of chess. Half of a player's pieces are interchangeable soldiers (the pawns), whereas the remaining ones start as pairs with special abilities (rooks, knights, and bishops) or have singular importance (the irreplaceable king and his great protector the queen). D'Angelo holds up different pieces one at a time and explains their roles. He demystifies the intimidating game by leaning on Bodie's and Wallace's prior understandings of the Barksdale operation. In turn, the world of formal rules and roles in chess provides a more abstract perspective on their everyday lives in the mercurial drug game. D'Angelo's allegorization of local institutions sketches a small corner of the kind of cognitive map that might "enable a situational representation on the part of the individual subject to that vaster and properly unrepresentable totality which is the ensemble of society's structures as a whole."[7] Mapping the Barksdale operation allegorically also evokes the series writers' efforts to track the victims of "untethered capitalism run amok" across five seasons. Simon and company want to pur-

D'Angelo tutors Bodie and Wallace on the rules of chess

sue how "power and money actually route themselves in a postmodern American city" in order to illustrate "why we as an urban people are no longer able to solve our problems or heal our wounds."[8] Although the writers uncover far more routing and wiring of what Fredric Jameson calls the "ensemble of society's structures as a whole" than D'Angelo's very local allegory, both mapping efforts ultimately lead to aggrieved and pessimistic conclusions.

"The king stays the king," D'Angelo teaches Wallace and Bodie (1: 3). Alluding to a different sporting game (bowling) to explain the literal and figurative meanings of chess, D'Angelo adds that the king in chess is "the kingpin. . . . Now he the man." Left to himself, the king as father figure is nearly as vulnerable as a pawn because "he ain't got no hustle." Unlike the other nonpawns, the king can only move one square at a time. "But the rest of these motherfuckers on the team, they got his back. And they run so deep, he really ain't gotta do shit." "Like your uncle," Bodie observes. D'Angelo silently agrees. He then holds up the piece that starts the game at the king's side: "Now this the queen. . . . Now she the go-get-shit-done piece." "Remind me of Stringer," Wallace adds. The pawns, D'Angelo continues, are the foot soldiers; they are also the figurative children in an organization ruled by the sentimental yet hard authoritarianism of a charismatic king (Avon Barksdale) and a more rationalistic and lethal queen (Stringer Bell). The pairing of Avon and Stringer on the chessboard transpose gender roles in that here the king stands for the romantic communal values of gemeinschaft (which the writers sometimes sentimentalize), while the queen stands for the economic abstractness and antiromanticism of gesellschaft (which the writers always disparage). Nevertheless, under either dispensation chess pawns still move "one space forward only, except when they fight." The king may have the queen and a whole team watching his back, but the pawns have no one shielding them from the game's brutality. Instead, they shield more powerful pieces. "Everything stay who he is," D'Angelo clarifies, "except for the pawns. . . . Make it all the way down to the other dude's side, he get to be a queen." Pawns may enjoy the unique opportunity of social advancement in chess but they begin with far greater vulnerabilities: "Pawns, man, in the game they get capped quick. They be out the game early." "Unless they some smart-ass pawns," Bodie notes, imagining himself rising in the drug game through hard work. Expecting major opportunities built on Avon's nepotistic favor, D'Angelo does not explicitly present the game as unfair in the chess allegory. That said, on another occasion he protests that "the game ain't got to be played like that" when crew members senselessly beat down some of their clientele (1: 3). The moment of protest foreshadows D'Angelo's later disillusionment with the game and the accompanying rhetoric of Barksdale family loyalty he comes to see as worthless.

D'Angelo wants his crew to start thinking more abstractly about their lives in the game.[9] His chess allegory is involuted, however, because he introduces chess (itself already a political allegory) as repeating the figures and moves of an institution that he and others constantly refer to as "the game." For D'Angelo, the notion of the (drug) game allegorizes the illicit drug economy as not merely a capitalist enterprise based on competition for markets, product, and profit but also an ensemble of rules, neighborhood loyalties, and traditions (such as the "Sunday truce") followed by a set of local Baltimore players. The first season of *The Wire* highlights the self-consciously sporting elements and localism of the game through the annual East Side–West Side basketball game. Suggesting the stability of their operations as social institutions worthy of neighborhood support, Joseph "Proposition Joe" Stewart (Robert Chew) and Avon Barksdale (Wood Harris) coach their teams and agree to bet a "clean six figures" on a nonviolent game played in public before a cross-neighborhood audience (1: 9). Alongside their other activities, these prominent business leaders are de facto community leaders.

Like a king on a chessboard protected by his subordinates, Avon directs his organization but is rarely seen acting in public. He does not personally handle any drugs or participate in gang hits (murders). His pawns (juveniles mostly immune to adult prosecution) handle the product at the level of street sales. The rooks on a chessboard are here "stash houses" and they move regularly to evade detection or theft; cell phones with prepaid minutes are used and then dumped before they can be traced; drug money is laundered into legal investments and enterprises; a downtown lawyer is retained to deal with police interviews, arrests, and court cases. If a criminal organization's leader holds onto power by intimidating others inside and outside his group with the threat of violence, the illegal conspiracy evades law enforcement through coded interactions and limited access points to valuable information. Lieutenant Cedric Daniels's Major Crimes Unit cannot even identify what Avon looks like until Lester Freamon quietly leaves his desk and uses his neighborhood contacts to obtain an old boxing poster featuring Avon's image. Ever the sportsman, Avon moved from the literal sport of boxing and its physical dangers to the figurative sport of the drug game and its dangers. Only rarely do the Barksdale leaders reveal their associations, as when several members of the Major Crimes Unit accidentally happen upon the cross-town basketball challenge. The investigators enjoy a long look at Barksdale acting peaceably in the sporting company of other felons. Most of the time Daniels's unit works to intercept the organizations' criminal calls via wiretapping and decoding a web of esoteric jargon through inference and deduction. Meanwhile, Stringer Bell tutors the Barksdale crew on how to thwart police surveillance by using code words or numbers for criminal activities when making contact on the phone.

Even with such specialized training, low-level employees in a drug conspiracy make little money—less than the minimum wage. They gain local social capital but are in a game where the chance of institutional advancement is very low. An economics best-seller turned to game language to discuss workplace motivation amid low compensation in the drug business and elsewhere. "An editorial assistant earning $22,000 at a Manhattan publishing house, an unpaid high-school quarterback, and a teenage crack dealer earning $3.30 an hour are all playing the same game," the authors wrote, "a game that is best viewed as a tournament." "In order to advance in the tournament," they continued, "you must prove yourself not merely above average but spectacular."[10] When the threats of violent self-endangerment or arrest rise, most teenaged drug dealers leave the tournament because they see the economic opportunities as too low to offset the potential costs. In the world of *The Wire*, by contrast, leaving the drug game is less abstract and simple because of family and peer pressure, employers' suspicions about snitches, and the difficulty of finding any other paying work. The pathos of the pawn's situation is that increased self-awareness and knowledge about the game only increase recognition of one's limited agency and constraint.

Imagined otherwise, a pawn's function in a chess game resembles that of a musical detail in a long-form scored composition. Both are small constituents of a larger whole that takes time to play or follow (hence the priority of allegory and narrative over symbolism and atemporality). The pawn progresses in chess by literally moving forward; most likely it will be vanquished and removed from play. A musical detail can be repeated and kept in play during a composition or transformed into something greater (like a motif or theme); most likely it too will fall away into silence. The composer stands above the musical narrative or composition orchestrating the details of a scored whole as the chess player knowingly sacrifices pawns, knights, and rooks for the sake of a final victory over the rival king. "The musical whole is essentially a whole composed of parts that follow each other for a reason," Adorno observed. "The whole," he continued, "is articulated by relations that extend forward and backward, by anticipation and recollection, contrast and proximity."[11] The class of musical compositions that interested Adorno could be read allegorically in terms of manifest narrative structures about parts and wholes and latent narratives about the movements of individual monads amid a social totality. "Without forcing the interpretation too far," Adorno wrote, "the detail can be understood as the representative of the individual, and the whole as that of the universal."[12] Imagining compositions as social allegories can encourage identification with the individual musical detail as a representative of the monadic individual longing for (and rarely finding) development, social harmonization, and relative autonomy. The individual detail in this picture, however, is hardly the sole author of its movement. If the theorist can only interpret the narrative of a scored composition by viewing it from the bird's-eye view needed to map allegorical structures, how are allegorized individuals or details to map their own possible relationships of "contrast and proximity?" We return then to the scene of D'Angelo allegorical lesson about chess pawns and advancement.

D'Angelo's pedagogical moment encourages Wallace and Bodie to recognize themselves as pawns on a chessboard and also to take the perspective of the unnamed player who uses them and other pieces in the game against another player. The king may be the alter ego of the player in chess, but in the drug game it is not the case that "the king stays the king." Somebody has to wear the crown, but it can circulate even as pawns and other pieces remain on the board. Here the allegorical parallelism between chess pieces and their representatives in the drug game falters in important ways. In the latter case, one might follow Marx and contend that there is an "*alien* social power standing above them." Standing above the game, this impersonal power emerges from the high and low pieces' "mutual interaction as a process and power independent of them."[13] Transcending any given king, this independent power keeps the game in play with an unending and colliding supply of new and old stock kings, pawns, and others. The rare pawn who becomes a queen underscores an ideology of equal opportunity among those with minimal social power. For D'Angelo, Wallace, and Bodie, the dawning of a divided perspective encourages questioning their relative institutional powerlessness amid an endless supply of new pawns. To think allegorically about their situation means temporarily detaching themselves from their everyday perceptions of personal autonomy in order to map their typical work activities amid the broader gamelike structures that constrict their agency. For each of the three characters in the scene of chess pedagogy, the imaginative leap to allegory and cognitive mapping will prove not only disillusioning but fatal.

When hopeful, D'Angelo and Bodie sit on the crushed velvet sofa and consider themselves "smart-ass pawns" who might rise to the power of a chess queen. The unusually empathic Wallace badly needs the income that dealing makes possible but is temperamentally unsuited to gang life. He contemplates a different life outside the game and confides to

D'Angelo, "I just don't want to play no more. I was thinking of going to school" (1: 9). D'Angelo enthuses that Wallace has the potential to end up at Harvard—an even less probable path than a pawn becoming a queen in chess. When D'Angelo protests to Stringer that Wallace should not be killed as a potential snitch, the ruthless queen overrules him. The businessman orders Bodie and Poot to murder their fourteen-year-old friend in the abandoned apartment where he looks after a number of younger children. Wallace's horrific murder by his coworkers is a turning point for *The Wire* and especially for D'Angelo. A pawn can imagine itself in the role of a more powerful chess piece like a king or queen, but it cannot force actual conditions to accommodate its imagining of a new life beyond the drug game and the family business. D'Angelo's disillusioning interpretation of *The Great Gatsby* in a prison reading group (led by real-life novelist and *Wire* writer Richard Price) marries his taste for allegorical interpretation to a newfound fatalism. He is speaking of Jay Gatsby but thinking of himself:

> [Fitzgerald is] saying that the past is always with us. Where we come from. . . . All this shit matters. . . . Like at the end of the book: boats and tides and all. You can change up. . . . But what came first is what you really are and what happened before is what really happened. . . . like all them books in his library. He fronting with all those books. . . . He ain't read near one of them. . . . that shit caught up to him. (2: 6)

The scholarship on class mobility in contemporary America shows that the literal facts of "where we come from" determine our fate more powerfully than one's idealized imaginings or efforts to reinvent oneself beyond the situation and the family one was born into. "What came first," D'Angelo concludes, "is what you really are." The utopian projection of an alternative self-fashioned identity in the present (Gatsby) or in the future (D'Angelo) is, finally, *not what is*. Shortly after agreeing with Fitzgerald's claim that there are no second acts in American life, D'Angelo is strangled to death in the prison library; his body is repositioned to indicate a suicide. Stringer secretly ordered the murder to silence Avon's independent-minded nephew. More generally, the trajectory of the novel-reading allegorist D'Angelo is that of "the problematic individual's journeying toward himself, the road from dull captivity within a merely present reality . . . towards clear self-recognition." As the young Lukács famously sketched the arc of utopian pessimism in the bourgeois novel, "after such self-recognition has been attained, the ideal thus formed irradiates the individual's life as its immanent meaning; but the conflict between what is and what should be has not been abolished and cannot be abolished in the sphere wherein these events take place."[14] As D'Angelo remarks about the distance between Jay Gatsby's low-born past and self-fashioned present, "that shit caught up to him." When he is murdered, the distance between D'Angelo's ideal of *what should be* and *what is* catches up to him as well.

Bodie's demise follows those of D'Angelo and Wallace. He refers back to the lessons of the chess scene as late as the fourth season: "I feel old. I been out there since I was thirteen. I ain't never fucked up a count. Never stole off a package. Never did some shit that I wasn't told to. I've been straight up. But what come back? . . . This game is rigged, man." "We like the little bitches on the chessboard," he admits to Jimmy McNulty (Dominic West). "Pawns," the detective adds (4: 13). McNulty will later borrow Bodie's phrase when he protests that the police "game is rigged" as well. The two eat lunch together in the Cylburn Arboretum, a public garden so peaceful that Bodie cannot believe they are still in Baltimore. Not much older than twenty, he has come to see the drug game as unfair to players like himself. As an employee, he has "been not merely above average but spectacular" and still he does not advance in the tournament. His loyalty and perseverance have not been rewarded over the years, and he is only losing position in the unprecedentedly brutal reign of Marlo Stanfield. Ruthless and quick-witted, Bodie proves himself to be the quintessential "smart-ass pawn" and a deserving contender in any fair tournament. Instead he remains an isolated pawn on a chessboard bereft of orderly advancement according to a rational and predictable institutional scheme. Allegorically reading the drug game as a rigged match where he sees himself as one of "the little bitches on the chessboard" provides Bodie with insight and disillusionment rather than expanded agency.[15] Once again, as with the disillusioned romanticism of D'Angelo before him or Lukács's generic protagonist, "the conflict between what is and what should be has not been abolished and cannot be abolished." The garden conversation with McNulty seals Bodie's fate. There will be no retreat from the game. One of Marlo's soldiers spots him leaving the detective's car at the police station. Though Bodie told McNulty nothing of investigative value, he is gunned down at his corner by Marlo's enforcers. At that point, all three characters from the first season's chess scene have been actively murdered by members of their own team in the chess tournament, a fate distinct from being passively sacrificed by one's king.

If the chessboard flickers with the possibility of upward mobility for a "smart-ass pawn," the thoughtful pawns of *The Wire* find all paths to that ideal blocked: chess's crystalline allegory of work and institutional life stands in stark contrast to the dynamism of "untethered capitalism run amok" in the drug game and elsewhere.[16] Bodie is not rewarded because the figures of authority on the chessboard are not stable enough to accommodate his patient project of orderly advancement. The chess lesson especially fails him when Marlo takes Avon's crown. No stable invisible hand exists to move Bodie and other "straight up" pawns toward their fair rewards in an efficient self-regulating market. Instead he experiences the shocks of a crisis-prone system in microcosm. While Bodie toils at his corner in the retail drug trade, his original king and queen end up dead or in jail within a few years and his last king (Marlo) has him murdered as a precautionary measure. The matter of rulelike stability in the literal chess game and its absence in the drug game turns our inquiry over to its second aspect: Avon Barksdale's regular utterance of the phrase "the game is the game" as a kind of authoritative proverb befitting a lawmaking king. Avon's practice of speaking in authoritative-sounding tautologies amounts to a holding strategy to keep present conditions in place. Beneath such formulas of tautological constancy, however, the institutional structures of *The Wire* are hardly stable. As the series' seasons unfold, the narrative leaves behind the relative consistency and localism of the East Side–West Side rivalry symbolized by the annual crosstown basketball game. Marlo (Jamie Hector) emerges as a more lethal avatar of Stringer's ruthless business logic; unrestrained by old relationships, the young leader seeks to finish off what now looks like the obsolete romantic communalism of old-school gangsters like Avon and Prop Joe. The death-dealing new king encapsulates his reading of the changing situation in a signature remark: "You want it to be one way, but it's the other way" (4: 4).[17]

The Kings of Tautology

Several important characters repeat a particular tautology across the five seasons of *The Wire*: *The game is the game*. As a magnet attracts iron filings, each utterance of the proverb draws toward it various considerations of work and its institutional settings. Tautological proverbs—such as *It is what it is; You gotta do what you gotta do; Business is business; Enough is enough;* and *Boys will be boys*—appear to repeat the basic logical principle of identity: *A equals A*.[18] At least as logical statements, tautologies make no formal claim to represent anything about the empirical world.[19] Wittgenstein once likened the logical tautology "to a wheel running idly in a mechanism of cog-wheels."[20] While many statements moving through language's "mechanism of cog-wheels" in everyday discourse make claims and designate or express attitudes, tautological proverbs appear to work like their logical counterparts that "run idly." Unconditionally true as logical claims, tautological proverbs like *It is what it is* seem to make no empirical claims about the world, and yet they are very popular in everyday conversation. These two facts are related and hint at why everyday tautologies are more than linguistic wheels spinning idly "in a mechanism of cog-wheels."

The productiveness of everyday tautologies emerges not at the site of logical abstraction but with the work of proverbs and clichés in ordinary language. "A cliché is not to be despised," Denise Riley urges. The "automatic comfort" of a well-received cliché "is the happy exteriority of a shared language which knows itself perfectly well to be a contentless but sociable turning outward toward the world."[21] The work of clichés in everyday talk extends beyond the relatively contentless talk often necessary to lubricate sociability or collegiality among peers who otherwise have little to say to one another. Tautological proverbs, Barthes observed, can come calling when other rhetorical tools seem to break down. Absent a supply of useful reasoned arguments, "one takes refuge in tautology."[22] Tautological proverbs and clichés here become blunt rhetorical weapons for underwriting power:

> Since it is magical, it can of course only take refuge behind the argument of authority: thus do parents at the end of their tether reply to the child who keeps on asking for explanations: *"because that's how it is"*, or even better: *"just because, that's all"*—a magical act ashamed of itself, which verbally makes the gesture of rationality, but immediately abandons the latter, and believes itself to be even with causality because it has uttered the word which introduces it. Tautology testifies to a profound distrust of language, which is rejected because it has failed. Now

any refusal of language is a death. Tautology creates a dead, a motionless world.[23]

Barthes here focuses on everyday tautologies and near tautologies as tools authority figures use when at "at the end of their tether" with subordinates.[24] Reason's failure incites a turn to *because that's how it is*, a phrase masquerading as a "gesture of rationality." In this picture, contentless linguistic wheels spin idly in the authoritarian tautologist's "dead, motionless world." By contrast, Avon Barksdale wields tautologies with conviction: in his hands, a cliché does not sound like a "magical act ashamed of itself." He means for assent to the proverb to reinforce his mastery of the game. When wearing the king's crown and at the top of the game, Avon would like to stop time with the atemporal tautology. During his turf war with Marlo, Avon thunders to his enforcers, "See how that shit got to be handled. The game is the fucking game, period!" (3: 6). When his institutional authority slips during Marlo's reign, the imprisoned Avon still favors the phrase as a sign of his interpretive authority. "The game is the game," he insists, before sometimes adding "always." "Always" is a way to hammer the phrase into place as noncontingent and nonnegotiable. "By eliminating all linguistic traces of the will of the superior," Adorno writes about similar utterances, "that which is intended is given greater emphasis." To wield tautologies and "old school-like phrases" along the lines of "that's the way it's done here," he continues, is to create the impression "that it is necessary to obey, since what is demanded already occurs factually."[25] Avon's signature phrase carries with it a sense of causal necessity. Things happen to be the way they are not because of the singular "will of the superior" but because *that is the way they must be.* Avon's impersonal utterance is an indirect speech act that implicitly refers to shared background and established rules in a relevant speech community. He leans on those rules as an external source of authority.[26] Avon's local knowledge lends him authority but also blinds him to how the rules of the drug business are changing.

Avon's signature tautology belongs to the class of clichés that readily link up with a high-power figure's posture of fatalistic realism. For the low-power players to whom Avon addresses his proverb, "possible resistance" is "eliminated simply in terms of logical form."[27] A grim

acceptance of the game's rules as immutable typically accompanies utterances of tautological proverbs like *Business is business* or *It is what
it is.* In order to save face "by eliminating all linguistic traces of the will
of the superior," a high-power figure might say *Business is business*
to displace responsibility for unpopular decisions onto the abstract and
nonmoral rules of the relevant institution or practice. In order to make
sense of disjunctions between *what is* and *what ought to be* (between
actual behaviors and one's disappointed hopes for alternative outcomes
or actions), low-power speakers can insulate themselves from the pain
of disillusionment by nodding fatalistically to one another that *it is
what it is.* Speaking his pet phrase to fellow gangsters reinforces Avon's
interpretive authority within a local speech community, but it can
hardly render that social world motionless. His injunction "always!"
may reveal some defensiveness about the chess king's authority and
the traditional rules of the game. The crime world of West Baltimore
is not an epic cosmos that stands still, despite Avon's desires for interpretive and institutional stability in a "totality of life that is rounded
from within."[28] He wants things to be one way, but ultimately they are
another way.

The statement *The game is the game* is not so commonplace as the
proverbs *Business is business* and *It is what it is.* When Avon utters
his signature tautology, its function is closest to the phrase *Business
is business* in terms of displacing moral responsibility (in this case, for
murder). He may prefer *The game is the game* to *Business is business*
because he presents himself as a traditional old-school gangster rather
than a businessman concerned solely with the bottom line. (As we shall
see, the distinction pries apart Avon's lifelong friendship and working
partnership with Stringer Bell.) Avon's signature phrase blends tautological simplicity with the obliquity of an allegory that finds its audience in a social context where neighborhood familiarity and assent
to tradition-bound ways of acting suggest a shared code hiding behind
a trivial tautology. At least formally, the generic allegory and the everyday tautology appear utterly unlike each other. If the garden-variety
allegory reveals that *A is not only A* (because the manifest narrative
references a latent prior narrative, albeit with discrepancies), a logical
tautology explicitly claims that *A equals A.* Meanwhile tautological
proverbs like *It is what it is* or *Business is business* rely on hermeneutic
assumptions about esoteric or second-order meanings. The tautological

proverb's apparently "contentless but sociable turning outward toward the world" assumes a shared understanding between a speaker and a designated listener about a phrase's manifest and implicit levels. When familiarity with an implicit level of signification is needed to understand an otherwise insignificant or nonsignifying tautological proverb, we find a structure similar to that of a generic allegory. The esotericism of tautological proverbs in everyday discourse resonates with a framing of allegory in terms of the "impossibility of reading."[29] If a listener does not already know the esoteric meaning beneath or behind a speaker's particular tautological proverb, the exoteric phrase falls flat or merely displays language "running idly" as an unreadable logical tautology, a phrase that gains no conversational traction. Allegorical depth marks the distance, then, between tautologies as matters of logical form and as convenient ciphers of esoteric knowledge. If one already knows the hidden esoteric meaning, then one does not need to hear the everyday tautology: passing around a tautology is a reminder and a performance of assent.

Avon's favored tautology reinforces a communal and familial shorthand about the game. Assent to the proverb seals acceptance of or resignation to the game's existential realities: the drug economy and its adjacent criminal conspiracies are enduring across time with a violent cycle of gangland consolidation, expansion, retreat, defeat, and regrouping. Typically, games are fictional, rule bound, and separated from the rest of life. The game about which Avon speaks is not separate from reality (it is only separate from the mainstream economy and the formal rule of law), nor is it the kind of make-believe or masquerade where one can slip out of one's game role by a simple change of clothing. Obliquity enters through the notion of gaming: which qualities and which other games does "the game" resemble? We have already noted Leavitt and Dubner's picture of drug dealing (as a kind of tournament where very few pawns or players advance) alongside the excessively hopeful pedagogy of D'Angelo's early chess lesson. The later Wittgenstein famously observed that the meaning of *game* as a noun is difficult to delineate because "similarities crop up and disappear" between games whenever one tries to clarify what unites all the instances of games. No single definition can cover all its examples: some games have long-established rules, others have no set rules whatsoever, others allow established rules to be adjusted for particular game instances, while others are only recognized as "games" in a figurative sense. Instead of a singular definition to capture all instances, "we see a complicated network of similarities overlapping and criss-crossing: sometimes overall similarities, sometimes similarities of detail."[30] Avon's signature tautology and Wittgenstein's observation remind us that games and talk about various activities as games are simply everywhere in *The Wire*. The games or sporting activities that are short and defined by explicit rules include at least the following: dice, boxing, gambling, dogfighting, poker, checkers, chess, pool, golf, basketball, football, and baseball. As we have seen, the sporting life is central to Avon's sense of himself as a traditional local gangster, a man in the family business. Fond memories of his own past as a neighborhood boxer inspire his sponsorship of Dennis "Cutty" Wise's boxing gym for neighborhood boys.

There are also more general and ongoing activities explicitly referred to as games by characters in *The Wire*: above all is the game of the illegal drug trade, but also detective work, political fund-raising, and other activities. Reflecting on the manipulation of statistics to demonstrate social progress and institutional success where reality tells the opposite, David Simon concluded that "the same game is played everywhere."[31] Less rule-bound gamelike activities include at least the following: policemen Clay Davis and others play make-believe with the unwitting real estate developer Stringer Bell; the detectives Jimmy McNulty and Lester Freamon play make-believe with the concocted story of a serial killer in order to continue the Marlo Stanfield inquiry (to which Bunk Moreland tartly responds, "I'm a murder police. . . . I don't fuck with no make-believe. I don't jerk shit around. I catch a murder, and I work it" [5: 6]); the police play "juking the stats" to demonstrate a reduction in major crimes by conveniently redefining what counts as such a crime; the teachers juke the stats by teaching students a test question in order to increase standardized scores rather than increase knowledge (an exasperated Colvin declares, "We pretended to teach them, they pretended to learn, and where—where'd they end up? Same damn corners" [4: 10]). A full accounting of games in *The Wire* would extend well beyond the scope of this essay.

Avon Barksdale is hardly the only character to utter, "The game is the game." The freelance enforcer Brother Mouzone (Michael Potts) says it when he expects to die after Omar has shot him twice in the chest. Mouzone will not beg for his life, but will slowly pronounce the monosyllabic phrase "The game is the game" one word at a time before adding that he is at peace with his God.[32] Mouzone accepts his possible death stoically even as he informs Omar, "You've got some wrong information" (2: 11) about the murder of Omar's boyfriend Brandon. Omar may answer "indeed" to Mouzone's statement that "the game is the game," but he is hardly a routine player. Omar's crimes against drug dealers—precisely the kind of robbery that could never be tried in the justice system—seem more like a trickster's sport than a means of financial enrichment or institution-building. Importantly, he never utters the phrase *The game is the game.* Omar's occasional tweaked statement, "It's all in the game," actively mocks gang members as the fearless hoodlum-with-a-conscience wreaks havoc on the predictable West Side rules of the game. Thus, he calls for an ambulance rather than let Mouzone die.

The most ruthless king, Marlo Stanfield, utters Avon's favored proverb—but only once. He asks the imprisoned Avon to facilitate a meeting with "the Greeks" so that Marlo can access their international heroin supply as a bulk customer. When the sociable Barksdale asks how things are, Marlo answers indifferently: "The game is the game." Avon responds with passionate assent: "Always!" Marlo utters the tautology to curry favor with the old-school gangster by showing a semblance of respect for an elder. The exchange underscores how different the two men are: the older one (only in his thirties) was raised locally in the family trade, while the young rising force is a social loner with no ties to an established community and no store of shared tautological proverbs and neighborhood traditions. Revealingly, Marlo roars an altogether self-concerned tautology that only mimics Avon's proverb of conservative institutionalism—"My name is my name!"—when he is jailed with Chris Partlow and Monk (5: 9). Avon is lucky to be an imprisoned "figure of authority" (as he puts it to Marlo) since his institutional position makes it more difficult for Marlo to enjoy the sight of watching Avon die. Marlo's disrespect and impatience with established authority figures coalesce in his signature statement: "You want it to be one way, but it's the other way" (4: 4). The obscure axiom shares an abstract flavor with Avon's signature tautology but with a different twist, as if to say, *You would like A to be A, but A is actually B.* Marlo utters the phrase to a convenience store guard who has caught him brazenly shoplifting a few lollipops. Marlo taunts the guard and later orders his murder. The verbal exchange between shoplifter and guard resonates with the young gangster's challenge to Prop Joe's authority and the wisdom of the purchasing "co-op" organized by Stringer Bell. One can imagine Marlo uttering his signature axiom in the face of each his elders in the Baltimore drug game as he takes pleasure in their murder.

"The street is the street. Always" (2: 12), Avon Barksdale's tertiary tautology, reinforces the primary one. His mode of authoritative speech via tautological proverbs about the game and the street as sites of permanence, conservative institutionalism, and rule-boundedness illuminates his growing alienation from Stringer Bell. In the first two seasons of *The Wire,* Avon and Stringer's joint venture B & B Enterprises suggests the reassuring circularity of a logical tautology: in the world of B & B Enterprises, *B will always equal B.* These two Bs are hardly identical, however, and Barksdale and Bell are increasingly divergent partners. When undetected, the business allows Stringer to move his and Avon's drug gains into potentially profitable legal businesses, most notably Baltimore real estate development. To move beyond the constrictions of Avon's relatively static world of local tautologies, Stringer reimagines Baltimore's drug game according to the abstract principles of textbook microeconomics. While Avon is in prison, Stringer starts to run gang meetings according to Roberts' Rules of Order (though without note taking). "We gonna handle this shit like businessmen," he clarifies at one point: "Later for that gangster shit" (3: 1). An economics class at the community college inspires Stringer to break from tradition and share some Barksdale territory with Prop Joe in order to gain access to the latter's superior product. Stringer also organizes a new informal cartel of local drug gangs so as to increase their wholesale purchasing power.

Avon rejects the paradigm shift as anathema to established traditions about how the game is played as a holistic institution or "a totality of life that is rounded from within." When Stringer defends the innovations and related matters in the abstract language of management-speak to deflect responsibility ("Every market-based business runs in cycles, and we're going through a down cycle right now"), Avon responds with an old-school gangster's tautological proverb: "This ain't about your muthafuckin' business class. It ain't that part of it. It's that other thing. The street is the street. Always" (2: 12). As he admits to Stringer in a discussion that intimates the dissolution of B & B Enterprises into its divided halves, "I guess I'm just a gangster, that's all" (3: 6). Stringer admits that the gangster game is not the only one he wants to play: "You know, Avon, you got to think about what we got in this game for, man. . . . Was it so our names could ring out on some ghetto street corner?

No, man, there's games beyond the fucking game. Avon, look, you and me, we brothers, B" (3: 10). Having a strong reputation on "some ghetto street corner" is of abiding interest to Avon as a local business and community leader. His partner, however, has peered at a broader panorama where success in the game of the Baltimore drug trade could lead toward broader economic opportunities untethered to the old neighborhood— games beyond "the game." When Stringer offers to betray his best friend and his secrets to the police, Major Howard "Bunny" Colvin presumes a tumultuous rift between the erstwhile best friends. "Nah, it's just business," Stringer counters truthfully (3: 11).[33] Left alone with his ambitions, Stringer's past business decisions catch up with him. Omar and Mouzone murder him in his unfinished investment property.

"Nature Don't Care. Nature Just Is."

For an approximation of Avon Barksdale's tautological language with telling differences on the law enforcement side of *The Wire*, we might close with Lester Freamon. The detective's colleagues praise him as "natural police" and a man who has "the stink of wisdom on him" (2: 7). At one point in season 4, Lester (Clarke Peters) and Bunk Moreland (Wendell Pierce) have advanced well into an evening of serious drinking when Lester begins to wax philosophical: "Age is age. Fat is fat. Nature is nature. . . . Pitiless. Nature don't care. Nature just is" (4: 4). The pronouncements resemble Avon's tautologies, though Lester is, as usual, showing only half of his hand. Unlike Avon, he does not resign himself to fighting (whether as a king or a pawn) in a world of institutional games. He is also delighted with nature's others—artifice, make-believe, and the nontautological realm of the imagination. In his world of refined dollhouse furniture, an armoire is an armoire but also something else—a toy or a valuable piece of individually crafted woodwork that could fit into a sock. Despite his fatalistic tautologies, Lester respects the difference between *what is* and *what is not*, and his tautologies do not reinforce the customs of Baltimore law enforcement, where a funhouse world of institutional games massages enforcement data to claim social progress and assuage politicians and voters.

Following orders by imaginatively "juking the stats" in order to advance one's career—another example of a "wheel running idly in a machine of cog wheels"—never appealed to Lester. Instead his tautologies evoke a more elemental vision of human existence as bare life: "Age is age," he says. "Nature don't care. Nature just is." Against the inflexibility of aging and physical death, institutions and their habits of second nature appear all the more clearly as the stuff of artifice, imagination, and contingency. A clerk managing a collection of lost and unclaimed objects may retreat into just such a world of private mastery and make-believe. Lester's success as a miniaturist is the residue of thirteen years of institutional death in the pawn shop. "The cleverer I am at miniaturizing the world," Gaston Bachelard once hypothesized, "the better I possess it." "But in doing this," he continued, "it must be understood that values become condensed and enriched in miniature."[34] In his first days with Cedric Daniels's Major Crimes Unit, Lester barely participates in the new group's activities and is taken for a useless "hump." He employs a magnifying glass not for detective work but to labor over his delicate tiny furniture. As Bachelard prophesied Lester's investigative genius, "miniature is one of the refuges of greatness."[35] Once his investigative powers are rekindled by Daniels's idealism and the opportunity to do real police work, Lester is willing to play with ideas and investigative possibilities beyond the restricted realm of the miniaturist or the cynical game of the institutional careerist.

"Cool Lester Smooth" (Detective Shakima "Kima" Gregg's nickname for him) has a rare degree of patience, intelligence, and ease with unorthodox thinking. While his last name scans easily as a signal of his identity as an unaligned free man, his first name captures the romantic nature of his freedom through an association with the genius musical improviser Lester Young, an unrivaled archetype of African American cool. The ghastly string of murders ordered by Marlo Stanfield, alongside the police department's refusal to continue that investigation, however, distresses the otherwise unflappable Lester. As the series winds to its conclusion, Lester loses his cool and transfers the full power of make-believe from the domain of miniatures to that of police work. He recognizes the turn within himself and unwittingly echoes Bodie's "I feel old" valedictory speech with the cue "I'm tired":

I've reached a point, Detective Syndor, where I no longer have the time or patience left to address myself to the needs of the system in which we work. I'm tired. . . . I'm going to press a case against Marlo Stanfield without regard to the usual rules. . . . If you have a problem with this, I understand completely. And I urge you to get as far fucking away from me as you can. (5: 6)

Lester fails to put Marlo behind bars; the homicidal gangster walks free as a millionaire. Nonetheless the detective ends up with a more enviable kind of forced retirement than the young gangster. Marlo's precarious legal triumph means that he has to immediately exit the game in Baltimore. His best friend and top enforcer Chris Partlow will serve a life sentence for all the murders Marlo ordered. Felicia "Snoop" Pearson has been shot dead by Michael Lee, who may become the next generation's Omar. Left alone on the streets, Marlo at first finds no old or new games to enjoy. His peak moment of pleasure may instead have been watching Proposition Joe's face crumble as Chris Partlow shot the elder gangster in the back of the head. Marlo is a rich man whose greatest pleasures may be behind him.

Even after helping to perpetrate a serial killer narrative built on pure "make-believe," Lester Freamon manages to exit the police force with his retirement pension intact. The retired detective looks comfortable at home pursuing his passion with building dollhouse miniatures and living with Shardene Innis, the much younger nursing student whose bravery helped put Avon Barksdale in prison. Upon meeting Lester and learning of his hobby, she had observed that it was sad that he had no dollhouse for all of his beautiful furniture. At the time Lester told her, "I just make 'em and sell 'em" (1: 8). Constructing period furniture miniatures was a way of standing apart from an everyday present of deadening tautologies. By the series' end, Freamon is playing house with Shardene and still building tiny furniture. Their apparent domestic tranquility, itself another fragile miniature, stands as a minor substitute for the thwarted victory in Lester's final criminal investigation. Against the series' concluding montage and its snapshots of a political "mechanism of cog-wheels" that spins but "runs idly" when it comes to powering social progress, the domestic idyll of Lester and Shardene—like the triumph of a recovering Reginald "Bubbles" Cousins dining with his sister and her child—miniaturizes social hope and holds it all the closer because of its fragility.

Notes

1. Where particular scenes or pieces of dialogue are discussed in this essay, I include the actor's name within parentheses (for the first mention only). Otherwise, only character names are given. All quotations are my transcribed approximation of the spoken dialogue; access to the printed scripts was not available.

Transcriptions are from DVD box set *The Wire: The Complete Series* (2008). Wherever dialogue is quoted, I note the season and episode numbers; for example, the sixth episode of the second season is rendered here as 2: 6.

2. David Simon, interviewed by Nick Hornby, *The Believer* 46 (August 2007): 71.

3. Duquan "Dukie" Weems, eager for an alternative to the drug game for which he is ill-equipped, inquires about working at the Sports Locker store. Poot tells him that he is too young. Homeless, out of school, and too young to work legally, Dukie must fend for himself on the streets. When seen in the series' closing montage, he is shooting heroin in an alley with another homeless garbage picker. Against such a despairing vignette, the good fortune of another bright West Side boy, Namond Brice, is enhanced for its rarity.

4. In some allegorical narratives, especially of the morally didactic kind, the latent narrative can be so close to the surface that the allegorical structure maintains a minimal degree of doubling and parallelism. The allegorical flavor of *The Wire* as a social critique is sometimes very obvious (e.g., the allusion to President George Bush's premature declaration of wartime victory in the episode "Mission Accomplished").

5. As the position and social power of the allegorist varies, so too will the political valence of allegorical interpretation. For a review of relations between allegory and power, see Gordon Teskey, *Allegory and Violence* (Ithaca, N.Y.: Cornell University Press, 1996).

6. Richard Pryor, . . . *Is It Something I Said?* Reprise Records, 1975.

7. Fredric Jameson, *Postmodernism, or the Cultural Logic of Late Capitalism* (Durham, N.C.: Duke University Press, 1992), 51. D'Angelo offers a "poor person's cognitive mapping," though (contra Jameson) conspiratorial paranoia is not his dominant note: see Fredric Jameson, "Cognitive Mapping," in *Marxism and the Interpretation of Culture*, ed. Cary Nelson and Lawrence Grossberg (London: Macmillan, 1988), 356.

8. Simon, interview, 72.

9. The long shadow of D'Angelo's allegorical chess discussion bears comparing to Tony Soprano's repeated therapeutic encounters with Jennifer Melfi on *The Sopranos* (1999–2007). Soprano's distrust of therapy stems from his habit of leaning on the fatalism of tautological proverbs to interpret his life and deflect personal responsibility. Melfi battles the murderous gangster's resistances against building a new interpretive frame or metalanguage for his past and present life: "Melfi wants to instruct Tony in how to make his life mean something other than what he thinks it means. She introduces him to allegory and symbolism and tries to push him beyond 'I am what I am' and 'it is what it is.'" Christian K. Messenger, *The Godfather and American Culture: How the Corleones Became "Our Gang"* (Albany: SUNY Press, 2002), 272.

10. Steven D. Levitt and Stephen J. Dubner, "Why Do Drug Dealers Still Live with Their Moms?" in *Freakonomics* (New York: William Morrow, 2005), 106. Their analysis leans on Sudhir Venkatesh's sociological study of the crack economy and gang culture in Chicago. A narrative account of this research, as told through Venkatesh's relationship with J. T., a young leader of the Black Kings gang, is in Venkatesh, *Gang Leader for a Day* (New York: Penguin, 2008).

11. Theodor Adorno, "Little Heresy," trans. Susan H. Gillespie, in *Essays on Music*, ed. Richard Leppert (Berkeley: University of California Press, 2002), 319.

12. Ibid., 320.

13. Karl Marx, *Grundrisse*, trans. Martin Nicolaus (New York: Vintage, 1973), 197.

14. Georg Lukács, *The Theory of the Novel*, trans. Anna Bostock (Cambridge: MIT Press, 1971), 80.

15. The "game is rigged" phrase stuck with David Simon, who wrote the teleplay for "Final Grades" (4: 13). "Much of our modern theater seems rooted in the Shakespearean discovery of the modern mind. [The writers of *The Wire* are] stealing instead from an earlier, less-traveled construct—the Greeks— . . . to create doomed and fated protagonists who confront a rigged game and their own mortality." Simon, interview, 71.

16. Along similar lines, see Gary Taylor's interpretation of Thomas Middleton's 1624 allegorical play *A Game of Chess*. Middleton's play, Taylor writes, "is not only an allegory, but also a critique of chess. Chess depends upon absolute distinctions, upon the maintenance of fixed visible categories created by precise rules. Like Nabokov's *The Defence*, Middleton's *A Game of Chess* combines this totally ordered universe with the disordered world of 'a dream.' . . . Dreams have no rules and no fixed categories. The very clarity and regularity of chess provide a background against which irregularities are conspicuously foregrounded. . . . In chess, players ought to obey the rules. But what if it were impossible to obey them?" Taylor commentary from *Thomas Middleton: The Collected Works*, ed. Gary Taylor and John Lavagnino (Oxford: Oxford University Press, 2007), 1827.

17. Similarly interested in matters of misrecognition of social reality, David Simon ruefully writes that the world of *The Wire* "is a world in which the rules and values of the free market have been mistaken for a social framework, a world where institutions are paramount and every day human beings matter less." David Simon, introduction to Rafael Alvarez, *"The Wire": Truth Be Told* (New York: Grove Press, 2009), 30.

18. When a quotation attaches to a particular character or characters, I place it within quotation marks. When a proverb or short phrase is attributed to no particular speaker in *The Wire*, I italicize it.

19. Ludwig Wittgenstein: "In a tautology the conditions of agreement with the world—the representational relations—cancel one another, so that it does

not stand in any representational relation to reality." *Tractatus Logico-Philosophicus* (London: Routledge, 1974), 4.462.

20. Max Black, *A Companion to Wittgenstein's "Tractatus"* (Cambridge: Cambridge University Press, 1964), 229.

21. Denise Riley, *Impersonal Passion: Language as Affect* (Durham, N.C.: Duke University Pres, 2005), 4.

22. Roland Barthes, *Mythologies*, trans. Annette Lavers (1972; repr., New York: Hill & Wang, 1986), 152.

23. Ibid., 153.

24. As Barthes hints, tautological reasoning sometimes maps onto class differences. Scholars of the contemporary American family have shown how social class maps onto different models of parental authority. College-minded and middle-class parents often model elaborate reason-giving and negotiation with authority figures (including themselves), whereas working-class and poor parents often model more passive acceptance of directives from authority figures (including themselves). The contrast speaks to Avon Barksdale's leadership style. See Annette Lareau, *Unequal Childhoods: Class, Race, and Family Life* (Berkeley: University of California Press, 2003).

25. Theodor Adorno, *The Jargon of Authenticity*, trans. Knut Tamowski and Frederic Will (Evanston, Ill.: Northwestern University Press, 1973), 88.

26. For a comprehensive analysis of proverbs from a linguistic perspective, see Neal R. Norrick, *How Proverbs Mean: Semantic Studies in English Proverbs* (Berlin: Mouton de Gruyter, 1985). Norrick shows that proverbs "are doubly indirect. First, they are quoted. As such they express observations not original with the speaker; the speaker need not take full responsibility for their form or content. Second, proverbs generate implicatures. The speaker means what he says on the literal level, but he means something more in context. It is up to the hearer to piece together the intended implicature" (27).

27. Adorno, *The Jargon of Authenticity*, 88.

28. Lukács, *Theory of the Novel*, 60.

29. Paul de Man, "Allegory (Julie)," in *Allegories of Reading: Figural Language in Rousseau, Nietzsche, Rilke, and Proust* (New Haven: Yale University Press, 1982), 200.

30. Ludwig Wittgenstein, *Philosophical Investigations*, trans. G. E. M. Anscombe (New York: Prentice Hall, 1973), 67.

31. The systemic corruption of institutional games in American society was a major concern of Simon: "You show me anything that depicts institutional progress in America, school test scores, crime stats, arrest reports, arrest stats, anything that a politician can run on, anything that somebody can get a promotion on. And as soon as you invent that statistical category, 50 people in that institution will be at work trying to figure out a way to make it look as if prog-

ress is actually occurring when actually no progress is. . . . I mean, our entire economic structure fell behind the idea that these mortgage-based securities were actually valuable. And they had absolutely no value. . . . But if you looked inward you'd see that the same game is played everywhere. That nobody's actually in the business of doing what the institution's supposed to do" (interview transcript, *Bill Moyers Journal,* PBS, April 17, 2009, http://www.pbs.org/moyers/journal/04172009/watch.html [accessed October 2009]).

32. One might imagine following Mouzone further: *The game is the game. I am at peace with my God, and with the game; as the game is the game, so God is God.*

33. When Stringer realizes that Clay Davis has stolen $250,000 from him, Stringer suggests that the Barksdale organization should assassinate Davis. Avon angrily chides his old friend: "What'd I tell you about playin' those fucking away games. They saw your ghetto ass coming from miles away, nigger. You got a fuckin' beef with them, that shit is on you" (3: 11).

34. Gaston Bachelard, *The Poetics of Space,* trans. Maria Jolas (Boston: Beacon Press, 1969), 150.

35. Ibid., 155.

PART TWO

Neoliberal Capitalism and the Urban Order

5

The Case against Kojak Liberalism

Carlo Rotella

In March 2008, a few days before the last episode of *The Wire*'s fifth and final season aired, Ed Burns, Dennis Lehane, George Pelecanos, Richard Price, and David Simon published an essay in *Time* entitled *"The Wire*'s War on the Drug War." It begins, "We write a television show. Measured against more thoughtful and meaningful occupations, this is not the best seat from which to argue public policy or social justice." But the authors do go on to argue public policy and social justice, starting with a thumbnail analysis of the damage done to urban America by the war on drugs: the deepening of racial divides, steep increases in incarceration rates, degradation of police work, and wholesale failure of politicians to buck the self-perpetuating logic of a permanent moral panic that their show dramatized so tellingly. They ask what "well-meaning, well-intentioned people" can do about this disaster.[1]

Feeling the need to come up with a better answer than writing a TV show, casting about for a response that has more evident effect in the real world, they pledge to always vote to acquit, no matter what the evidence, when serving on a jury charged with deciding a nonviolent drug case. It's a small but tangible thing one can do, they argue, to begin undermining the pernicious effect of a war on drugs that has become a war on the poor. In support of this call for jury nullification in protest of a government incapable of "repairing injustices," they cite Thomas Paine on civil disobedience and Harry Blackmun's principled refusal to tinker with the machinery of the death penalty, and they claim a historical precedent in the case of John Peter Zenger, who in 1735 was acquitted of seditious libel against the royal governor of New York when a jury decided that Zenger had indeed broken the law but that the law was unjust. They close the essay with a call to readers to follow their lead by voting to acquit all nonviolent drug offenders. "And when the lawyers or the judge or your fellow jurors seek explanation, think for a moment on Bubbles, Bodie, or Wallace"—fictional characters they invented who have enlisted viewers' sympathy. "And remember that the lives being held in the balance aren't fictional."[2]

The essay is a public attempt, unscreened by the mask of fiction, to win free of the suffocating logic of the war on drugs, which for decades has succeeded in monopolizing the political mainstream and pushing dissenters to a far margin occupied by bleeding hearts, stoners, libertarian cranks, and hairsplitting lawyers for the defense like *The Wire*'s own Maurice Levy. As self-conscious inheritors and defenders of the New Deal tradition—"liberals," if that word still means anything in American political discourse—the writers maneuver in their essay to escape a nasty ideological trap set by the war on drugs and the larger war on crime from which it descends, a trap that has snared two generations of Democrats and moderate Republicans: you have to prove that you're "tough on crime" before you can set about attempting to sustain the premises of the welfare state, even though the acceptable ways to establish your bona fides—endorsing "zero tolerance" crimewar measures like mandatory minimum sentences for drug offenses and the drastic expansion of the prison system—oblige you to support policies that only further overburden the welfare state, further decreasing its viability.

So Simon and company do not lack for courage or intellectual ambition, but their argument is unconvincing. When they ask what well-meaning people can do about the social disaster they decry, they respond, "for five seasons we answered lamely, offering arguments about economic priorities or drug policy, debating theoreticals within our tangled little drama. We were storytellers, not advocates; we ducked the question as best we could."[3] This gets it exactly backward. Jury nullification is, rather, a pretty lame response to the war on drugs, the kind of adequately theorized "practical" measure that plays well in a manifesto but not in real courthouses. Their high-minded moral justification for flouting the laws of the land would only encourage armed antitax crackpots, antiabortion extremists, and other unwelcome bedfellows eager to foment widespread violent social chaos in the name of principle. And picture yourself explaining to a judge or fellow jurors that the moving example of Bodie, an imaginary person played by the actor J. D. Williams, inspired you to vote to acquit the nonfictional offender in the dock before you. Williams also played a gangster named Froggy in the blaxploitation parody *Pootie Tang*, so maybe you could add that you did it for Froggy's sake, too.

And the writers, in their overly modest eagerness to dispense with mere fiction and get to policy, mischaracterize their own show. *The Wire*, as the response of a group of storytellers to the war on drugs, is anything but lame. At least for its first four seasons, before Simon's beef with the newspaper business upset the balance and reduced the fifth season to mere high-end TV melodrama, the show did not offer arguments or debate theoreticals with the didactic stiffness typical of self-consciously "political" popular culture. Rather, it was a superlative piece of genre work distinguished by its sustained success in mating a fresh and sophisticated synthesis of crime-show formulas to a humane exploration of how compelling characters lived the consequences of the war on drugs. It was a "tangled little drama" in the best sense: the many vivid characters' intersecting lives seemed no less real, and in fact far more real, for having been arranged so elegantly to highlight the contours of a nuanced analysis of the war on drugs. That analysis embraced politics and culture, addressing not only governmental policies but also a set of ancillary routines for telling crime stories. This all helps explain why academics love *The Wire* so immoderately: it's first-class genre fiction that also advances a coherent analysis, and neither quality hamstrings the other.[4] The opposite, in fact. The analysis disciplines and complicates the signature pleasures of the genre, and the show's innovations in genre present just the right formal devices to advance the analysis.

— — —

In the last third of the twentieth century, the war on crime claimed so much ideological real estate that there was almost nowhere left to stand for a person who didn't want to volunteer for the lunatic fringe. The notion of a war on crime—and a subsidiary war on drugs—was of a piece with what Christopher Wilson characterizes as "a broader American political disenchantment with liberal, root-cause approaches to social problems," from FDR's New Deal to LBJ's War on Poverty; but, as both

Wilson and Stuart Scheingold argue, the notion of crime as a permanent crisis deserving special treatment rapidly came to "transcend the familiar struggle between liberal and conservative policies."[5] The rise of crime control orthodoxy to nearly unquestioned domestic preeminence came at a time when the assumptions and agenda of the aging New Deal order were increasingly discredited and the political coalition that had supported them was breaking up in struggles over the Vietnam War, the civil rights movement, the urban crisis, and the urban fiscal crises and depression of the 1970s. Urban liberals, especially, were squeezed into a tight corner by compulsory universal conscription in the war on crime.

One apparent solution for them was to become what the columnist E. J. Dionne called "Kojak liberals." Dionne coined the term in 1993 in a column that urged streetwise urban Democrats to emulate the detective lieutenant played by Telly Savalas: "tough as nails" but with "a heart of gold." What that meant in practice, he argued, was to go back to doing the "things that local government knows how to do—putting cops on the street, picking up the garbage, keeping libraries open and the parks clean"—and get out of the business of doing "things it doesn't know so much about," like providing social service programs intended to correct for distributive inequities. Crime, he assumed, should always come first on their list of issues they could address. If there was a war on, then law and order was like defense in wartime—sacrosanct, essential, prior to all other concerns, including seeing to the needs of the inner-city poor and a middle class forever threatening to decamp to the suburbs.[6]

Kojak liberalism seemed like a way for refugees from the wreck of the New Deal order to function in a political climate that made enlistment in the war on crime mandatory for any realist, but it turned out to be a trap. Making war on crime was not simply one item on a list of things that cities could do well; it increasingly shaped federal policy, too, and hamstrung the ability of all levels of government to address any other item on the list, no matter how golden-hearted the motivation for putting it there. For example, proponents of the war on crime favored order-maintaining tactics such as stiff mandatory penalties for even low-grade drug offenses (according to a logic that famously made smoking crack cocaine, a "ghetto" behavior, a much more serious offense than putting coke up your nose the middle-class way); such draconian sentencing put more adults in jail, taking them out of the regular workforce and making it harder for them to help support families, which in turn helped to put a new round of kids on the street, a situation to which the state would have to respond with law-and-order measures (always the first item on the list of things to do) rather than social services, and so on—a cycle that only increased demands on governments less and less able or willing to provide services other than policing, prosecution, and incarceration. "Zero tolerance" approaches to getting tough on crime might feel like a decisive response to lawlessness, but they also ensured that there would be a limitless supply of fresh asses to kick and names to take. Simon, a former crime reporter, and Burns, a former police officer and teacher, and others like them came to believe passionately that the war on crime, in which Dionne urged post–New Deal Democrats to enlist as their best chance to save the urban poor, only made things worse for the poor.

The war on crime also played out in the America imagined by Hollywood, which had its own favored tactics. In the crime-story boom of the 1970s and 1980s, the police procedural's great subject was street policing, the day-to-day business of managing informants, gathering local lore, shadowing suspects, and otherwise exploiting one's knowledge of the lay of the land (hence the generic climax of the period, the chase through streets and alleys, with wah-wah pedal and woodblock accompaniment). This was especially true of the depiction of the war on drugs within the larger war on crime. William Friedkin's influential synthesis of documentary feel with classical Hollywood storytelling in *The French Connection* (1971), a fictionalized account of a big NYPD heroin case, set the stylistic and thematic template for scores of movies to come, and also for TV shows like *Kojak*, *Police Story* (and other shows derived from Joseph Wambaugh's writing), and *Hill Street Blues* and its pluralist-ensemble cousins—a body of crime stories that used street policing as a figure to consider the tenuous viability of a social contract frayed by serial urban crises, a difficult but possibly workable arrangement between police and citizenry.[7] There was also a competing head-busting, shoot-'em-up strain in the era's treatment of street policing, most prominent in urban action fantasies on the Western-derived model of *Dirty Harry*—*SWAT*, for example, or *Hunter*, in which former football star Fred Dryer ritually repeated his signature tag line, "Works for me" while visiting summary justice upon punks and psychos. The two strains of fictional street policing, which one might think of as "left" and "right" parts of a greater whole, had in common an interest in imagining the conduct of the war on crime as a series of engagements fought in an evocatively detailed urban landscape, with a social cost measured in casualties among both the police and the policed.

In the 1990s, another element of police procedural, the interrogation room, took center stage. *NYPD Blue, Law & Order,* and other such shows did not devote as much effort to mapping a richly imagined street, instead turning a greater part of their energy indoors to the drawing-room dramas of the box, as the interrogation room is called. In the box, police officers proved their virtue and efficacy by creatively working around or violating the rights of suspected criminals. They allowed suspects to believe things that weren't true, lied to them, shook them up by stage-managing confrontations with witnesses, tried to prevent them from lawyering up, threatened them, and sometimes just lost it—or made a calculated decision to value the greater good over the letter of the law—and beat the necessary information or confession out of them. The box was not a new element of police procedural (there's a deliriously strange moment in Friedkin's movie *Cruising* [1980], for instance, when a giant police officer wearing only boots, a jock strap, and an undersize cowboy hat enters an interrogation room and wordlessly begins slapping a suspect), but it acquired new importance in the genre in the century's last decade. Christopher Wilson links the rising presence of the box on TV to changes in the management of real police work—including diminished resources, greater managerial oversight of detectives, and the renewed focus on clearances-by-confession occasioned by the CompStat style of statistics-driven law enforcement—but he also acknowledges the box's telegenic qualities. It's a setting "well suited to the medium of television," a handy space in which to both explore character and "reinforce an aura of police implacability, even inescapability" in endless reruns of the confrontation between highly focused, technically expert state power and a pandemic criminality that shelters behind the protections accorded to the rights of individual citizens. Wilson argues that the box took center stage in a "post-liberal" moment ushered in by decades of war on crime, a moment in which even hard-line ancestral Democrats subscribed to the logic of treating police work as intelligence-gathering in a time of war, which led to valorizing police deception and other end runs around a suspect's *Miranda* rights. It was *Homicide,* after all, a TV adaptation of a book by the future jury-nullification advocate David Simon, that popularized "the box" as a term of art and helped move interrogation to center stage in the genre.[8]

The Wire offers the genre a new formal and thematic synthesis, assimilating and synthesizing street policing and the box by framing both with a third element, the wiretap, which introduces a conscious theme and aesthetic of structural analysis. If street policing is about the social contract—maintained with great difficulty in "left" versions, permanently abridged by evildoers and therefore defensible only with righteous violence in "right" versions—and the box is about the necessity of narrowing individual rights in a time of crisis brought on by war, then the wiretap is about piecing together the relations of power that shape the city. Wiretaps, too, had been around in the genre for a long time. There's one in *The French Connection*, for instance, foregrounded in a sequence in which the cops put in long hours with headphones and coffee, sifting through the banal domestic trivia of a local gangster's life to find the break they need, which comes in the form of a phone call from a Frenchman with a lot of heroin to sell. But until *The Wire* the wiretap had not been fully exploited by police procedurals as a way for an investigation to peel away layers of surface crime to open up the strata of deep crime, turning an account of police work into a dissection of social and political order.

In *The Wire* that structural analysis subsumes street policing and the box, so that even the cleverest bit of streetwise technique or interrogation ruse becomes implicated in the larger account of what is most deeply wrong with the city. Jump-outs, raids, chases, box tricks, and the like may be lots of fun to watch, but they dramatize Kojak liberalism at its most futile. In *The Wire*, hauling in corner boys and dope fiends on minor charges and then trying to sweat confessions out of them is a Sisyphean waste of time and energy for the sensitive, thoughtful cops who are skeptical about the war on drugs as well as for the gung-ho true believers who can't see beyond the fleeting authoritarian satisfaction of busting heads. It's make-work dumped on all of them as a result of their superiors' embrace of the police equivalent of the U.S. military's obsession with body counts during the Vietnam War. And it's worse than a simple waste of time: the kind of low-level arrests that result from such make-work—the tangible product of all that thrilling action the genre provides in heaping loads in both fictional dramas and reality programming—can actually interfere with the laborious, research-intensive piecing together of workable cases against drug kingpins and their allies situated well off the street in the upper reaches of the city's power structure. Viewers can momentarily lose themselves in the familiar adrenaline rush that comes with lights-and-sirens and screeching brakes and drawn guns, just as they can lose themselves in the pleasures of the box, but *The Wire* relentlessly returns them from this fugue state of genre joy to the sobering realization that the standard methods of waging the war on drugs are only making worse the problems the war is nominally supposed to address.

— — —

Building the case against Kojak liberalism in a TV drama involves assembling both a critique of policy and an aesthetic brief that recognize the power of conventional crime-story forms—like street policing and the box—but also identify their limits. *The Wire* uses the figure of the wiretap to enframe and condition the genre pleasures of police procedural by constant recursion to structural analysis. To see how that formula for social procedural works as storytelling, I want to examine how the show sets up its array of genre materials in season 1 and sketches out what it's going to do with those materials.

HBO's house style encourages throwing away the first few episodes of a season, at least as most TV writers or executives would see it. HBO dramas make a fetish of patiently laying the groundwork for complexity to come, resisting the temptation to deliver clockwork payoffs to viewers who have been trained by network television to expect that each hour of a police drama, for instance, will provide narrative closure in the form of investigative climaxes ("It had to be you, Bob, because nobody else had access to both the vial of rare Sumatran frond mold and the nondairy creamer") and/or action sequences ("Freeze! Police!"—vroom vroom bang bang kiss kiss). The emphasis on long-form storytelling favors a slow, sexy, novelistic build, which in the case of *The Wire* suggests an analogy not to Dickens, as is proposed in season 5 by a pompous newspaperman who represents the kind of journalism that substitutes sentiment for legwork, but to Zola's twenty-novel Rougon-Macquart series, a taxonomy of Second Empire France that serves as a model not only of social scientist realism but also of hardboiled proto-noir.[9]

Episode 1 of season 1 of *The Wire* begins with blood on the street and a dead body. Evidence gathering is under way for a case that needs solving—street policing in progress—but the death of Omar Isaiah Betts, aka Snot Boogie, turns out to be of purely thematic importance. It's a sort of parable, and it's not there to get us started on figuring out "who shot Snot," as McNulty puts it, or what brilliant stratagem the cops will use to break the case. Rather, it gives McNulty and a corner boy who was Snot's friend the opportunity to suggest the relationship between surface crime and deep crime—that is, between the symptomatic, solvable surface crimes that drive the plot and the chronic, structural, world-ordering deep crime the cops can't do anything about. Snot Boogie's habit of trying to rip off the local crap game every Friday night finally got him killed, and when McNulty asks why the neighborhood guys ever let Snot play at all, if they knew that sooner or later he'd grab the money and oblige them to chase him down and beat him up, the friend says, "Got to. It's America, man." With stakes in place—the investigation of murders and drug deals (surface crimes) will reveal something about money and power and the ideology of freedom of opportunity that, taken to an empty extreme, justifies their uneven distribution (deep crime)—we're ready to roll opening credits.[10]

After the credits we go to Judge Phelan's courtroom, where D'Angelo Barksdale is well on the way to beating a charge of murder because the city's overextended police and legal forces are no match for his uncle Avon's criminal organization, and from this scene to the sort of ultimately futile street-level bust that amounts to little more than shoveling shit against an overwhelming tide. Carver and Herc, the show's emblematic duo of loyal foot-soldiers in the war on drugs, are partnered with Kima to do the dangerous grunt-work that provides much of the genre's standard visual excitement. After a tense guns-drawn sequence in which they confiscate drugs and guns from a car they staked out on an informant's tip, we go back to court just in time to see D'Angelo acquitted. From the opening scenes of episode 1, then, the juxtaposition of business as usual on the street and in court appends a shadow of structural analysis to the simple genre pleasures associated with watching cops nail crooks.

So far, we are filling out the map of genre terrain surveyed by *The French Connection* and other movies of the 1970s: criminals will get off, and the more important the criminal the more likely that he walks. During a conversation with Judge Phelan, McNulty nails down the point by dismissing "street rips" (of the sort that Kima and the boys have just excitingly performed) as petty make-work, like "community policing and all that," which occupies the time that officers should be spending on taking down the Barksdales and other major players. The police press harder and harder to win the war on drugs, risking their lives and expanding their powers in a futile attempt to keep up with free-market gangsters (when Judge Phelan reminds him that they live "in a nation of laws," McNulty replies, "I thought it was Baltimore"), but they always catch the wrong people, those so low in the criminal hierarchy that they might as well be victims.

We then move back to the station to consider in more explicit detail the ideology of the war on drugs. After the bust, as Herc and Carver idly watch Kima toil through an arrest report using an antiquated typewriter, Carver waves away the necessity of all such paperwork, claiming, "We are an effective deterrent in the war on drugs when we are on the street."

HERC: "Fuckin' motherfuckers up, right?"
CARVER: "Indeed."
HERC: "Fuck the paperwork. Collect bodies. Split heads."
CARVER: "Split 'em wide."
HERC: "The Western District way."
CARVER: "A'ight."

They deliver these units of ideological boilerplate with knowing irony, but the tragedy of Carver and Herc is that they're also not kidding at all; they have no other way to imagine their jobs than with the conceptual resources afforded to them by the war on drugs. The amalgam of party-line cant and tribal Western District ritual, sealed with a fist bump, is all the equipment they can call on for the task of describing and legitimating the police work they do. Kima suggests the poverty of their conceptual resources with her comment on their exchange: "You heroic motherfuckers kill me. Fightin' the war on drugs, one brutality case at a time." It's not like Kima has a better way to think of police work, and she takes similar pride in upholding the honor of the police force by winning every battle on the streets, even if each such victory makes it all the more inevitable that they will lose the war, but she has a little more analytical distance from what they all do—a capacity for grasping the big picture that will, in time, enable her to learn from Lester Freamon that the paperwork dismissed by Herc and Carver is in fact the one path to doing the far more meaningful police work necessary to identify and net the big fish. Prompted by Kima, Carver shows the first flash of what will over the next few seasons develop into his own increasingly sophisticated understanding of the inadequacy of the Western District way, which only makes worse the social conditions it's supposed to address. "Girl," he says, "you can't even call this shit a war." Herc asks, "Why not?" Carver says, "Wars end." Herc writes down the bon mot, but, a headbusting street hero to the end, he never does figure out its full import.

— — —

Having in episode 1 put a frame of cautionary analysis around the joys of watching street policing on TV, season 1 then does the same for the box. In episode 2, Bunk and McNulty soften up D'Angelo in an interrogation room at the office of the homicide division by showing him a picture of Bunk's kids, telling him they're the now-orphaned children of William Gant, an upstanding citizen who has been killed by the Barksdale organization because he testified as an eyewitness to one of their murders. The detectives have D'Angelo weepy and reeling, and even get him to write a letter to Gant's imaginary children saying that he's sorry for their loss, before the Barksdales' lawyer, Levy, arrives to interrupt the virtuoso performance. So far, it feels like business as usual in the box as TV imagines it, but while most cop shows revel in the joys of getting around *Miranda* and treat the arrival of defense counsel as the end of the party, *The Wire*'s habitual return to the scale of larger structuring conditions delimits the pleasure of watching such a scene of virtuosic box work. There's a certain queasiness to the comedy of the moment when the soft, bald Levy, angrily hauling the sheepish gangster D'Angleo by his elbow out of the police station, reaches up to smack him on the back of his shaven head while reminding him that if D'Angelo doesn't do, say, or write anything when he's in the box, then in the natural course of things Levy can very probably mobilize enough money and leverage to get him off. Given the larger structuring truths of which Levy's reminding his client, it's clear that while tricking D'Angelo into remorse was an inspired piece of work by his interrogators, it didn't accomplish anything.

And that's the cops at their best in the box. Often, they're not anywhere near that good. In episode 4, Carver and Herc screw up a canned routine when Carver, who is playing the sympathetic interrogator, loses his temper. "You're supposed to be the good cop!" shouts Bodie, a veteran participant in such scenes and a stand-in for consumers of them, as the detectives throw off all pretense and descend on him to put in the boot. That episode is full of formal reminders that on this show even the most generic pleasures of the crime genre—like deceptive fun and games in the box—come enframed by a larger analysis that makes the viewer suspicious of them. Part of the show's formal profile is to always be jumping to the big picture. There's a lovely match-on-grossness, for instance, a visual rhyme between the water in a mop bucket in the detention center from which Bodie escapes and the contents of Herc's coffee cup as he complains about being on another shit detail, that suggests that both corner boy and cop are obliged to put up with unpalatable substances that flow downhill from people with real power (a subject that Herc and Carver discuss in scatalogical detail in episode 1). There's a deft camera uptilt that takes us abruptly from the projects—where a viewer trained by *Cops,* gangster movies, and hiphop videos could happily hang out forever, watching corner boys do telegenic business—to the downtown skyline and then, after an edit, to Judge Phelan and the deputy commissioner talking about the Barksdale case as a political football. There's also a fair amount of interpolated surveillance camera video in this and other early episodes, a post-9/11 stylistic touch that reminds us that what we see—and our enjoyment of it—is conditioned by who owns what, who knows what, who sees what. In the context of such recursions to structure, it's no longer possible to just sit back and revel in the spectacle of cops busting heads on the street or finding clever ways to get around criminals' rights in the box, or in the equally familiar spectacle of bad boys selling drugs and shooting rivals and otherwise cutting up rough.

When the wiretap finally goes up, it becomes the plotline and formal element that organizes everything else. Having been trained by the opening episodes to always be questioning our pleasures—*That was a really exciting raid,* the ideal viewer thinks, *and the cops look like they were really into it, and I hope there's another one soon, but I wonder if we all bought the pleasure of the raid at the cost of messing up the case against Avon and Stringer*—we're primed to look to the wiretap to pull together the elements of structural analysis already moving through the show from the outset. By the time Lester explains how things work to Sidnor and Prezbo in episode 9, "You follow drugs, you get drug addicts and drug dealers; but you start to follow the money, and you don't know where the fuck it's gonna take you," he's confirming what the show's form and content have already prepared us to understand. "More than the drugs," he says, "it's the money that matters," and the way to trace the money is through mind-numbing paperwork—poring over corporation charter papers, records of political contributions, and real estate transactions—that reveals the true structure of power in the city, the layer of deep crime. Like Sidnor and Prezbo, part of the viewer's genre-trained mind is thinking, *Oh, no, this looks like confusing and boring work. Can't we just get back to good old street rips?* But the *Wire*-trained viewer's genre mind is also thinking, *This is the real police work right here, the part for grownups. Everything else is cheap thrills, misdirection, and noise.*

The seasons that follow pay off this setup. Season 2 deepens the economic picture via an account of Baltimore's postindustrial transformation as seen from the waterfront. It's tempting to see *The Wire* as *Homicide* plus *The Corner*, but in at least one way the TV show is greater than the sum of those two excellent books. Using the tools of TV drama, such as long shots of characters framed against a waterfront in transition from blue-collar redoubt to a drug depot and site of renovated housing for service professionals, *The Wire* delivers the sense of the economic and political big picture that Simon and then Simon and Burns were unable to sketch convincingly in prose. Where the otherwise admirably disciplined nonfiction books reveal a weak point, resorting to the purple-dictioned generalities of a bad metro columnist whenever faced with task of putting the spiraling negative effects of the war on drugs in a larger historical context ("We can't stop it." Paragraph. "Not with all the lawyers, guns, and money in this world," and so on), the fictional TV show delivers sharp-edged analysis with the tools at its disposal: framing, editing, and resonant lines of dialogue voiced by characters about whom we care.[11] "You know what the trouble is, Brucie?" says Frank Sobotka, connecting the dots between a corrupt political culture, the booming drug trade, and the undermining of the working class by the collapse of the industrial economy. "We used to make shit in this country. Build shit. Now we just put our hand in the next guy's pocket."

Season 3 fills out the account of the city as a political system, and arrives at an analytical climax in the story of the rise and fall of Hamsterdam, the show's most fully realized diegetic critique of the war on drugs. The emotional climax comes in season 4, which traces the arrival on the street of a new generation of kids failed by the failing welfare state. The arc of Carver and Herc through it all serves as an object lesson. Herc never learns any way other than the Western District way, and ruins other characters' lives by doing what he thinks is the right thing: blowing the whistle on Major Colvin's Hamsterdam experiment, for instance, or letting a suspect in the box figure out that it was Randy who snitched to the police about a murder. Herc is Kojak's similarly smooth-headed early-twenty-first-century descendant, except he patrols the streets in an age that doesn't really allow for hearts of gold to do anything more than occasionally make a decent gesture (Herc's respectful chat with Bodie's grandmother, for instance) between episodes of enforcing the ruinous policies of the war on drugs. It makes perfect sense that Herc ends up as a private consultant, making good money off a bad system. Carver, by contrast, apprentices himself to Major Colvin and comes to understand the lessons of Hamsterdam, which leaves him in the emblematic situation of dedicated public servants with a sufficiently big-picture perspective on their work: pounding the wheel of his car in frustration after delivering Randy to a group home that will, inevitably, either destroy him or deliver him onto the street as a hardcase corner boy. Or, if Randy gets lucky, he might become a cop.

— — —

In his spoken commentary on the DVD version of episode 1 of the first season, David Simon notes that it was Ed Burns who wrote Carver's memorable line about the war on drugs: "Wars end." Simon adds that Burns is "entitled" to have written it after having fought in two losing wars, first as a soldier in Vietnam and then as a police officer in the war on drugs. The New Deal order spent much of its remaining force in these long, bloody pyrrhic stalemates. That is the historical and political big picture against which *The Wire*'s action is set, and in interviews the writers of the show are explicit about their interest in that big picture.[12]

Burns told me, "The three of us, David and George and myself, are not that happy about the war on drugs." Discussing their essay in *Time*, he added, "The point of the article, basically, is that people are fed up with it. We wanted to make it permissible to talk about that." He pointed out that Kurt Schmoke, who was mayor of Baltimore from 1988 to 1999 and turns up on *The Wire* in a small role as a health commissioner, was "crucified for questioning the war on drugs." Like the essay in *Time, The Wire* set out to make it all right to ask such questions. "The police have become an army of occupation," Burns, the former soldier and cop, said. "If you keep ignoring it, it won't go away." Simon added, "We were simpatico, politically. We wanted to highlight the fact that the drug war is actually destructive to law enforcement. We were not trying to affront good police work."

For Dennis Lehane, the chance to address the big picture in politically simpatico company was part of the attraction of signing on to write for *The Wire*. "I felt that a lot of 1980s crime fiction was shit and it wasn't about anything," he told me. "It was, 'Let's have nine serial killers.' I felt it has to be about something, some kind of social document. If there was a place where we all agreed, it was that the war on drugs was a farce, a de facto war on the poor that drove our incarceration rate through the roof."

Lehane and the others were trying to make a way between unacceptable paths of least resistance, choosing instead to blaze a fresh trail through the political culture. "I'm not a knee-jerk liberal," Lehane said. "I grew up in Boston under busing. We're not Kojak liberals"—he got the term from me, in the conversational back-and-forth—"and we're not knee-jerk liberals." In writing a good TV show that keeps these standard options at arm's length, he said, "the trick is to have a moral vision without becoming didactic about morality." For instance, "You don't read George [Pelecanos] without feeling his anger about gun control, but it's complicated. I don't think George is antigun in a crude way"—witness the scene Pelecanos wrote for *The Wire* in which Omar and Brother Mouzone discuss the properties of their respective firearms in a Western-style standoff in an alley—"but we've gotten to a level of lunacy in this country where gun people use the exact opposite argument on drugs."[13]

When I asked Pelecanos how explicit he and his fellow writers were in story meetings about their politics, he said, "It's always in the air. You don't want to let it get into the show"—in didactic form, he meant, agreeing with Lehane—"but it's there. Bunk's line about 'The bigger the lie, the more they believe it,' now that's about the war." Bunk delivers the line when he's gloating at the end of the opening set-piece of the first episode of season 5, after he and his partners have tricked a gullible suspect by pretending that a photocopier is a lie detector. When the invasion of Iraq began in 2003, Pelecanos was in Dayton, Ohio, on a book tour. "There's footage of the bombing on TV, and everyone in the hotel sports bar is cheering. I just had to go up to my room and get away from that. The line comes out of that."

The Wire registers its own status as a post-9/11 crime story in a number of formal and thematic ways: the omnipresence of camera surveillance in the visual scheme of the show and in the plot (as in the farce surrounding Herc and Carver's lost camera, for instance); the feds' increasing obsession with terrorism as the only crime they care about; surveillance as a larger and larger part of what the state does with its expanded powers. And, most centrally of all, the prominence of the wire itself has a strong post-9/11 feel. As the cops monitor chatter on the network and connect up the cells of foot soldiers to the intellectual authors of the ruin of Baltimore, it's hard to escape the analogy between the war on drugs and the even less rhetorically persuasive war on terror (how do you fight a war against being afraid?)—two permanent drop-everything crises that justify even more governmental abandonment of crucial duties to the citizenry in the name of delivering them from evil. This is how, finally, the motif of the wire enframes itself. In addition to contextualizing street policing and the box and showing up their limits, *The Wire* also trains the viewer to mistrust and suspect the pleasures of the wire—the primal joy of eavesdropping and voyeurism, the analytical thrill of breaking through to the layer of deep crime and coming to understand how power is organized in the city. The wire lets you, like the show's most astute investigators, apprehend the secret logic of the world of the text with revelatory clarity, the kind of lightning-strike insight that made Dashiell Hammett's Flitcraft feel as if "somebody had taken the lid off life and let him look at the works."[14] But there's nothing you, or McNulty and Lester and the rest, can do to change that secret logic. And when the wire comes down, as it always must, the evidence is boxed up and filed away in the depths of police bureaucracy, and the unsolved and apparently unsolvable deep crime exposed by the wire is hidden again from view.

Notes

1. Ed Burns, Dennis Lehane, George Pelecanos, Richard Price, and David Simon, "*The Wire*'s War on the Drug War," *Time*, March 5, 2008, http://www.time.com/time/nation/article/0,8599,1719872,00.html.

2. Ibid.

3. Ibid.

4. On academics' love of *The Wire*, see, e.g., Drake Bennet, "This Will Be on the Midterm: You Feel Me?" *Slate*, March 24, 2010, http://www.slate.com/id/2245788/.

5. Christopher P. Wilson, *Learning to Live with Crime: American Crime Narrative in the Neoconservative Turn* (Columbus: Ohio State University Press, 2010), 4 and 15.

6. E. J. Dionne, "Saving Cities: Is 'Kojak Liberalism' the Answer?" *Washington Post*, June 15, 1993.

7. I offer an extended argument about *The French Connection* as a pattern-setting posturban crisis crime story in *Good with Their Hands: Boxers, Bluesmen, and Other Characters from the Rust Belt* (Berkeley: University of California Press, 2002), 105–66.

8. Wilson, *Learning to Live with Crime*, 49–60.

9. The Rougon-Macquart novels are full of social analysis of the kind that William Julius Wilson, a big fan of *The Wire*, could love, but there are also many crime stories, some of which now read like robust precursors of noir. Perhaps the best example is the subplot in *La Bête Humaine* in which a husband fixated on the idea that his wife has a hidden fortune is slowly murdering her, despite her paranoid inspection of everything she eats and drinks, by slipping rat poison into her enemas.

10. For more on deep crime and surface crime, see Rotella, *Good with Their Hands*, 119.

11. David Simon and Edward Burns, *The Corner: A Year in the Life of an Inner-City Neighborhood* (New York: Broadway Books, 1997), 57.

12. I interviewed Simon, Burns, Lehane, and Pelecanos in the spring of 2008 in the course of writing a magazine story on Pelecanos: "Crime Story," *Washington Post Magazine*, July 20, 2008, 8–15, 22–26.

13. While he lasts, Omar is *The Wire*'s great unframed pleasure, the exception that proves the rule. A creature of pure genre who inhabits his own personal Western fable, he moves with duster aflap through the world of the text with a freedom denied all other characters, a freedom that serves to highlight the constraints placed on all the others by the dictates of social realism and the show's rigorous analysis of power. Omar's true neighborhood of origin is not in West Baltimore; it's the syllabus of a film course on the Western that both Simon and Pelecanos took, a couple of years apart, when they were undergraduates at the University of Maryland.

14. Dashiell Hammett, *The Maltese Falcon* (1930; New York: Vintage, 1972), 66.

6

The Wire: Bush-Era Fable about America's Urban Poor?

Peter Dreier and John Atlas

No television show about urban life has received as much praise as *The Wire*, a dramatic series about Baltimore that was broadcast on HBO for five years, ending in 2008. The entire show is now available in a five-CD set.

Although not a major commercial success with viewers, it was a huge hit with critics, who applauded its gritty depiction of urban life. The show won praise from reviewers across the political spectrum—from the *New York Times* to the *Wall Street Journal*, from the liberal *American Prospect* to the libertarian *Reason* magazine. Jack Dumphy, a columnist for the right-wing *National Review*, wrote that *The Wire* is "still the best show on television." *Slate*'s Jacob Weisberg called it "the best TV show ever broadcast in America." Novelist Stephen King, writing in *Entertainment Weekly*, called the show "a staggering achievement."

The show was a sociological treasure chest. The main focus of *The Wire* was life on the mean streets of Baltimore's inner city, especially its African American neighborhoods, and particularly the world of the gangs that controlled the city's drug trade. But each season, the show focused on a different aspect of life in Baltimore—the police, the docks, city hall, the schools, and the daily newspaper. The show juggled over sixty-five vivid characters. The large ensemble cast (disproportionately African American actors) included cops, teachers, reporters, drug dealers, dockworkers, politicians, and other characters in the real dramas of a major American city. Each year of the show, at least twenty-five of the characters had important parts. The writers wove these settings and characters into the show throughout its five-year run. As a result, viewers got a sense of how people were shaped by the larger system—their relationships with each other and with the web of institutions.

This wasn't just a formulaic cops-robbers-and-lawyers show (like *Law & Order*). Some critics compared *The Wire* to a great literary novel. Unpredictable plot twists, deft foreshadowing, and complex characters justify that judgment. Like most great stories, the main characters were morally ambiguous, but so finely etched that we cared about them. Even the gangsters were complex personalities, not the stereotypes typical of TV crime dramas. We ended up taking sides in gangland battles, rooting for Omar, Proposition Joe, and Bodie, and wanting Marlo annihilated. Unlike other TV crime shows, *The Wire* allowed viewers to see the characters and situations from multiple perspectives, not just through the point of view of the police and prosecutors.

David Simon, the show's creator and chief writer, is a former *Baltimore Sun* reporter; the other major cowriter, Ed Burns, is a former Baltimore cop and schoolteacher. Before writing *The Wire*, Simon wrote two books about Baltimore—*Homicide: A Year on the Killing Streets* (the basis for the excellent NBC television series *Homicide*, which he served as a writer), and (with Burns), *The Corner: A Year in the Life of an Inner-City Neighborhood* (which Simon adapted into an HBO miniseries, *The Corner*). Both books are full of sociological insights about urban life.

The writers paid attention to detail. The workplaces, neighborhoods, language, and events portrayed in *The Wire* had the kind of verisimilitude that justifies the torrent of praise. The show really captured Baltimore's nuances, flavor, language, and culture. Police detectives drank "Natty Boh"—National Bohemian, a beer originally brewed in Baltimore. And the dialogue rang true. Snoop, second in command to drug thug Marlo, explained to a hesitant gang member how she'd retaliate if he didn't cooperate: "We will be brief with all you motherfuckers—I think you know." Another drug kingpin, Avon, locked in jail and eager for stories in the street, asked Marlo: "What about you? How you been?" Marlo shrugs: "You know. The game is the game."

But in most ways, *The Wire* could have been about any older American city, facing the realities of the past decade—the loss of blue-collar union jobs, a shrinking tax base, racial segregation and the concentration of poverty, street gangs and the drug trade, and troubled schools.[1]

The show's two creators had a political agenda. They wanted *The Wire* not only to examine the realities of urban life, but also to provoke moral outrage. In interviews during and after the show's five-year run, they explained that they considered *The Wire* to be a form of muckraking reporting. Simon said he considered himself a "gadfly" and called the show "a political tract masquerading as a cop show" and a "critique of what . . . has gone wrong in America."[2] They didn't simply want to entertain. They wanted to expose injustice. They wanted to get people upset—perhaps upset enough to actually do something about the conditions portrayed in the show.

But if that was their goal, they failed. They failed not because the show wasn't upsetting, but because it portrayed urban life as hopeless. They portrayed the characters in the show as victims of a "system" beyond reform.

The show's writers may have thought that they were presenting a radical critique of American society and its neglect of its poor, its African Americans, and its cities. But there's nothing radical about a show that portrays nearly every character—clergy and cops, teachers and principals, reporters and editors, union members and leaders, politicians and city employees, social workers and everyday people—as corrupt, cynical, or well intentioned but ineffective.

In an interview, Simon observed that "*The Wire* is dissent."[3] But when asked, "Do you think change is possible?" Simon answered, "No, I don't. Not within the current political structure."[4] This view is reflected in the show. All writers make choices about what to include and what to exclude. This is called "artistic license." But those choices have consequences. *The Wire* was the opposite of radical; it was hopeless and nihilistic. The city portrayed in *The Wire* is a dystopian nightmare, a web of oppression and social pathology that is impossible to escape. *The Wire*'s unrelentingly bleak portrayal missed what's hopeful in Baltimore and, indeed, in other major American cities.

The Wire's last season ends with a critique of the press for failing to tell the true story of the innercity. Simon criticized the *Baltimore Sun* for its inadequate reporting about poverty and its decision to drop its poverty beat in the early 1990s.[5] In *The Wire*, however, Simon made the opposite error. He was so determined to expose Baltimore's problems that he provided viewers with an unrealistically negative picture of the inner city. In five seasons, the show didn't even hint at the possibility that residents, if well organized and strategic, can push powerbrokers to change policies and institutions to make the city more humane and livable. The effective organizing work over the past two decades of progressive union, community, and environmental groups in many cities and metropolitan areas—including Baltimore—is entirely missing from *The Wire*.[6]

In this regard, *The Wire* is similar to much of American sociology, which, despite its reform impulse, is better at describing the various forms of inequality and injustice in society than at identifying the political opportunities that make mobilization and reform possible. Sociologists are typically sensitive to examining what's wrong, but not as useful at offering solutions. There are, of course, many important exceptions to this characterization, but, in general, sociologists—even the radicals among them—are typically more comfortable emphasizing the structures of oppression over human agency, political strategy, and public policies that promote greater fairness, equality, and opportunity.

The Wire was broadcast from 2002 through 2008—the George W. Bush era. During that period, America faced the biggest concentration of income and wealth since 1928. A growing number of Americans—not only the poor but also the middle class—found that their jobs, their health insurance, their pensions, even their homes were increasingly at risk.[7] The cost of housing, food, health care, gas, and college tuition rose faster than incomes. During Bush's presidency, the number of Americans in poverty increased dramatically—from 32.9 million (11.7 percent of the population) in 2001 to 37.3 million (12.5 percent) in 2007—many of them among the growing army of the "working poor."

These conditions *should* provoke outrage. But simply being aware of these outrageous conditions doesn't guarantee that middle-class Americans, faced with their own economic insecurities, will identify with and make common cause with the poor. For that to occur, they need to believe three things:

First, that the plight of the poor is the result of political and social forces, not self-inflicted by the poor themselves

Second, that lifting up the poor will not come at the expense of middle-income Americans

Third, that the problems of the urban poor—and the magnitude of urban poverty—*can* be solved

In other words, they need some sense that all, or most, Americans share a common fate. They also need some sense of hope that things can change for the better. Hope springs from a combination of political leadership and grassroots activism.

Each of these three conditions has taken root in the past decade. Polls show that more and more Americans want the government to address the issues of poverty, housing, health care, and the environment. Even before the nation's economy took a sharp nosedive in late 2008, a growing number of Americans, including those in the middle class, believed that the widening gap between the rich and everyone else is a serious problem that government should deal with.

Since welfare reform was enacted in 1996, pushing more and more low-income people into the workforce, Americans have changed their views about the poor. They now increasingly view poverty through the prism of work and working conditions. They view people who remain in poverty despite working as the "deserving" poor. As a result, polls reveal that a vast majority of Americans want to raise the federal minimum wage so that it is above the poverty level—in other words, they believe that work should be rewarded. The popularity of Barbara Ehrenreich's book *Nickel and Dimed*, the challenges to Walmart (the world's largest employer, with a large low-wage workforce), and the remarkable success of the "living wage" movement in about 200 cities all reflect an upsurge of concern about poverty. Polls also show that support for labor unions has reached its highest level in more than three decades.

What does this have to do with *The Wire*? Three things:

First, to the extent that *The Wire* helped raise awareness of these problems—and the systemic nature of the urban crisis—it deserves all the praise it received. No other major industrial nation has allowed the level of sheer destitution that we have in the United States. We accept as "normal" levels of poverty, inequality, hunger, crime, homelessness, and inadequate and unequal school funding that would cause national alarm in Canada, western Europe, or Australia. *The Wire* brilliantly portrayed these realities, putting a human face on the "urban crisis."

Second, *The Wire* showed how people cope with "the system" and the overwhelming obstacles they face in just trying to get by or do their jobs. It showed how even people with good intentions and some idealism face enormous hurdles. By exploring the dysfunction of many key urban institutions—including politics and municipal government, the schools, the criminal justice system, and the media—*The Wire* revealed how urban politics is often a struggle over crumbs, whether the issue is funding for schools, police, housing subsidies, or drug rehab programs.

But third—and most important—*The Wire* failed to offer viewers any understanding that the problems facing cities and the urban poor are *solvable.*

To bring about the change that the show's writers hoped for, people need to feel not only that things *should* be better but that they *can* be better. *The Wire* offered viewers little reason for hope that the lives of the people depicted in it could be improved not only by individual initiative but also (and primarily) by collective action and changes in public policy. It offered viewers no hint that in Baltimore there was a small but growing movement to mobilize urban residents and their allies to address these problems—a movement that exists in every major city in the country and that has borne fruit in many ways.

The Wire's portrayal of Baltimore buttresses the myth that the poor, especially the black poor and the black working class, are helpless victims, unable to engage in collective efforts to bring about change. In other words, *The Wire* reinforced the notion that the harsh status quo cannot be changed.[8]

The Wire was populated by low-income African Americans and a handful of working-class and middle-class people whose jobs—cop, teacher, social worker, government bureaucrat, reporter, minister—involve relating to the poor as "problems" or "clients" rather than as fellow citizens.

The show virtually ignored Baltimore's black working class. Although the show portrayed African Americans in a wide range of occupations (police administrators and cops, principals and teachers, union leaders and dockworkers, social workers and clergy, editors and reporters), almost all of the African Americans living in Baltimore's ghetto were depicted as dangerous criminals, drug addicts, welfare recipients—an unemployed underclass—culturally damaged, a class of people whose behavior and values separate them from respectable society.

Much of the Baltimore we see in *The Wire* focused on the residents of the low-income black neighborhoods. In 2006, blacks comprised 65 percent of the city's population. Among them, 23 percent were poor.[9] True, many were jobless. Baltimore has been hemorrhaging jobs for decades, an issue that *The Wire* addressed in its second season, when it looked at the decline of the city's port. As a result, finding a job has become a problem, especially for African Americans. The black unemployment rate in Baltimore in 2006 was 13.7 percent, more than double the white rate of 5.7 percent. In 2006, 42,300 black Baltimoreans were jobless. That's a big number, but that means that 86.3 percent of Baltimore's black adults in the labor force *were* working.

Virtually absent from *The Wire* were the working poor—those who earn their poverty in low-wage jobs. Among the 180,000 Baltimore residents who worked full-time, 38 percent earned less than $30,000. Among the 105,266 African Americans in Baltimore working full-time, almost half (46 percent) earned below $30,000.

The show offered a few small rays of hope by portraying some characters as people who were able to maintain their dignity and pride amid enormous turmoil. One such character was Bubbles, a recovering heroin addict and homeless person who displays an incredible will to live and extraordinary survival skills. *Slate* magazine's Jacob Weisberg lauded this aspect of the show. *The Wire*, he wrote, "is filled with characters who should quit but don't, not only the boys themselves but teachers, cops, ex-cops, and ex-cons. . . . This refusal to give up in the face of defeat is the reality of ghetto life as well. Feel me: It's what *The Wire* is all about."[10]

But the few heroes depicted in *The Wire* were individualist renegades and gadflies. These include cops like James McNulty and Lester Freamon and the stick-up artist Omar, as well as the social worker Walon (a Narcotics Anonymous sponsor played by the singer Steve Earle), the Deacon (an influential West Side clergyman played by Melvin Williams), and Dennis "Cutty" Wise (whose boxing program may stop a teenager from succumbing to a life of drugs).

Unlike unions and community organizing groups, the few do-gooders portrayed in *The Wire* didn't seek to empower people as a collective force. They tried to help individuals, one at a time, rather than trying to reform the institutions that fail to address their needs. One person alone, no matter how well intentioned, can't save a school system, create jobs, or make a neighborhood safer.

But Baltimore *was* (and *is*) filled with labor and community activists who were doing just that—mobilizing people to reform *institutions*, to change the *system*, to change the relationships of *power* in the city. Those people were *completely absent* from the show over the entire five years and sixty episodes.

Baltimore's recent history is filled with examples of effective grass-roots organizing that Simon and Burns could have used to portray a different slice of the city's sociological and political realities.

For example, in 1994, a community group known as BUILD (Baltimoreans United in Leadership Development) led a campaign that mobilized ordinary people to fight for higher wages for the working poor. One of those people was Valerie Bell. She lived in a small row house in Baltimore. With just a high school degree, she secured a job with a private, nonunion custodial firm that contracted with the city to scrub floors and take out the garbage at Southern High School. Baltimore was trying to cut costs by outsourcing jobs to private firms. Bell earned $4.25 an hour with no health benefits. Like so many others who earned a minimum wage each month, Bell coped with how to pay the electricity bill, groceries, and the rent.

BUILD put together a coalition of churches and labor unions and lobbied the city to pass a "living wage" law that would increase wages above federal poverty line. The law would apply to employees who worked for private firms that had contracts with the city. It would affect 1,500 workers, hired by private bus, security, and janitorial companies. The ordinance would force wages up from $4.25 to $8.80 an hour over three years, and then increase each year to account for inflation.

At some risk to herself, Bell organized other custodians to join the living wage campaign. When the company discovered Bell's activities, it fired her. Undeterred, Bell stayed active with BUILD and helped gather petition signatures and organize demonstrations. BUILD recruited academics who produced studies showing that it made no sense for the city government to save money in the short term by underpaying workers, who then had to resort to a variety of government-supported homeless shelters and soup kitchens to supplement their low wages. Working with BUILD, Bell and others put so much pressure on the city, they convinced Mayor Kurt Schmoke to support them. As a result of this grassroots organizing effort, Baltimore passed the nation's first living-wage ordinance. The current rate is $9.62. In 2007, community and labor activists led a successful campaign to get the state of Maryland to enact a state living wage law—the first state in the country to do so.

Economists estimate that the Baltimore living wage law puts millions of dollars into the pockets of the city's working poor each year, and has had a ripple effect pushing up wages in other low-paid jobs in the city. Following Baltimore's lead, there are now similar laws in about

200 cities across the country. The political momentum created by these local living wage victories changed the political climate at the national level. In May 2007, President George W. Bush reluctantly signed a bill increasing the minimum wage from $5.15 to $7.25 over two years—the first increase in the federal minimum wage in almost a decade.

For thirty years, BUILD—which is part of the Industrial Areas Foundation network founded by organizer Saul Alinsky and which has affiliates in many cities—has been dedicated to transforming Baltimore's struggling inner-city neighborhoods. BUILD has not only won the nation's first living wage campaign, it also has built hundreds of affordable housing units called Nehemiah Homes (named after the biblical prophet who rebuilt Jerusalem and modeled on a similar program in New York City).

BUILD also created a network of after-school youth programs called Child First. That program began in 1996 with city and private money, and provides free after-school care for over 1,000 children every year at the city public schools. Child First is an academic enrichment program. The program involves parents, staff, administrators, church members, and other community members to help students, a real "it takes a village" approach. Child First trains parents to take part in their kids' education by volunteering at schools and coming together to discuss how they can improve the school system. Volunteers tutor students in math and English, help them with study skills, and nurture their artistic talents.

During the 2007 election, BUILD signed up 10,000 voters as part of its "Save Our Youth" campaign. Every candidate for city council and mayor, including Mayor Sheila Dixon, committed to the agenda, which included doubling the number of summer jobs for young people and funding neighborhood recreation centers.

In December 2007, after several years of working with Dixon (as a city council member and then as mayor) to renew the run-down section of Baltimore known as Oliver—where much of *The Wire* was filmed—BUILD persuaded the city to transfer 155 abandoned properties to the community group, which will either rehab the homes or tear them down and build new ones, then sell them to working-class homebuyers. "BUILD is making steady progress in eliminating blight throughout the Oliver neighborhood, where 44 percent of properties are vacant," said Bishop Douglas Miles, fifty-nine, pastor of Koinonia Baptist Church.

A native Baltimorean, Bishop Miles, BUILD's cochair, grew up in public housing projects. He's been involved with BUILD for thirty years. Under his leadership, Koinonia Baptist Church initiated a number of innovative ministries including an after-school program called Project Safe Haven, a juvenile alternative sentencing program that has saved many teenagers from the fate of a life in and out of jail.

Bishop Miles, who watched every episode of *The Wire,* was outraged at the way the church community was portrayed. "*The Wire* ignores all the good work the faith community had done," he complained.

BUILD isn't the only group in Baltimore engaged in successful grassroots organizing.

The fourth year of *The Wire* focused on Baltimore's school crisis through the lives of several young boys barely coping with problems at home and lured by the illegal drug business. At one point in the show (episode 50, "Final Grades"), the boyish but cynical Mayor Thomas "Tommy" Carcetti lobbies Maryland's governor to help bail out the city's bankrupt public school system.

Missing from the storyline is what actually occurred in 2004 when two groups—ACORN and the Algebra Project—mobilized parents, students, and teachers to pressure Mayor Martin O'Malley (now Maryland's governor) to ask for state funds to avoid massive layoffs and school closings.[11]

ACORN, a community organizing group, built a coalition that included public employee unions and the Algebra Project (a group founded by civil rights icon Bob Moses to organize young people around school issues). The community and union activists hit the streets and filed lawsuits to get more money pumped into the school system.

In November 2003, ACORN members rallied at City Hall to deliver Maryland ACORN's second annual "Turkey of the Year Award" to Mayor O'Malley for his plan to balance the school district's budget at the expense of Baltimore students' education, in part by laying off a thousand school employees. The next month, ACORN organized a confrontation at a board of education meeting. With hundreds of ACORN members attending, and one member shouting through a bullhorn, ACORN took over the meeting before police hauled them out of the room.

The protests were part of a months-long campaign of agitation that forced O'Malley to come up with the money and avoid unnecessary layoffs and a state takeover.

"The system is in meltdown," Mitch Klein, an ACORN organizer, told us. "Cutting funds is like the Baghdad version of putting back together the Baltimore city public schools."

School reform is only one of several issues that Baltimore ACORN—an affiliate of a national organization with chapters in over 100 cities—has addressed. Its young organizers have identified and trained tenant leaders to wage a campaign to clean up hundreds of lead-contaminated rental units. ACORN's tenants organized a rent strike to pressure slumlords to remove lead hazards in thousands of apartments. ACORN's members also closed corner stores dealing drugs, improved the city's housing code enforcement program, and pressured the police department to assign more foot patrols to the low-income Cherry Hill section of Baltimore.

Banks have persistently redlined Baltimore's minority neighborhoods or engaged in abusive, discriminatory predatory lending practices, leading to a recent wave of widespread foreclosures. Lobbied by ACORN and other community groups, Mayor Dixon and the city council sued Wells Fargo Bank in January 2008 for targeting risky subprime loans in the city's black neighborhoods that led to a wave of foreclosures that reduced city tax revenues and increased its costs of dealing with abandoned properties. It was the first lawsuit filed by a municipality seeking to recover costs of foreclosure caused by racially discriminatory lending practices.

"Some things I can't accomplish by myself," said Sonja Merchant-Jones, a former public housing resident who is active in Baltimore ACORN, "but together we've been able to confront elected officials, banks, and the utility companies, and get them to meet with us, negotiate with us, and change things. But I'm disappointed that I never see things like this on *The Wire*."

Robert Mathews is a sixty-four-year-old janitor in an eleven-story office building in downtown Baltimore. He rents a small house in Montebello, one of Baltimore's most troubled neighborhoods, with his wife and two grown sons. The former merchant marine has been a deacon in his church for many years and a mentor for many of the church's youth. He takes them on trips and counsels them when they appear to be heading in the wrong direction. For almost three decades, Mathews has also been a union activist, utilizing the same skills to counsel, mentor, and organize his fellow low-wage janitors across the city.

After thirty years cleaning office buildings, he was making $9.10 an hour.

To win a better contract, in December 2007 Mathews helped lead a campaign of thousands of janitors in Baltimore, Philadelphia, and Washington, D.C., among them 700 cleaners, most of them African American, at over forty Baltimore buildings, including the high-rise Candler, Legg Mason, and Bank of America buildings downtown.

After months of protesting, picketing, threatening to strike, and negotiating, the janitors—part of the Service Employees International Union's Justice for Janitors campaign—won a 28 percent pay increase. The janitors also won up to two weeks vacation and employer-paid family prescription drug coverage. The agreement added dental and vision benefits to the employer-paid health plan.

Mathews, who remembers when Baltimore's schools, movie theaters, and restaurants were segregated, participated in civil rights protests in the 1960s. "To make change, you have to take a stand," he told us.

Mathews only occasionally watched *The Wire.* He was offended by its bad language, but also by its unrealistic depiction of the Baltimore he's lived in his entire life. "It's more negative than positive," he said. "The people on the show don't have anything to live for. The young people have no vision. If you want change, you have to believe things can change."

These real-life organizing campaigns by BUILD, ACORN, and SEIU's Justice for Janitors were reported in the *Baltimore Sun* and by local TV and radio stations. Yet David Simon, the show's creator, found no room to tell any of these stories in the sixty episodes of *The Wire* over its five-year run.

Rob English, a thirty-eight-year-old organizer for BUILD, is hardly a romantic radical. He served for four years as a platoon leader in Somalia.

Referring to *The Wire,* he said: "The show does an excellent job of telling one side of the story. But it's missing all the pastors, parents and teachers, principles, young people who are doing amazing work, radically trying to change and improve Baltimore."

People like Valerie Bell, Bishop Miles, Sonja Merchant-Jones, Robert Mathews, and Rob English are committed activists who have persisted in their organizing efforts through victories and disappointments. They never succumb to cynicism or corruption. The people organized by BUILD, ACORN, the Algebra Project, SEIU, and other community, labor, and environmental justice groups maintain a sense of hope and possibility in the face of difficult odds. And, slowly and steadily, their organizations have won significant victories that improve the lives of Baltimore's poor and working-class residents.

These community activists are not superheroes or naive idealists. They are ordinary people who sometimes manage to do extraordinary things. What distinguishes them is their patience, political savvy, street smarts, empathy, faith, and people skills required to build strong organizations that can mount grassroots organizing campaigns. They harness what organizers call "cold anger" and turn it into outrage against injustice rather than indiscriminate rage.

They do not expect to turn Baltimore upside down. Rather, they mobilize people to win small, concrete victories that improve people's living and working conditions, and whet their appetites for further battles. They challenge the city's political and business establishment and seek to get Baltimore's power players and institutions—employers, landlords, politicians, police chiefs, school superintendents, and others—to the bargaining table, where they can negotiate on a somewhat level playing field. They don't always win, but by their persistence and their ability to recruit people to join them, they have to be taken seriously by the city's powerbrokers.

They know that there are limits to what can be accomplished in one city—that many of the problems facing America's cities can only be solved with changes in federal policy. They recognize that organizing people in their communities and workplaces is a precondition for mobilizing people from across the country into a broader movement for social justice.[12]

Those who lead union- and community-organizing fights have the same foibles and human weaknesses we witnessed in the characters in *The Wire*. But incorporating their stories into the series would have shown a different aspect of Baltimore, one in which the poor and their allies seek change, not charity, and learn how to marshal their collective power. Unfortunately, community activists and leaders like these didn't exist in the Baltimore depicted in *The Wire*. Without them and the organizations they belong to, we were left with a view of Baltimore's poor as people sentenced for life to an unchanging prison of social pathology. This, in fact, was how *The Wire* viewed the poor.

David Simon, *The Wire*'s creator, told *Slate* magazine, "Thematically, [*The Wire* is] about the very simple idea that, in this postmodern world of ours, human beings—all of us—are worth less. We're worth less every day, despite the fact that some of us are achieving more and more. It's the triumph of capitalism."[13] He added, "It's the triumph of capitalism over human value. This country has embraced the idea that this is a viable domestic policy. It is. It's viable for the few."

But Simon's worldview—at least as it revealed in *The Wire*—is hardly radical. He generally views the poor as helpless victims rather than as people with the capacity to act on their own behalf to bring about change. He may think he's the crusading journalist exposing injustice, but, based on the show, he's really a cynic who takes pity on the poor but can't imagine a world where things could be different.

It is probably no accident that *The Wire* ended its five-year run just as the Bush era was ending. The zeitgeist of the Bush era was a culture of fend-for-yourself cynicism, with no agenda to address the needs of cities like Baltimore. It appears that Americans may be ready to feel hopeful again, as evidenced by the election of Barack Obama.

Perhaps, a year or two from now, Simon or another writer will propose a new series to TV networks about the inner workings of the White House and an idealistic young president, a former community organizer, who uses his bully pulpit to mobilize the American people around their better instincts.

This president would challenge the influence of big business and its political allies, to build a movement, a New Deal for the twenty-first century, to revitalize an economy brought to its knees by Wall Street greed, address the nation's health care and environmental problems, provide adequate funding for inner-city schools, reduce poverty and homelessness, and strengthen the power of unions and community groups.

In May 2008, Simon and Burns received an award from the Liberty Hill Foundation, a Los Angeles organization that provides funding for cutting-edge grassroots community, environmental, and labor organizing. In accepting the award, they offered congratulations to the activist groups whose leaders were represented in the audience.

Simon said, "*The Wire* spoke to a world in which human beings—individuals—matter less, a world in which every day, the triumph of capital results in the diminution of human labor and human value. Is that world an accurate depiction of America? I hope not. But we live in interesting times, and perhaps the only thing that is left to us as individuals is the power to hope, and to commit that hope to action."

Unfortunately, that attitude was not evident in *The Wire*. But in that statement, Simon reflected a new spirit of possibility that is a precondition to transforming the country.

Notes

1. See William Julius Wilson, *More Than Just Race: Being Black and Poor in the Inner City* (New York: W. W. Norton, 2009); William Julius Wilson, *When Work Disappears: The New World of the Urban Poor* (New York: Alfred A. Knopf, 1996); Douglas W. Rae, *City: Urbanism and Its End* (New Haven: Yale University Press, 1993); Peter Dreier, John Mollenkopf, and Todd Swanstrom, *Place Matters: Metropolitics for the 21st Century*, 2nd ed. (Lawrence: University Press of Kansas, 2004); David Ranney, *Global Decisions, Local Collisions: Urban Life in the New World Order* (Philadelphia: Temple University Press, 2003); Steve Greenhouse, *The Big Squeeze: Tough Times for the American Worker* (New York: Alfred A. Knopf, 2008).

2. "*The Wire*'s David Simon," KQED's Forum, December 4, 2008, http://huffduffer.com/ Clampants/1278.

3. Margaret Talbot, "Stealing Life: The Crusader behind *The Wire*," *New Yorker*, October 22, 2007.

4. Meghan O'Rourke, "Behind *The Wire*: David Simon on Where the Show Goes Next," *Slate*, December 1, 2006, http://www.slate.com/id/2154694. In a 2006 speech, Simon said, "I am wholly pessimistic about American society. I believe *The Wire* is a show about the end of the American Empire. We are going to live that event. How we end up and survive, and on what terms, is going to be the open question." http://immasmartypants.blogspot.com/2007/12/on-behalf-of-human-dignity.html.

5. Lawrence Lahanan, "Secrets of the City: What *The Wire* Reveals about Urban Journalism," *Columbia Journalism Review*, January–February 2008.

6. In recent years, a number of social scientists and journalists have documented that upsurge of grassroots organizing across the country. See, for example, Heidi J. Swarts, *Organizing Urban America: Secular and Faith-Based Progressive Movements* (Minneapolis: University of Minnesota Press, 2008); Lowell Turner and Daniel Cornfield, eds., *Labor in the New Urban Battlegrounds: Local Solidarity in a Global Economy* (Ithaca, N.Y.: Cornell University Press, 2007); Manuel Pastor, Chris Brenner, and Martha Matsuoka, *This Could Be the Start of Something Big: How Social Movements for Regional Equity Are Reshaping Metropolitan America* (Ithaca, N.Y.: Cornell University Press, 2009); William

Julius Wilson, *The Bridge over the Racial Divide: Rising Inequality and Coalition Politics* (Berkeley: University of California Press, 2001); Mark Warren, *Dry Bones Rattling: Community Building to Revitalize American Democracy* (Princeton, N.J.: Princeton University Press, 2001); Richard Wood, *Faith in Action: Religion, Race, and Democratic Organizing in America* (Chicago: University of Chicago Press, 2002); Robert Gottlieb, Mark Vallianatos, Regina Freer, and Peter Dreier, *The Next Los Angeles: The Struggle for a Livable City*, 2nd ed. (Berkeley: University of California Press, 2006); Daniel Clawson, *The Next Upsurge: Labor and the New Social Movements* (Ithaca, N.Y.: Cornell University Press, 2003; Samuel Freedman, *Upon This Rock: The Miracles of a Black Church* (New York: Harper Collins, 1993); David Reynolds, ed., *Partnering for Change: Unions and Community Groups Build Coalitions for Economic Justice* (Armonk, N.Y.: M. E. Sharpe, 2004); Paul Osterman, *Gathering Power: The Future of Progressive Politics in America* (Boston: Beacon Press, 2002); Marion Orr, ed., *Transforming the City: Community Organizing and the Challenge of Political Change* (Lawrence: University Press of Kansas, 2007); Gregory Squires, ed., *Organizing Access to Capital: Advocacy and the Democratization of Financial Institutions* (Philadelphia: Temple University Press, 2003); Marshall Ganz, *Why David Sometimes Wins: Leadership, Organization, and Strategy in the California Farmworker Movement* (New York: Oxford University Press, 2009); Peter Dreier and John Atlas, "The GOP's Blame ACORN Game," *The Nation,* November 10, 2008; Peter Dreier, "A Progressive Moment or a New Progressive Era? Community Organizing, the Labor Movement, and Progressive Politics in the Age of Obama," in *Where Do We Go From Here? American Democracy and the Renewal of the Radical Imagination,* ed. Mark Major and William Thompson, (Lanham, Md.: Lexington Books, 2010); and John Atlas, *Seeds of Hope: The Untold Story of ACORN, America's Most Controversial Community Organizing Group and How It's Changing America* (Nashville: Vanderbilt University Press, 2010).

7. Jacob S. Hacker, *The Great Risk Shift* (New York: Oxford University Press, 2006).

8. This is typical of how the media in general report on urban affairs. See Peter Dreier, "How the Media Compound Urban Problems," *Journal of Urban Affairs* 27.2 (2005): 193–201.

9. In 2006, 19.5 percent of Baltimore's residents—and 27.5 percent of its children under eighteen—were poor, according to the U.S. census.

10. Jacob Weisberg, "*The Wire* on Fire: Analyzing the Best Show on Television," *Slate,* September 13, 2006, http://www.slate.com/id/2149566.

11. Laura Vozzella, "Allies, Foes of Mayor Swap Sides over Loan: O'Malley's Schools Plan Praised by Labor, Activists; Business Leaders Worry," *Baltimore Sun,* March 15, 2004; Liz Bowie, "Trustee Suggested for City Schools: Grasmick

Bombshell Comes at Funding Hearing," *Baltimore Sun*, August 5, 2004; John Gehring, "Velvet Glove, Steel Hand," *Education Week*, January 14, 2004; John Gehring, "Studies, Sit-ins Earn ACORN's Activists Voice in Education," *Education Week*, February 18, 2004; "Blacks Support for ACORN Grows," *Sun Reporter*, January 8, 2004.

12. *The Wire* left it to the viewers to put the problems of Baltimore in a wider context. Although the United States has many serious problems that are disproportionately located in cities, these are national problems. Local governmental policies are not their cause. Even the most well-managed local governments on their own don't have the resources to significantly address them. A good example is the current mortgage meltdown. Baltimore sued Wells Fargo for its predatory lending practices. But the problem extends far beyond Baltimore. It was caused by the failure of the federal government to regulate the financial services industry. Only the federal government can address the issue of regulating banking practices. Similarly, only the federal government has the resources to provide adequate funding for housing, public schools, health care, child care, and environmental cleanup; and to address the shortage of decent jobs that is ultimately at the root of Baltimore's crisis, from the docks to the ghetto to the inner suburbs.

13. O'Rourke, "Behind *The Wire*"; Mark Bowden, "The Angriest Man in Television," *Atlantic*, January–February 2008, http://www.theatlantic.com/doc/200801/bowden-wire.

7

Tales of the Neoliberal City: *The Wire*'s Boundary Lines

Liam Kennedy and Stephen Shapiro

As noted in the introduction to this book, David Simon views *The Wire* "as a vehicle for making statements about the American city and even the American experiment."[1] That these two concepts are conjoined in Simon's perspective is suggestive of a particular view of the city as a crucible and laboratory of national concerns. This is an idea of the city that has a long lineage in American culture and representation: it valorizes the city as a space of encounter in which the dramatic intersections of different narratives and identities reproduce an imaginary citizenship. *The Wire* refashions this idea for the contemporary city and produces a belated imagining of the "making of Americans" as an urban process.[2] In this chapter we will examine how the show both critiques and reimagines this process, with particular focus on its treatment of neoliberal forms of urban governance.

"It's All Connected'

The Wire's opening scene can be read as projecting these concerns. The white cop McNulty arrives at a crime scene where the victim, Snot Boogie, has been killed having tried to rob a dice game. McNulty sits down next to a black Baltimorean and asks why Snot Boogie was allowed to return constantly to the contest if the players knew that he would always try to grab the money. The informant replies: "Got to. This America, man." Indeed, the series' first screen image reinforces this axiomatic claim. Our first view of *The Wire*'s Baltimore is literally the street with a streak of blood set off by a harsh (police siren) light. The color code of red, white, and the pavement's darkish blue, combined with the clanging opening sequence song, implying the bang following a rocket's red glare, suggests that we are being invited to view the ensuing urban procedural as a forensic dissection of the root features of national mythology and motivation. The "tragedy" of the tale that McNulty hears, but does not reply to, is, of course, that "the game" (a keyword for *The Wire*'s cosmography) is structurally loaded against the individual. Snot Boogie has the right to try, but no matter how agile he may be in this mundane casino, eventually the house will take everything back in the most fatal way. The significance of this scene as a symbolic framing device is accentuated by its anomalous nature, for it is exceptionally disconnected from all that follows—neither the "crime," Snot Boogie, nor the informant is mentioned again—but this only emphasizes the significance of the scene as a primal scene of "the American experiment," a "game" of repeated, delusionary promises.

There is something retrograde in this ambition to read the city as a national space at a time when it has become more difficult to describe a national experience in urban terms or evoke a shared historical consciousness of the city. Simon's ambition to dramatically present the city as a totality is also an attempt to reenchant his audience's jaded fascination with the city as the indispensable center of (post)modernity. The Baltimore of *The Wire* is an imagined totality, which is intended to symbolize desires and anxieties around the meanings of nationhood, citizenship, urbanity, and justice in the United States. As such, the show both comments on and reproduces a common desire for "legibility" in urban representation.[3] This is notable in its multinarratives, spanning and entwining different urban formations and lives, and in its ambition to reveal the barely visible routings of power and capital in the urban order. The show attempts to provide new narrative and media techniques to gain a many-windowed perspective (to use longtime Baltimore resident David Harvey's terms) on the lived systems and institutions that contemporary capitalism creates, redefines, and leaves aside as obsolete.[4] In this respect, we may understand the linking plots, connected in part by the technology of "the wire," as fused chronotopes, mediating the distinctive temporal and spatial coordinates of neoliberal urban governance and its discontents.

However, this sense of totality and connectivity—"It's all con-

Opening shot of season 1, episode 1.

nected" is a key refrain in the show—is also an illusionary construct that glosses the limitations of a heuristic imagination and a left-liberal critique as commensurate to understanding neoliberal urbanism. Throughout the show, as the plotlines unfold, *The Wire* also unfolds ideological and formal contradictions and limitations of the crime story as a template for understanding urban America in the twenty-first century. To some extent, the creators are aware of this and draw attention to exhausted genre conventions. At the same time though, *The Wire* is caught up in the conditions and contradictions of its own powerful social critique, and its appeal may in part be symptomatic of the capitalist moment it critiques. This is to recognize that all cultural production is symptomatic of the "conditions of possibility" within which the producer(s) work and which are set by a given stage of capitalism.[5] The significance of *The Wire* as a cultural production must include comprehension of the political economy of its making, dissemination, and reception (for example, as HBO product) as well as the nature of its powers of representation and critique. This is not to gainsay its critical agencies and capacities, nor its utopian moments. *The Wire's* totalizing imperative—at once mirroring and critiquing the totality that is contemporary capitalism—is a form of dialectical representation that is rarely so expressively formulated in televisual terms. As such, it drives a progressive critique of the conditions of capital's power and modes of governance. But it also gives rise to tensions and contradictions that illustrate the blindness as well as the insight of this critique.

These limitations are apparent in the show's use of established genres and narrative forms. Simon frequently refers to Greek tragedy and Anglo-European naturalism as core influences on the show's presentation of power, the deterministic environment of the city, and its fated effects on individuals. At the same time, he describes the world of contemporary capitalism as "postmodern" and asserts that *The Wire* "depicts a world in which capital has triumphed completely, labor has been marginalized and monied interests have purchased enough political infrastructure to prevent reform. It is a world in which the rules and values of the free market and maximized profit have been mistaken for a social framework, a world where institutions themselves are paramount and every day human beings matter less."[6] If this account might fit Fredric Jameson's definition of the postmodern moment as the period in which capital has overcome any geography of uneven development, it also does not necessarily match to the Baltimore that viewers are led through.[7] Nor is it comfortably represented by naturalist modes of narrative, plot, and character representation, and the discord between the mode of representation and its object indicates the difficulties the show has in cognitively mapping the forms and effects of neoliberal urbanism.

Simon's perception of postmodern capitalism and its institutions correlates with what is now commonly referred to as neoliberalism. Neoliberal economics stands as the particular and newly dominant phase of capitalism defined by a set of core strategies involving the reestablishment of social inequality, the privatization of public resources, the deregulation of markets by disabling the State's protective oversight, the financialization of everything into movements of fictitious (or speculative) capital, and the acceleration of disempowerment of any collective form of representation, but especially that of labor (unions) through a tactical deployment of individual liberty, the freedom of consumer choice in a world composed less by consensual negotiation than by selfish competition that is often predetermined for the benefit of an elite crony-cartel, and the embrace of entrepreneurial risk, as the "rational choice" for organizing even the most basic of life choices, such as housing and service utilities, health, education, and so on. In urban terms, it refers to the sociospatial restructuring of the city in the interests of a deregulated, speculative capital that seeks out "spatial fixes' for excess accumulation and thereby displaces and devalues established social formations and landscapes. Under these conditions of "creative destruction," urban governance involves new strategies of social control, policing, and surveillance, and managing social reproduction.[8]

Many of these elements do appear as thematic touchstones and recurring events within the series, as with the abiding concern with the gentrification of Baltimore's laboring-class neighborhoods and use of "development" as meaning the appropriation and refinement of urban neighborhoods for speculative, privatized housing for a new elite, rather than the broad enfranchisement of populations through civil rights campaigns. The show also foregrounds social obsolescence and in particular the criminalization of the urban poor—key components of neoliberal doctrine—as everyday facts of urban governance, but seeks to put human faces on this "other America." This governance is also pronounced in the surveillance and regulation of urban social life—most obviously, the surveillance of drug dealers and others by the police—and in the fiscal constraints on policing and correlative depiction of policing as quantitative administration, obsessed with enumerated "turnover" and "results."

Yet while *The Wire* represents key aspects of neoliberal urbanism, it also produces confused and confusing messages about this mode of capitalism. The show's overarching concern would appear to be anger at the corrosion of regulatory state and state apparatus institutions by capitalist interests, and the resulting feature that what were once social institutions no longer function to ensure the social contract that properly behaved individuals will be protected. In this sense, Simon's postmodern complaint can be understood as anger at neoliberal capitalism's deregulation of the urban institutional matrix, which once allowed its social map to be intelligible through the rational procedure on which the detective genre depends. Yet if this is *The Wire*'s point, it often either sidesteps it or buries the "lede." (The repeatedly staged complaint that the FBI has been in dereliction of its duty to pursue criminals because its resources have been dedicated to the "War on Terror" does not clearly indicate a new form of capitalism as the fundamental problem.) *The Wire* also foregrounds a much more classically modern-era complaint abut the stifling effects of institutional bureaucracy, its inefficiencies (particularly as a springboard for the entrepreneurial or self-motivating), and the ways in which its concerns for its own survival allow for a new psychopathology of organizational careerism and self-protective deadwood sitting on its hands waiting for the pension clock to ring.

The mixed nature of *The Wire*'s complaint against a definition of dominant postmodernism/neoliberalism and a dominant modern-era/monopoly/Fordist capitalism, we contend, both captures its peculiarity within the period's television and highlights the outline of its visionary boundaries. Periodization is partly what is at issue here, for the show seems to promise to map the historical totality that is neoliberal urbanism, but is also in thrall to a vision of earlier modes of capital-labor relations—most obviously in the romance of a white ethnic city that has all but disappeared.

"Every Piece Matters"

The golden era of HBO (and its cable associates) dramatic broadcasting was defined by hewing repeatedly to a particular theme, regardless of historical period or location: the tale of the small (family) business or unit that was losing its struggle against incorporation within or obliteration by the competitive pressures of a larger organization. This fear of succumbing to the overdetermining pressures of a larger monopoly or corporate unit (however broadly defined) was personified by the angry breathing of a male protagonist who frequently could not articulate his anxiety even while audibly performing an embodied belligerence and then spasmodically erupting into manual violence or projections of this blood sport with the fascination with relics of the grotesquely traumatized body. Hence *The Sopranos*, *Deadwood*, *Six Feet Under*, *Rome*, Showtime's *The Shield*, and so on. In many ways, it was HBO's version of its own self, even while accurately resonating with and then amplifying many of its subscribers' concerns about a swiftly globalizing marketplace that undermines past certainties and is placing increasing pressure on purchasing costs of a middle-class identity as signaled by the status markers of housing, health care, and (higher) education.

The Wire continues this theme while also differentiating itself, signaled by its mixed genre form. It awkwardly combines the conventions of the generic detective novel and hard-boiled procedural noir. The show's overall arc follows the lines of noir as McNulty ventriloquizes and stages serial murder, even while also seeking to maintain the fiction of the detective's outside objectivity.[9] The mixed nature of Simon's complaint and the series' form is less an instance of incoherence than a disturbance that illuminates the keys to its perspective. For what distinguishes The Wire from other small-unit-under-threat shows is its claim to be uninterested in competing for the wealth that it otherwise dedicates itself to following via its path of circulation. Yet this lack of interest itself becomes the source of its noirlike incrimination because its desired hoard is not the desire for money to be speedily accumulated and invested as capital, but information to be slowly cumulated and packaged as a heuristic. The surveillance team that is re-created at the center of each series is analogous to a team of (academic) researchers. The zoology that The Wire captures is less that of the racialized ghetto than of the behavioral spectrum of researchers, some of whom remain dedicated to their pursuit, some of whom convert their careers along the lines of careerism and the institutional politics of administration, and some of whom slumber toward retirement, years before the event. The analogical proximity of The Wire's procedural to analytical research results from the series' most clearly defined and asserted value: the need for autonomy of artisanal craft in the face of interference from bureaucratic desire for mass production and time-resource efficiency measures.

Despite the pressures to remove red ink from the gridded board in the homicide unit, there is the constant refrain of praise for "natural (or real) police," a self-defining elite determined by their dedication to the inefficiency of artisanal diligence, an ideal exemplified by Lester Freamon's patience in the pursuit of results and the vexed respect for "giving a fuck when it's not your turn" despite, and often in direct antagonism to, institutional requirements for achieving turnover targets. It is a truism that The Wire gives dignity to the black underclass by illustrating the comparable structure and pressures within the institutions of the drug trade and the police, a world in which individuals must shape their personalities into personas that fit the social game's conventions. Yet the halo of equality is greatest among the figures who recognize their ostensible antagonists' dedication to their craft, a focus enunciated as having a "code" or personalized compass of behavior different from "the game's." The code is best seen in its willingness to resist the larger institutional or corporate management even if it means facing career and/or self-obliteration, a move performed repeatedly by *The Wire*'s characters and staged multiple times in the show as "pissing in the tracks of an oncoming train." Stringer Bell never becomes more compelling, despite his ruthlessness, than when he displays chesslike long-term focus and craft ("nicely played" is the phrase McNulty and he exchange). Similarly, Proposition Joe first appears to the viewer as an absurd figure during the East-West Baltimore basketball game as he wears a suit to mimic corporate management. He gains dignity, instead, when shown as a careful, reflective craftsman, literally a worker with his hands in a functioning repair shop.

The idealization of individualized craft's dedication to use-value rather than the institution's pursuit of exchange-value and quickly achieved turnover is not unique in contemporary culture. Every episode of *CSI*, for instance, must legitimize the forensic team by enacting the solitude of the laboratory as the place where "old-school" and "real" artisanal concentration on skillfully manipulating difficult techniques and esoteric instruments stages the utopian escape of those with trained skill from the otiose pressures of dim-witted officials and office managers who damn the artisans as residual obstructions to the forward motion of results, rather than refinement. Yet the fetish of archaic craftwork as quasi-aristocratic resistance of the skilled elite to the large-scale industrial production of public institutions belongs to the procedural convention as far back as Poe's "chevalier" Dupin and Sherlock Holmes's chafing of the bureaucratized, urban police. What separates the condescending attitude of *The Wire*'s craft workers from these earlier models, however, is the dedication to transgenerational mentoring. Where earlier forms of the craft detective require a sidekick, the latter's purpose is only to record the master's brilliance. In *The Wire*, training of the apprentice into the mysteries of the craft stands as a model of social organization that competes with the plot of career advancement through learning how to trade in the market in favors. Craft mentoring is deeply (male) homosocialized (which is perhaps why Kima can last as a detective, while Beadie does not, because the former does not scramble training with heterosexual desire, while the latter does) and is often placed in opposition to lineage succession via "blood" family and ethnic relations. Artisan mentoring emerges as *The Wire's* most successful model of overcoming the tribalism of racial divisions, such as seen with Pryzblewski's tutelage by Freamon or Bubbles's "schooling" of Johnny or "bushy-headed" McNulty's by Bunny and then Bunk. Conversely, kinship is rejected as the sphere where mentoring often fails (mainly because the family is seen as too easily capitulating to the easy pursuit of money—McNulty's seeming complaint at his ex-wife). Maury Levy's welcoming of Herc as "family" by the end of season 5 is to be heard as a sickening victory of the sly opportunism of those antiartisans who take shortcuts.

Leslie Fiedler long ago noted the recurrence within nineteenth-century American culture of narratives wherein a lower-status, older black mentors an impulsive, white naïf, and this model recurs within contemporary productions in films such as *Pulp Fiction, Seven,* and *Die Hard.*[10] While *The Wire* does repeat this pattern, it does not allow it to dominate its vision of craft training as a mark of realness, since *The Wire* presents instances of extrafamilial mentoring between blacks (Omar's schooling of his lovers and gang associates, Michael's training by Chris Partlow, and, in one of the most accurate depictions of a seminar room's frustrations, Stringer Bell's running of the meetings in the funeral home as a community college classroom, where Bell wants his authority confirmed as a skilled teacher, rather than family-based ruler, of men) and across the white ethnicities (the Greek Spiros's affection for the Polish Nick). Rejecting biological production and social reproduction through bureaucratic licensing in favor of an elite's training, craft work is seen as a modern overcoming of the feudalized bloodlines of ethnicity and family, but also uses its defiant celebration of learned skill to reject the Taylorized bureaucratic organization's mass production of posts and the politics of promotions.

The celebration of a self-selecting, but trained elite of dedicated craft workers as a model for social organization and mechanism for the creation of urban dignity has limitations, though, as Richard Sennett argues in *Respect in a World of Inequality* (2003), a work contemporaneous to *The Wire.*[11] Like the series, Sennett's theme is the search for a mechanism for the granting of dignity for those caught within the long duration of generational poverty and spatial constraints of low-income public housing. Sennett's work begins with a reflection on his own childhood in Chicago's Cabrini-Green projects and its transformation away from its historic roots as a mixed-race housing compound. While his single-parent mother moves out of the projects and he advances from a foreshortened musical career into a prolonged and celebrated academic one, Sennett recalls returning to Cabrini-Green on a panel of successful graduates designed to explain to its current youthful residents "how to get there from here" (a question Dukie plaintively asks in *The Wire,* without ever being answered), how to escape the vortex of the ghetto. Sennett's larger argument for the Toquevillian collective performance of self-administration has its limits, mainly in his almost total avoidance of the pressures of drugs and gang violence that *The Wire* richly details. But *Respect in a World of Inequality* usefully cautions against the craft ideal as a model for social amelioration. For "craft" leads the individual to an inward-oriented language of perfectionism as a device for the discrimination of others through shameful judgment on the motivations of others. The craft ideal's assumption that merit and talent should be free from the regulations forming social groups leads to an aggressive dismissal of others in a stereotypical masculinist fashion. These are the features that neatly characterize McNulty, but also his easier-to-digest associates, like Freamon and Bunk.

The crony institutional structure that rewards tribal coherence and the ideal of individualized craft are not, however, the only models of possible social organization that *The Wire* presents. A third way appears in social (or community) service, a parainsitutional ethic that can exist in both public state bureaucracies and private corporation-like structures, while also seeking to behave in ways not reflective of the dominant values of either. The public service ideal involves the activity of those who tirelessly work, often in the lower grades of management, pragmatically within but not compliant to the corroded (public) institution in order to protect and provide for individuals to the degree possible. Examples of the public service ideal include the deacon (Melvin Williams), who is mainly responsible for finding job placements for ex-convict Cutty, Assistant Principal Marcia Donnelly, the unnamed Catholic Worker soup kitchen manager, and Walon leading the AA meetings, along with a host of minor other characters, such as the Baltimore City Community

College economics instructor (who unwittingly aids Stringer Bell). In *The Wire*, it is the community service characters that act as the real forces who are able to link figures in need through different settings. The artisan, on the other hand, increasingly sees his own institutional setting as deserving autonomy and lacking the need to interact with other social institutions, thus creating the very gaps in the social fabric through which characters like Randy and Bubbles fall. In this light, it is significant that while the police have no means to identify Barksdale, he is made recognizable by the boxing poster from community groups. The community service workers succeed partly because they both protect their superiors and respect their manager's best intentions, while also learning how to juke the system in sustainable ways. Unlike McNulty's hair-trigger betrayal of the chain of command, Donnelly makes a point of telling Bunny that the school principal is a good man that needs protecting, and she is also the one whom the deacon directs Cutty to for work, since Donnelly has preserved part of the janitorial budget for truancy work. Unlike McNulty's offbook allocation of departmental resources to solve crimes in season 5, Donnelly's improvisation will not blow up in her face.

The distinction between craft and community service is one also felt palpably in the wake of *The Wire*, which has received grateful reception as a spur for real-life nonprofit projects, especially for black youth, such as Sonja Sohn's Baltimore community initiative ReWired for Change. Interestingly, nowhere is the racial divide (and rejection of Simon's fatalistic vision) more palpable that in the response by the cast, where the white actors seem collectively less personally transformed by *The Wire*'s implications than the black cast members, who testify both to the specialness of their personal experience on the set and its acting as a catalyst for spending energy away from their career and toward public service.

Yet while the community service ideal is arguably more successful within *The Wire*'s narrative, it is also consistently de-emphasized, if not marginalized. The interior lives of the communitarian characters are rarely presented to viewers, and they are rarely scripted in ways that articulate their motivation. Indeed, any immersion into their believability is often undermined through casting choice, such as the controversial use of a real-life Baltimore drug lord for the deacon or the exceptional use of a recognizable star with Steve Earle's Walon. Cedric Daniels says

of his ex-wife Marla that she used to live through the events of his career, and this functions as a metareflexive comment since we, the viewers, do so as well. Yet when she begins to be involved as an agent of
community representation, we are positioned as seeing her as part of
the problem rather than an attempted solution. It is a truism that *The
Wire* reflects a masculinist culture and has difficulty presenting the
lives of women with as much complexity as it does of the men. Kima,
for instance, is significant only because Simon admits that they wrote
the character as if she were a man. But *The Wire*'s gender division is not
simply a patriarchal inability to contemplate the other sex's structures
of feeling, since gender acts as the medium for the show's distinction
between social maneuvers. For the community service model is routinely feminized (even when carried out by men) and presented as disabled (literalized with the paraplegic state delegate Odell Watkin or the
HIV-positive, recovering addict Walon). It is not just that Simon is most
comfortable with narrating the tale of the underrecognized, frustrated
male intellectual/artist (a move that is continued through *Generation
Kill* and wholly surrendered to in *Treme*), but that this gendered figure
carries out a particular devaluation and refusal of the communitarian
project.

The refusal to extend recognition (and screen time) to the community service ideal exists, however, to limit the horizon of the social in
two ways. Firstly, as Dreier and Atlas note in their essay in this book,
The Wire is reluctant to show the existence of grassroots activism, beyond social service ones.[12] The historical background of black civil rights
is erased from the background and only appears tangentially in season
2 with the convention that the stevedore union leadership will rotate
between the races. The black empowerment of the Nation of Islam appears through Brother Mouzon, but only as an organization complicit
with, rather than resistant to, the drug trade. In a larger sense, there
is a larger political constraint involving more socialist forms of state
organization. The rejection comes obliquely, since to denounce it directly would also begrudgingly acknowledge it as a possible alternative.
In a world where the craft workers believe that "every piece matters,"
we are twice presented with the comedic scene of McNulty and Kima
failing to negotiate the construction of Ikea furniture, a process that
requires separating out all the pieces immediately to know in advance
where they will go. Flat-pack furniture stands as a metonym for the left-

center "Swedish model" of combining a free market with high taxation and statist control. Similarly, the denunciation of Rotterdam's port as monstrous (possibly a backhanded comment on Paul Verhoeven's own Rust Belt procedural, *Robocop*) does not ask the question of how labor might work with the state rather than in opposition to it. While not as many jobs would have existed as Frank Sobotka might have wanted, the Rotterdam option would have saved the job of Johnny Fifty Spamanto, who reappears in the homeless encampment in season 5.

The American rejection of Eurosocialist or communitarian ideas explains why "modern" institutions are valorized within Simon's liberalism, a nostalgic yearning for a state run by meritocratic elites that grants a place for capitalism, so long as the free market does not attempt to infiltrate the sociopolitical sphere of artisan elites. The complaint in the series is not about capitalism, only about a late stage of capitalism ("postmodernism"). For this reason, the coda that Lester hears is not that he should have focused on the bankers, but the lawyers, as if corrupted institutions, rather than class exploitation, is the fundamental problem in contemporary America. For unlike the TV show *Breaking Bad*, which presents its lawyer, Saul Goodman, as a weak buffoon, *The Wire* makes a point early on of indicating that Maury Levy was president of the local bar association and therefore not one to be trifled with. It is *The Wire*'s refusal to push beyond its definitional boundary that results in its petit bourgeois ideal finding solace with a properly functioning free market, typified by Lester Freamon, who ultimately becomes a kind of property developer, rehabilitating and then selling dollhouse furniture (assumably to clients not from the Baltimore hood) and succeeds in the Dickensian ideal of reclaiming a "fallen woman" with a good heart into the ideal of home and institutional work as a nurse. If the naturalist genre was willing to confront a larger panorama of capitalism, Simon's retreat to the Greeks as his informing texts indicates his reluctance to break that boundary.

"Back in the Day"

The Wire's confused representation of periodicity is strongly reflected in the turn to memory within the show's narratives and it's more general treatment of a fatalistic environment of decaying urbanism. To be sure, the Baltimore of *The Wire* symbolizes "deindustrialization" within a broader, national community of memory. What is less clear, however, is who are the subjects and objects of this symbolism, both within the world of the show and among its projected viewers. While the show demystifies elements of the procedural genre, it also mystifies the investments—affective and economic—that popular television has in representations of urban decline.

For Simon, "Baltimore" represents the symbolic order of a national identity that is strained and fractured, but was once more whole, held together by forms of work and community that have all but dissolved under conditions of neoliberalism. He appears fascinated not only by the forces and results of the dissolution but also by the remnants of the earlier (imaginary) urbanism. A repeated visual motif of *The Wire* is a long, panning shot of decaying row buildings. In his DVD commentary on episode 1 of season 3—which begins with a scene of demolition, the implosion of the Franklin Terrace housing project—Simon expresses what sound like spontaneous feelings about a later shot of abandoned row houses:

> I love this shot. This is what was at stake. This is the Baltimore that. . . .
> I mean, I love row houses, and if you're from around here you know that
> they've destroyed and gutted and bulldozed a lot of the vacant ones . . .
> and even though they're vacant . . . you just want to think that one day
> they're all going to come back . . . it's just so sad.

Simon's fragmented commentary indicates a confused perspective on the abandoned environment as a space of loss. Does he mean to envisage a renewed neighborhood, or is this a lament for those who are gone? Is he referring to an earlier age of race and capital formations in this urban space, or to the present? Who is being forgotten/remembered in the representation of such abandoned spaces? Whose memory can reenchant these spaces? This is also to ask: what are the imaginative investments of cultural producers and viewers in creating and consuming representations of urban decline?[13]

These questions once again underline issues of periodization and historicity. On the one hand, in its own temporal unfolding—its deliberate slowing of time (as conventional serial narration)—*The Wire* invites the viewer to fill in historical ellipses, restore time to perceptions of ghetto space, and confront the longevity of the ghetto as a structural condition of urban governance. On the other hand, the connections between past and present are often rendered opaque or dissolved by the sense of loss that permeates the narrative and is awkwardly plotted in character developments and relations across ethnic and racial lines. This generalized sense of loss also suffuses the landscapes of the show and renders Baltimore a space of memory, an uncanny *lieux de memoires,* replete with gothic references to abandoned buildings full of ghosts.[14] When, at the end of the last series, McNulty says to a homeless man, "Let's go home," he expresses both an impossible dream and a fitting closure to a show that mourns a lost urbanism. He also brings us full circle, echoing the compulsive, fatal investment in the game that Snot Boogie lost.

The Wire registers considerable ambivalence about the power of memory work to reclaim or maintain alternative urban imaginaries or as a resource for critical explanations of historical processes. In a rare moment of explicit national history commentary, stevedore Frank Sobotka relates a tradition of union betrayal at the federal level to an uncomprehending Bunk. This outburst helps explain the slow train of eroding labor influence and self-control that Sobotka has spent the majority of his life, rather than simply the late 1990s, experiencing. Almost before he actually had children, then, he began to feel the need to preserve an inheritable lifeworld for them to occupy. Yet despite Sobotka's longer frame of time, most of the characters in *The Wire* explain their current feelings of insecurity more as a result of the loss of collective memory than as the result of a long, structurally influenced unraveling of popular power. "Back in the day" is both the plaintive slogan of social erasure and incomplete mechanism of explanation. The loss that the drug trade is listed as causing indicates the experience of violence to time itself, where the known rules of behavior in the neighborhood that provide protective body armor for survival are considered to be constructed by Time, rather than society, and consequently ephemeral and unreliable. The complaint about the loss of time, rather than bodies or social relations, is usually pitched simply as one generation's disregard for the prior one (another reason why *The Wire* usually presents families as locations for disappointment rather than extramarket protection). Marlo Stanfield's refusal to accept the compacts of those older than himself and his accomplishment of Cheese's nephew's betrayal of Proposition Joe looks to destroy the memory of the past as much as does the personnel of the older standing order.

"Back in the day" is perhaps a more appropriate strapline than "It's all connected" to describe *The Wire's* urban imaginary. It is the axiom of an enervated urban perspective that simultaneously romanticizes the past and acknowledges the failures of resistance and explanation in the present. Several authors in this volume refer to the limits of interpretation encoded in the show's reflexive treatment of the procedural genre. Rotella argues that *The Wire* lets us "apprehend the secret logic of the world of the text" but adds that there is nothing we can do to change the world represented. Kraniauskas identifies the "narrative limit" of the show as the space of fictitious capital, the "pure money" of neoliberal accumulation. These limits may be seen as a recognition of the limits of critique confronted by the speculative forms of neoliberal accumulation. On this reading the failure of detection is symptomatic of the conditions of this accumulation; capitalism is the "unsolvable deep crime," in Rotella's words. Or they may be seen as a consequence of Simon's efforts to retrofit a genre that is asynchronous with its object. Or perhaps it is the fatalism of his own vision that is most limiting. *The Wire's* final message, as seen in the concluding montage, is that time does not matter, for the dominant social order means that all of the structure's positions will return even if the specific characters change: so Omar is replaced by Michael, and so on. The tautology of repetition, as Anderson notes in his essay ("the game is the game") works to deny the importance of historical reflection and any striving to recover and remember the past. Once again, Snot Boogie is our guide.

Yet the show does present a differing viewpoint with its chief philosopher of historical continuity and transformation within that continuity: Slim Charles. Slim Charles is both aware of the futility of trying to maintain the past exactly as it was ("the thing about the old days: they the old days") and willing to adapt to the new times by moving from West Side Baltimore (Barksdale) to East Side (Proposition Joe). On the other hand, he recognizes that the fundamental logic of the drug trade remains even if its form (of production and distribution) alters. When an out-of-time Cutty remarks on how the "game" has changed, Slim Charles tersely replies, "Game's the same, just got more fierce." It is not that the past is simply irrelevant for Slim Charles; he is, after all, the one who "sentimentally" acts as the sword of vengeance by murdering Cheese in Joe's memory after Cheese has delivered an antinostalgic polemic that emphasizes "the moment" and "deep structure" ("It's just the street, and the game, and what happened here today") without moral regard to the past. Instead, as Slim Charles (at times reluctantly) moves upward in the hierarchy of drug leadership, seen in the last montage as now replacing Joe and Marlo as he sits with Spiros to discuss distribution, he appears to understand what Simon does not, that each cycle of capitalism shares certain features, even while it constantly revolutionizes its mode of production. Perhaps it is this realization that makes Slim Charles ultimately one of the most successful players in the game, moving ever upward in his institution in ways that seem to be destined for longevity rather than notoriety.

Slim Charles, however, is exceptional in his understanding of historicity. For most of the characters, temporal analysis gets truncated, yet simultaneously preserved, in the compensatory mechanism of narrative language itself. A similar relation is explained in *Candyman* (1992, Bernard Rose), which was shot within and concerns Cabrini-Green projects. The film is ultimately a tale of a white woman's resistance to patriarchal authority as she inhabits the history of experienced violence by the black community. Early in the film the woman, Helen Lyle, an ambitious graduate student, explains the project's myth of Candyman, a spectral presence who appears after his name is said three times before a mirror: "An entire community starts attributing the daily horrors of their lives to a mythical figure." The prophylactic turn to gothic as a compensatory language, to both say what is happening before their eyes and not risk the danger of saying, likewise appears with the explanation that Chris Partlow is making zombies in the terraces (instead of saying what is latently realized, that these houses are haunted not by the undead but by "decomps" created by drug violence). Like *Candyman*, *The Wire* seems to suggest that blocked structural analysis finds its way out through the production of the vibrant slang and phrasing that most viewers of the show find magnetizing and quickly begin themselves to emulate through repetition. The mirroring of the obvious, but with a twist that is epitomized in the phrase "true dat" suggests that the language of the neighborhood has a dual function to both sustain in a subterranean fashion the realization of social dynamics and historical linkage and cap it from being extended into an explicit form of declaration, which might be dangerous and revolutionary. The ambivalent nature of language, as both a key to decoding and an instrument best left contained, is epitomized most clearly with the figure of Officer Caroline

Massey, the black officer who first appears in season 3 as one who must translate ghetto slang, even to other black officers. Massey, again, is one of the peripheralized characters in *The Wire*. She is never given either a backstory (of how she came to be attached to the unit) or included in any summative trajectory (and does not seem to be present at the various bar wakes, the scenes of institutional esprit de corps). Many fans of the show will struggle even to recognize the character's name, let alone presence. Yet Massey suggests that in the absence of structural analysis, it will be language and florid narrative that will hold, uphold, and constrain collective memory.

Collective memory, though, can miss the ways in which the best parts of the past are enrolled into the changes of the future. John Lanchester notes that despite its "Balzacian . . . scope and achievement," *The Wire* "still missed out on one of the worst disasters to affect Baltimoreans in decades": the wave of mortgage foreclosures due to subprime real estate loans during the 2002–8 boom.[15] By 2010, more than 33,000 householders in Baltimore had lost their homes, with many of these in the show's African American West and East Baltimore neighborhoods. Homelessness was not simply caused by a familiar practice of gentrification, the displacement of ethnic neighborhoods by wealthier whites, but by newer forms of neoliberal speculation due to the predatory lending by banks that manipulated programs designed to aid nonwhite home ownership. The blowout caused by resulting foreclosures has caused the city of Baltimore to file several lawsuits against lending practices that specifically targeted nonwhites' desire to purchase homes within their own neighborhoods, in ways that reconfigured racial disempowerment within new neoliberal predicates.[16]

Antony Bryant and Griselda Pollock raise the enigmatic role of Bunny Colvin as *The Wire* gives no background to what allowed Colvin to differentiate himself from Wee-Bey (or high-school Bunk from Omar) or all the other "invisible citizens" who likewise escape the undertow of the drug trade.[17] The absence of the past's differentiations, however, still leaves Colvin's rescue of Namond as one of the few instances of how a character can go from "here to there." While season 4 ends with Namond looking out from Colvin's home onto a departing car, which allegorically sounds the tentacles of his drug past departing, the viewer does not realize that Colvin's neighborhood, and Namond's future, was simultaneously under threat due to the bankers' own version of Hamsterdam, a reverse redlining that was ensnaring even the middle-class African American community within subprime mortgages. The problem with *The Wire*'s own inability to recognize the differences between gentrification and subprime has to do with Simon's dogged insistence on the authenticity of nostalgic memory over ongoing analysis of a city in dynamic capitalist restructuring. As one web commentator notes, Simon takes events from 1990s Baltimore (the time of his journalism) and has them enacted in the first decade of the new century (the time of *The Wire*'s broadcast), thus displacing a focus on contemporary pieces of lives and real estate that were being moved about on the urban gameboard.[18]

"True Dat"

Early in 2011, the new Baltimore police commissioner claimed that *The Wire* had severely damaged the city's reputation, describing it as "a smear that will take decades to overcome." In response, Simon argues that "*The Wire* owes no apologies. . . . As citizens using a fictional narrative as a means of arguing different priorities or policies, those who created and worked on *The Wire* have dissented.'[19] This certitude about the role and capacity of the citizen-as-dissenter is a clear reformulation of Simon's vision of the show as a commentary on "the America experiment" and a vision corrective of the skewed representations of contemporary American urbanism. As such, *The Wire* may be viewed as something of a distended jeremiad, calling the nation back as well as forward to a more unified national purpose. The imagined citizenship of this call is in part the projection of its documentary format, a format that Simon has long favored, believing that such representation of the lifeworlds of others presages forms of ethical apprehension and social knowledge. This reflects a tradition of American documentary production that runs from the late nineteenth century, one that holds that documentary modes of representation function to "model" liberal-democratic citizenship; they both mirror and shape relations between liberalism and democracy, between public and private spheres, and between the individual and the state.[20] Central to the development of documentary representation in the United States is the belief that it functions as a critical mirror of American history, revealing the discrepancies between the nation's ideals and its real conditions. Simon endorses this documentary ethos, and *The Wire* maps and models ideas of liberal-democratic citizenship, critically and symptomatically, at a time of crisis for its once-sustaining paradigms of the nation-state and of liberal capitalism.

This is to say, once again, that the show advances a belated critique in its efforts to cognitively map neoliberal urbanism. Belated and fatalistic as it is, it is also utopian in allowing us a fitful apprehension of historical processes that shape the neoliberal moment. If it does not fully envision alternative urban futures, yet it powerfully illustrates why they are needed and the failures of the state and of mainstream popular culture to imagine them.

Notes

1. David Simon, "*The Wire*: A One-Hour Drama for HBO," http://kottke.org.s3.amazonaws.com/the-wire/The_Wire_-_Bible.pdf, September 6, 2000, 2.

2. We allude to Herbert Gans, *The Urban Villagers: A Study of Second-Generation Italians in the West End of Boston* (Philadelphia: University of Pennsylvania Institute for Urban Studies, 1959).

3. To render the city "legible" has varied, overlapping meanings in different forms of urban representation: for planners, it means making the city integral and governable; for cultural producers, it means making it coherent and knowable. The classic account is Kevin Lynch, *The Image of the City* (Cambridge: MIT Press, 1960).

4. David Harvey, *The Limits to Capital* (Chicago: University of Chicago Press, 1982).

5. As we have argued elsewhere, all cultural studies have to seek to define their study with reference to four different, but intertwined, layers or valences. These are the object of study's relationship to the features of capitalism in theoretical abstraction (such as the law on value, the tendency of the rate of profit to fall, etc.), the continuing, material features of capitalism in actual practice from its onset through to the current moment, the phases that have different dominant practices in sequentially expanding periods (the era of handicrafts, the era of manufacture, the era of large-scale industry, etc.), and finally the particular features of an object within a world-system of time and place formed with reference to the other three aforementioned layers. Since all four aspects must be accounted for, the failure to do so can lead to cultural criticism often being unable to explain the ways in which eighteenth-century affairs are both linked to and different from twenty-first-century ones in capitalist societies. Yet the effort of differentiation often provides an avenue for evaluating a cultural ob-

ject's achievements and limitations, its resistances and capitulations. Stephen Shapiro, *The Culture and Commerce of the Early American Novel: Reading the Atlantic World-System* (University Park: Penn State University Press, 2008), 29–30.

6. David Simon, introduction to Rafael Alvarez, *"The Wire": Truth Be Told* (Edinburgh: Canongate, 2009), 30.

7. Fredric Jameson, *Postmodernism; or, The Cultural Logic of Late Capitalism* (Durham, N.C.: Duke University Press, 1991).

8. For neoliberal urbanism, see Harvey, *The Limits to Capital* and David Harvey, *Spaces of Neoliberalization: Towards a Theory of Uneven Geographical Development* (Stuttgart: Franz Steiner Verlag, 2005) and *A Brief History of Neoliberalism* (Oxford: Oxford University Press, 2005), and Gérard Duménil and Dominique Lévy, *The Crisis of Neoliberalism* (Cambridge: Harvard University Press, 2011).

9. The generic detective novel or procedural within the bourgeois marketplace posits an objective analyst who seeks to resolve a crime. Yet since the outrage is only the contingent manifestation of a more latent and larger crime, usually involving class conflict, which the detective cannot resolve or even openly comment on, the tension between reestablishing the surface harmony of society as it ought to be through the device of police administration and the representation of the actual structurally determining social conflict, which is unreported, let alone challenged, results in the detective internalizing this contradiction and recording it instead through personalized psychic disorders and physiological damage (drug and alcohol self-abuse being the main modes of choice). Noir or hard-boiled procedurals seek to escape the sanitizing effects of the crime and urban procedurals that are acceptable to the middle class by representing social contradictions through contaminated narratives, wherein the detective's pursuit of the solution becomes a matter of self-revelation as the analyst finds her- or himself increasingly implicated *within* the crime and thus increasingly unable to achieve the prophylactic security of distanced surveillant. In noir, the detective's presence is itself the crime. Such tales come closer to explicit social critique, even when they ultimately remain trapped within or submissive to the hegemony of conventional permissibility.

10. Leslie Fiedler, "Come Back to the Raft Ag'in, Huck Honey!" *Partisan Review* 25 (1948): 664–71.

11. Richard Sennett, *Respect in a World of Inequality* (New York: W. W. Norton, 2003).

12. Sonja Sohn confirms Drier and Atlas's argument as she relates that while working in Baltimore with ReWired for Change she found to her surprise that many in the Baltimore "nonprofit world" were angry that their community work was not represented. "Race and Justice: *The Wire*," Harvard Law School,

April 12, 2011, http://www.law.harvard.edu/news/spotlight/civil-rights/ogletree-race-and-justice-the-wire.html.

13. Since the early 1970s, urban narratives in many genres have (re)told the stories of ethnic or racial secession and passage as powerfully motivated processes of remembering and forgetting. See Liam Kennedy, *Race and Urban Space in American Culture* (Edinburgh: University of Edinburgh Press, 2000), 53–55 and 129–30.

14. Laura Lippman, mystery novelist, *Baltimore Sun* reporter, *Wire* cameo journalist, and David Simon's wife, reinscribes this turn as she writes, "The Centers for Disease Control will tell you that Baltimore is the off-and-on capital of syphilis, but the true local malady is nostalgia, a romanticizing of our past that depends on much glossing and buffing, as if our history was just another set of marble steps to be cleaned," in her "Introduction: Greetings from Charm City" to her edited short-story collection *Baltimore Noir* (New York: Akashic Books, 2006), 13. This collection is part of Akashic's city-titled noir series, which uses gothic boosterism to celebrate a locality's "spirits" by narrating the perverse charms of its social and individual dysfunction. Lippman's collection is a post-*Wire* paratext, with contributions from David Simon and Rafael Alvarez. Her own contribution to the book, "Easy as A-B-C," revises Baltimore legend Edgar Allen Poe's "The Black Cat," while also silently referencing a story line in *The Wire*'s season 2. The story has a first-person narrator, a married building contractor, who has an affair with, and then murders, a yuppie woman in the course of his renovating her recently purchased Locust Point row house, which had been his grandmother's and his childhood residence. The narrator disposes of the corpse by covering it with lime (like Chris Partlow) and bricking the corpse in the basement fireplace. Locust Point is the Sobotkas' neighborhood, where Nick fails to purchase his aunt's old home. With its dislikable female victim, the story differs from Lippman's usual Baltimore fiction, typified by their strong women, which is perhaps also why she was enrolled to defend *The Wire*'s marginalization of women with "The Women of *The Wire* (No, Seriously)," in Alvarez, *The Wire*, 54–60. "Easy as A-B-C," though, follows *The Wire*'s moves as it stages class envy and seemingly spontaneous violence against an agent of gentrification, but then overlays class struggle with the connotations of white aggression against the rise of nonwhites, as Lippman echoes Poe's own tale of a black domestic's revolt and her story's introductory complaint about the influx of Latino workers into Baltimore's manual craft trade and the fascination with a woman alluded to as of foreign ethnicity. Sobotka is brought down by "The Greek," who is never brought to justice for dead women in a can; Lippman's narrator gets away with likewise killing of a woman with "darker eyes that made me think of kalamata olives" ("Easy as A-B-C," 17–28).

15. John Lanchester, *IOU: Why Everyone Owes Everyone and No One Can Pay* (New York: Simon and Schuster, 2010), 67–68.

16. "Baltimore Is Suing Bank over Foreclosure Crisis," *New York Times*, January 8, 2008, and "Bank Accused of Pushing Mortgage Deals on Black," *New York Times*, June 6, 2009. See also Elvin Wyly, "Things Pictures Don't Tell Us: In Search of Baltimore," *City* 14.5 (2010): 497–528.

17. Antony Bryant and Griselda Pollock, "Where Do Bunnys Come From? From *Hamsterdam* to Hubris," *City* 14.5 (2010): 709–29.

18. "Spike," comment on "DVD Reviews: *The Wire*, Season Two," November 20, 2007, http://pandagon.blogsome.com/2007/11/20/6344 (accessed September 4, 2011). Simon never hesitates to recite a declension narrative about the failure of contemporary journalism to pursue holistic exposes, but he also is prey to a certain ideal of journalism that understands investigative journalism is primarily dedicated to the revelation of political decision-making rather than structural analysis of contending economic forces.

19. "'Wire' Creator Responds to Top Cop's Criticism," *Baltimore Sun*, January 18, 2011, http://weblogs.baltimoresun.com/news/crime/blog/2011/01/simon_responds_to_bealefelds_c.html (accessed February 18, 2011.

20. See Robert Hariman and John Lucaites, *No Caption Needed: Iconic Photographs, Public Culture and Liberal Democracy* (Chicago: University of Chicago Press, 2007).

8

Elasticity of Demand: Reflections on *The Wire*

John Kraniauskas

Can't reason with the pusherman
Finances is all that he understands.
  —Curtis Mayfield, "Little Child Runnin' Wild"

David Simon and Edward Burns's TV series *The Wire* (HBO, 2002–8) opens with a killing and builds from there, over five seasons and sixty hours of television. What it narrates is the present life of a neoliberal-ized postindustrial city, from the critical perspective of its bloody "cor-ners," the bloody corners of West Baltimore, USA.[1] *The Wire* is a con-tinuation of Simon and Burns's earlier series *The Corner* (HBO, 2000), a docudrama, or quasi-anthropological reconstruction of real lives, di-rected by Charles S. Dutton. In fact, in many ways it is a combination and development of two previous TV series: *The Corner* (based on Si-mon and Burns's book *The Corner: A Year in the Life of an Inner-City Neighborhood*, 1997) and NBC's cop show *Homicide* (based on Simon's book *Homicide: A Year on the Killing Streets*, 1991).[2]

Corners are where everyday drug business is carried out. They are violently fought over and defended as what remains of the local econ-omy is bled dry and addiction extends. They are the places, in other words, where the stories of the "invisible hand" of the market and/or "originary" capital accumulation are played out. This is the local, ev-eryday street experience of (illegal) capitalist globalization. It provides the pathetic script for the character Bubbles (drug addict and police in-formant), which is literally written into his body, making him the fig-ure of maximum affective intensity in the film text.[3] They are places of labor, too, including child labor: the "corner boys." Finally, they are places of intense state scrutiny and surveillance.

The "wire" that gives the program its name is a bugging or wiretapping device, fundamental to the narrative structure of each one of *The Wire*'s seasons. It is the main technological means of secret intelligence gathering, sought and deployed by the police to listen to, identify, and decode the telephone messages circulating between the drug dealers. In this respect, *The Wire* presents itself as a police procedural, centered on the detective work involved in juridically justifying and then deploying the bugging technology required. In a sense, looking for and acquiring such a device defines the operation as involving serious police work: patient investigation and interpretation and the like. Unlike the police-procedural pedagogic norm, however, *The Wire* critically foregrounds technological underdevelopment and uneven distribution, educating its viewers into a culture of everyday police bricolage and ingenuity, very different from the hyperbolic scientific know-how of *CSI* and its many imitators.

The activities of pushing and policing in *The Wire* mark out a territory that is racially and socially divided, crisscrossed and sutured (constituted in antagonism); in other words, wired. Crime at one end, joined to the law at the other; it constitutes "a whole way of life."[4] In this respect a work of urban anthropology, *The Wire* nonetheless turns its corners so as to accumulate characters, stories, and "adventures." It expands and opens out onto the world, charting encounters, much like the novel in its chivalric, educational, and realist historical modes. However, here it is a TV camera-eye that travels, explores, and frames the city, emplotting its sociocultural environments (in particular, their racialized, gendered, and class divisions), activating, in Franco Moretti's words, their "narrative potential," which is to say, their relations of power, their "plots"[5]—but only so as to return, repeatedly, to illuminate its point of departure, the streets, and its principal object of attraction, the everyday experience and effects of the trade in drugs and its policing. Like other works of detective and/or crime fiction, *The Wire* relays and establishes the political and cultural contours of the contemporary, at speed. Indeed, in this sense, it fulfills one of the prime historical functions of the genre.[6]

As *The Wire* voyages out from the low- and high-rise housing projects whose corners it films, accumulating and weaving together its stories, it accretes social content as part of its overall moving picture. This is conceived primarily in terms of a set of overlapping institutions and their hierarchized personnel: the police (both local and federal), the port authority and trade union organization (in season 2), the city administration, its juridical apparatus, and its shifting political elites (especially from season 3 onward), the local educational state apparatus (season 4), and the local city newspaper (in season 5). It is important to note that these are all places of work. Work is a structuring ideologeme of the series, as it was previously of *The Corner*—with its dealers—and more recently of Simon and Burns's disappointing subsequent series about U.S. soldiers in Iraq, *Generation Kill* (2008), with its "grunts."[7] They are also sites of political power-play, concerned, like *The Wire*'s "auteurs" themselves, with establishing their own standpoint with respect to the dramas played out and filmed in the streets. Thus *The Wire*'s own TV camera consciousness produces itself, as it were, in counterpoint to the multiplicity of institutional perspectives it reconstructs, taking the side of the dominated, that is, of the "workers" portrayed in each case (this is what provides for the moments of identity between the frontline police and the corner boys—Bodie, Michael, Namond, Randy, Dukie, Poot—dramatized particularly in season 4). *The Wire*'s populist images are, to use Sartre's words, "act(s) and not . . . thing(s)."[8]

Season after season, over years of progamming, *The Wire*'s looping narrative methodology transforms and enriches its own story and perspective. There is, however, a tension here that drives its realist compositional logic—and which its long-running televison format invites—that is both formal and analytic. *The Wire* attempts to resolve the enigmatic character of the social that grounds the crime and/or detective fiction form through an accretive looping logic that incoporates *more and more* of the social (through its institutions), but that thereby simultaneously threatens to overload and diffuse its televisual *focus* on what is most compelling: the dramatization of the political economy of crime as the key to the understanding of contemporary neoliberal capitalist society (in Baltimore) and its policing. As the series develops and gathers in more institutions, increasingly the dramas occur as these overlap—police with city hall and school, newspaper with police, for example—rather than in and between drug dealers and police. Inverting the procedure of the classic police-procedural film *The Naked City*

(Jules Dassin, 1948), instead of zooming in on one of "8 million stories," the series zooms out, arguably too far, attempting to show them all. The paradox of *The Wire*'s accumulative compositional strategy—and the epistemological and aesthetic problem it poses—is that the more of the social it reconstructs, shows, and incorporates into its narrative so as to explain the present, the less socially explanatory its dramatic vision threatens to become.[9] Although, alternatively, this compositional paradox might also be read as constitutive of all form-giving in an unreconciled (that is, class) society.

Crime Scenes

It is as if *The Wire* had been produced in response to questions initially posed by Walter Benjamin in his "A Small History of Photography" (1931) regarding the photographic mediation of the experience of the modern city. Noting how the journalistic—and quasi-cinematic—work of photographers like Atget was increasingly able "to capture fleeting and secret moments" that thus demanded explanation (he refers specifically to the emergence of the use of captions in this regard), Benjamin asks, "is not every square inch of our cities the scene of a crime? Every passer-by a culprit?" And further, "Is it not the task of the photographer . . . to reveal guilt and to point out the guilty in his pictures?"[10] Three-quarters of a century (of technology) later, this is where the first episode of *The Wire* begins, with a crime scene in a Baltimore city street, one of many.

The opening scene of *The Wire* is both generically conventional and narratively surprising. It is also intensely televisual. A crime has taken place, and *The Wire* takes us to it immediately, opening directly onto a bloodstained street in close-up, bathed in the flashing red and blue lights of police vehicles, and to the sound of their sirens—images familiar to TV viewers from reality cop shows and local news programs. But if *The Wire* begins TV-like, it soon becomes cinematic: the camera scans and tracks, revealing the dead body of a young man. It then pulls back, encircling and framing the scene (thereby producing it) in which the key elements of its juridical and cultural coding—that is, the wired (bloody) territory of the series' diegetic space—are crystallized: from a dead black African American young man, the victim of a ridiculous and arbitrary crime, we pass on to an African American witness, who tells its story, and then to a white Irish American police officer, who listens and chuckles at its utter banality.[11]

The streets of *The Wire*'s crime scenes thus constitute a central social space of encounter where, to put it in Althusserian terms, social power is transformed and normalized by the state apparatus qua machine, institutionalized as law, and actualized as force.[12] The police are the main agents of this process, of course, and homicide detective McNulty, the main star of the show, is at his post asking questions and making his presence felt. Most importantly, thanks to the invisible presence of the camera, audiences magically become privileged viewers of the crime scene too, positioned alongside the police at work for the state in the form of the local city, and given immediate access to look upon and accompany the process of crime interpretation. So far, so generically conventional: *The Wire* is a traditional work of detective fiction, adopting a critical (that is, a "workerist") police perspective that McNulty embodies.

What is narratively surprising about *The Wire*'s first scene, however, is that the crime that opens the series has no particular significance for it, except in its generality, and will be neither reconstructed nor emplotted into its interlocking narratives. The death of the young man holds no mystery for the police and will not be interpreted and tracked. (This is to be expected in this part of town; it has been socially and culturally coded that way.) It does, however, register an important, although banal, truth that is significant for the relation the series establishes between narrative form and its own historical material: the excess of history over form. *The Wire* thus signals, on the one hand, its own partiality and, on the other, its consequent status as a work of narrative totalization that is always already incomplete. In this sense, the program emerges not only from a realist desire to accumulate social content, as noted above, but also from a modernist acknowledgment of its own narrative limits (imposed by narrative form) and thus not so much as a representation as an invention. The first killing functions as just one of a continuous, repetitive series that compositionally divides *The Wire*'s overarching narratives off from the history that determines and contextualizes it. It stands in for all the victims associated with the commercialization of drugs that precede the stories told across the five seasons, for all those that will follow them, as well as for the collateral damage, those victims that accompany the telling of the stories dramatized in *The Wire*, episode after episode.

It is possible to identify other such series too, although these are built into the narratives that make up *The Wire* over time, season after season, imposing, for their appreciation, a discipline on its viewers that is specifically televisual: they have to stick with it, for years (or for countless hours of DVD watching). For example, there is a series of insider witnesses, many of them doomed by their contact with the police, especially with McNulty; and a series of wakes for members of the force who pass away, which ends with McNulty's own symbolic one, when he leaves the profession at the conclusion of the final, fifth season. He will be replaced. So if one series—of killings—opens *The Wire*, another—of deaths—brings it to conclusion. McNulty's institutional death, meanwhile, finally reveals *The Wire*'s central articulating narrative: from the beginning, its first crime scene, it tells the story of McNulty's way out, the "death" of a policeman.

"Like detectives," writes John Ellis in *Seeing Things: Television in the Age of Uncertainty*, "we are rushed to the scene of the crime hoping to make sense of what happened from the physical traces that it has left." Ellis is not describing *The Wire* here, or a program like it, but deploying the conventional hermeneutic of detective fiction to account for a general effect of contemporary televisuality—which also, it so happens, describes the TV experience of tuning in to a program like *The Wire* and being "rushed to the scene of [a] crime."[13] Ellis's description of television form connects with Benjamin's account of photography. As is well known, the revelatory potential of photographic technology, in which once-hidden historical determinations are brought into the light of day by the camera demanding explanation, underpins Benjamin's notion of the "optical unconscious." In this way, the camera's ability to capture reality in photographs is associated with a modern hermeneutic—one that Carlo Ginzburg links to art criticism (the discovery of forgeries), psychoanalysis (listening out for signs of the unconscious), and detection (revealing criminal intent)—in which captured scenes may be read as "symptoms" of something else (a criminal capitalist economy, for example) and thus demand close scrutiny and interpretation.[14] Such technological developments are deployed and advanced by the state too, in surveillance operations, like those portrayed in *The Wire*.

These involve not only new visual technology, but devices geared specifically for sound. For it turns out that there is also a "sonic" unconscious, made available for scrutiny today by mobile phones. This is what McNulty and his colleagues seek to access by "wiring" and grabbing the messages exchanged between corner boys and drug dealers. Ellis, meanwhile, is interested in camerawork, but more than just with its recording function: combining aspects of both the cinema and radio, with television the camera has become a broadcasting and transmitting device too. In the words of Rudolf Arnheim, "television turns out to be related to the motor car and the aeroplane as a means of transport of the mind."[15] This is how "we are rushed" to other places, such as West Baltimore's corners, or how other places are tele-transported to viewers, as scenes, as they relax in living rooms and bedrooms. Television, in other words, appears to overcome both the distance between its subjects and objects and their different times, making them co-present in viewing; and not just mentally, as Arnheim suggests, but sensually too—sounds and images touching and tugging at the body through eyes and ears. Ellis refers to the new social form of looking produced by contemporary television as "witnessing," and to television form itself as a kind of dramatic "working through" of the materials thus broadcast in an era of information overload: they are managed and formatted into genres (from the news, to sports programs and soaps), dramatized and put into narrative, serialized and scheduled.[16] Again, Ellis might also have been describing *The Wire* and its first scene, whose last shot is a close-up of the dead victim, his blank wide-open eyes staring out from the TV screen at the tele-transported viewers; and in the background, the witness and the detective, working through.

There is another crime scene in the first season of *The Wire* that is destined no doubt to become a classic of its type. In contrast to the first scene, however, this one, although approaching abstraction in its sparseness, is full of significance for the articulation and unraveling of its narratives and dramas. It involves McNulty and his partner "Bunk," and a disenchanted middle-level drugs dealer D'Angelo Barksdale (known as "D"), the nephew of West Baltimore kingpin Avon Barksdale. The latter is the prime target of McNulty and his associates' police investigation, the object of the wire, and remains so across three of *The Wire*'s five seasons. Despite all the surveillance, however, information- and evidence-gathering is difficult, since Barksdale and his crew are deadly, ruthlessly shoring up any possible weakness or leakage in their organization. Like so many subaltern outlaw groups, the Barksdale crew have internalized and replicated statelike repressive structures that are ferociously hierarchical, and, within their own terms, strategically meritocratic.

Even before McNulty and Bunk arrive at the murder scene, viewers know that Avon has had one of his girlfriends killed (she had threatened to give him away and talk). We know this not because it is a crime that is shown and witnessed, but because in a previous scene he tells the corner boys he organizes. As noted above, *The Wire* is made up of a number of proliferating narratives, and moves between and through them transversally. As it jumps from scene to scene, it travels between different characters, the social spheres they inhabit and work in (institutions), and their locations (streets, offices). Thus all narratives are interrupted and crossed by others, looping back and forth, such that at and through each level—episode, season, and series—*The Wire* resembles a collage or a montage of segments. This is the relation established between the scene of D's "narration" and the scene in which McNulty and Bunk reconstruct his crime. However, what happens before, at the level of narrative emplotment, happens *simultaneously* at the level of its story. These scenes, like others, are part of a constellation of mutually dependent segments with a shared temporality, but distributed across different spaces. This means that viewers know Avon is guilty before McNulty and Bunk do, but who then—in their decoding of the crime scene—work it out and catch up, such that by its conclusion characters and viewers become co-present again at the level of knowledge as well as that of action. But if *The Wire*'s polydiegetic and segmentary character may be described as either novelistic or cinematic, its televisual character should not for that reason be ignored.

Indeed, it has been suggested that the segmentary quality of the television moving image is definitive of its form: originally anchored in domesticity, distraction, and the predominance of the glance over the cinematic gaze. Interrupted viewing (by adverts, for example) is constitutively inscribed into both the medium and into television form itself, most obviously in news programs and soaps. Being an HBO production, however, whose broadcasting is advert-free, *The Wire* is able both to put such segmentarity to use as a compositional strategy and simultaneously to subvert the temporality of its viewing. This is because, for the most part, its compositional segmentarity works to extend the action and narrative continuity *beyond* the fixed temporality of the episode, undermining the latter's semiautonomy within the series (as maintained even by *The Sopranos*), slowing down and spreading the action and stories it portrays beyond episodic television time (and its scheduling), giving the impression, at times, that "nothing happens." At this level, *The Wire* dedramatizes the serial form from within. This experience of "slowness"—which contrasts markedly, for example, with the hectic deployment of segmented scenes in 24[17]—may be one of the reasons why *The Wire* has attracted so few viewers on television, although it is a success on DVD and "on demand" platforms.

This other crime scene may be only a short segment, but its significance flows through season 1 and into season 2.[18] It knots their narratives. This is underlined by the inclusion of another brief segment within this constellation of scenes in which Lester—McNulty's partner on the wire detail—identifies a phone number he has picked up off the wall at another crime scene (where the romantic character Omar Little, a kind of urban cowboy, has stolen one of Avon's stashes), which he identifies as linked to a corner phone used by "D" at work.[19] Through composition and editing, all of these discrete segments feed the central narrative: they become part of the story in which, first, the wiretap is justified and put to use and, second, "D" is persuaded to give up his uncle-boss Avon (and is then murdered in jail).

The scene is a kitchen in a house that has been stripped bare and wiped clean. It has become a white box. And in such a space, the detectives' reconstruction of the crime is almost a work of performance art. Bereft of forensic technology, they use their bodies, their pens, and a tape measure like *bricoleurs* to reimagine the crime, the trajectory of the bullet, the position of the shooter as he taps the window ("tap, tap, tap," as "D" has already described it) and shoots the young naked woman as she turns to see who is there. This is the work of the imagination, and in its eccentric performance both Conan Doyle's Sherlock Holmes and Poe's Dupin are parodically evoked. Most important for this reconstruction, however, are the photographs of the barely clothed dead victim that McNulty and Bunk scrutinize for clues and place about the room so as to visualize the event—for this work of detection is also the work of fantasy. McNulty and Bunk perform the scopic drive. Whilst scrutinizing they only enunciate one word and its derivatives— "fuck!"—over and over again as they realize how the murder was committed, reaching a climax of discovery—"fucking A!"—as they find the

"Fucking A!"

spent bullet in the fridge door and its casing in the garden outside. It is as if the discovery were a restaging of the primal (crime) scene.

"Fucking" and detection intertwine. In a sense this is just an extension of the sexualized homosociality that characterizes the office of the homicide division of the Baltimore Police Department run by Sergeant Landsman, its principal promoter. But it also says something about McNulty and Bunk's own addictive relationship to their work: they do not spend time together drinking so as to forget and obliterate their experiences as police; on the contrary, they do so to maintain and extend it, and in fact to obliterate everything else, the rest of their private, non-police lives.[20]

Adam Smith in Baltimore

The main conflict within the police institution in *The Wire* is that between its upper bureaucratic echelons with more or less direct access to the political elites (associated with city hall) and the working detectives in the homicide (McNulty) and narcotics ("Kima" Greggs, "Herc" Hauk, and Ellis Carter) divisions joined to form a special detail in the pursuit, first, of Avon Barksdale (seasons 1–3) and, then, of his "succesor," Marlo Stanfield (seasons 3–5).[21] Under the command of Cedric Daniels, they are joined by a variety of marginalized officers such as Lester and Prez. The "brass" imposes targets and, therefore, arrests. In Lester's version, they "follow the drugs" and arrest low-level drug dealers and addicts. But keeping minor criminals off the streets helps the mayor. For their part, the detectives "who care" (such as McNulty, Lester, Kima, and Daniels) want to build cases against the kingpins inside and outside the state, and "follow the money," exposing economic and political corruption. In this context, the struggle to legally justify the wiretap becomes a political one, requiring legal justification and the allocation of resources (and finally the goodwill of the mayor). It is hindered at every turn.

However, *The Wire*'s principal interest lies in the way in which the conflicts inside the state apparatus are mirrored—across the wire—within the criminal, drug-dealing community and its political economy. This includes not only the influence of the police on the illegal, subalternized capitalist economy, but also the ways in which the latter, through bribery, loans, and money laundering (I am thinking particularly of the character Senator Clay Davis in this regard) underwrites upper echelons of the local state and economy through the circulation of its accumulated wealth—at which point it becomes finance capital.[22] The intracrime conflict presents itself on the ground as a struggle between fractions for territory and corners (between the East Side and West Side of Baltimore) and takes three main forms, each of which is associated with a particular economic logic and specific characters: "Proposition" Joe, Avon Barksdale and Marlo Stanfield, and Omar Little.

The first form involves an attempt to overcome the struggle between competitors. In this context, the character of Proposition Joe (who comes to the fore in seasons 4 and 5) is important since he represents a tendency toward the formation of a kind of Baltimore cartel, a cooperative of dealers, which can manage quality, prices, and security. For some, however, this delegation of business administration sounds suspiciously like monopoly, and undermines the pursuit of self-interest, self-reliance, and, thereby, control. Avon and Marlo, who represent a second street-level, "competitive" form of doing drug business, are suspicious of Proposition Joe's corporate, conference-room style (he is finally assassinated by Marlo's henchmen toward the end of the series), preferring instead to impose their own more neoliberal economy. The third form is a romantic version of the second, and is represented by Omar, the transgressive outlaw's outlaw (and thus McNulty's criminal mirror-image and sometime ally). Taking advantage of the mistrust generated between the corporate and competitive styles, Omar uses guerrilla tactics to trick and rob all the local kingpins. On the one hand, Omar becomes a local myth in his own (albeit brief) lifetime; on the other, he violently debunks the myth of original accumulation.[23]

The tension between these regimes of accumulation is what drives the segmented narratives of *The Wire* as they loop across and through each other. The narrative loops connecting the different dramatic scenes may thus also be thought of as narrative cycles: from the cycle of capital accumulation as it passes through commodity exchange, which takes place on the streets (or in prison), to the cycles of finance and capital investment, which take place mainly in offices (or restaurants and luxury yachts). This is why the policing that McNulty and Lester struggle against constitutes a racist disavowal on the part of the state. The imposition of a policy based on targets and the pursuit of street crime (that is, of corner boys and drug addicts), which ignores the circulation of money capital, involves, in the first place, the fabrication of the otherness of the criminal "other" (a racist production of difference) and, second, the deployment of the resources to insist on it. The flow of money, however, tells us that the supposed "other" is in fact constitutive of the state in the first place. This is why drugs money is "laundered."[24] Lester and McNulty pursue the money—so much so that, in the end, they almost break the law[25]—to reveal its origins and, particularly, its ends. In other words, they are involved in a radical act. Taking the side of the "working" detective within the police institution, from scene to scene and location to location, *The Wire* follows the money too.

Nevertheless, the narrative pursuit of money through the cycle (or loop) of accumulation from the streets into finance only goes so far, and this narrative limit constitutes the generic limit of *The Wire* as a work of crime fiction. Crucial, here, is another important character in the series, "Stringer" Bell, the key to McNulty and his colleagues' surveillance operation, via "D." He is murdered at the end of season 3 by

Omar and Brother Mouzone (a hit man from New York) with the tacit agreement of Avon Barksdale.

Stringer Bell is Avon's second in command, the manager of the business (he counts the money), a close associate and friend (he advises him to have "D" killed)—indeed, he is the "brains" of the outfit (much as Lester is for the wiretap detail). Avon is a more charismatic leader with a keen sense for the uses of violence as a strategy of power and drugs commerce. Inside the partnership of Barksdale and Bell (Stringer eventually dies under a sign for "B & B Enterprises") there coexist in increasing conflict two of the above logics of accumulation associated with commodity exchange, on the one hand, and corporate finance and investment, on the other. *The Wire* traces this conflict in Stringer's attempts to consolidate the "cooperative," with a reluctant Avon following him right into the offices of Baltimore's luxury apartment redevelopment projects in which he invests (with the help of Senator "Clay" Davis, among others)—until he is shot, when Avon decides against the world of finance capital. *The Wire* follows suit, abandoning the compositional strategy of looping in and between accumulation cycles linking the office scenes of finance with commodity exchange on the streets. Instead, it returns to foreground the battle for corners and corner boy allegiances in the streets, where accumulation begins, and where *The Wire*'s story over seasons 1 to 3 is replayed across seasons 4 and 5—this time between different crews and different kingpins: Proposition Joe and his nemesis Marlo Stanfield.

The significance of Stringer Bell's story as a limit both for the narrative of *The Wire* as a whole and for its narration is given in a very brief scene—starring McNulty and Bunk again—at the beginning of the last episode of season 3. It repeats the conflict of accumulation regimes as a problem of police interpretation. Stringer has just been killed and the detectives find an address they did not know about in his wallet. They go and are uncharacteristically stunned into silence by what they (do not) find. They wander in to Stringer's open-plan designer apartment, and just stare, as if it had become stuck in their eyes (it refuses to open up and become an object for them). "This is Stringer?" asks (states) McNulty; "Yeah!" replies Bunk. Their scopic prowess has clearly reached its limits: the more they scan the apartment, the more unreadable it becomes. Bunk stands in the middle of the living room as if there were nothing to be decoded, no clues, none of those traces on which his and McNulty's subjectivization as detectives depends. McNulty and Bunk

"This is Stringer?"

have reached the limits of their considerable interpretative powers and find no pleasure—no crime—in the scene. This is because Stringer has "laundered" his lifestyle and wiped his apartment clean, so that it would seem to have nothing whatsoever to do with crime—that is, the drugs business, the murder that he administers, the violence of the exchange of commodities he coordinates—nor with the "culture" associated with it. McNulty goes over to a bookshelf and looks at the books. He takes one down and glances at it and asks: "Who the fuck was I chasing?" (as if to the viewers, since they know more than he) and puts the book down again. At which point the frustrated detectives turn and leave. The scene is never mentioned again, never returned to and "looped" into the narrative. However, just as they turn away, the camera detaches itself from their perspective and becomes momentarily autonomous—this is *The Wire*'s TV camera consciousness at work again—to concentrate the viewer's gaze momentarily on the title of the book McNulty has discarded. It is Adam Smith's *The Wealth of Nations*.

The detectives do not pick up on Stringer's particular knowledge, even though McNulty had previously followed him to a college where he studies business administration, specifically the idea of "elasticity of demand." It is clear in class that Stringer's practical knowledge of the market in heroin has given him a head start on his peers since he already appreciates, as he tells the teacher, the importance of the creation of consumer demand, of feeding desire, so as to sell more and more commodities of a particular type. This feeding of consumer desire has its correlate in Stringer, an addict too, since the elasticity of demand also feeds his own desire: to accumulate.

The late Giovanni Arrighi taught at Johns Hopkins University in Baltimore, although it is by no means certain that Stringer Bell attended his lectures. We might speculate, however, at what might have been the result if, like *The Wire*, rather than looking to China in his study of the contemporary world economy, Arrighi had turned instead to the local "wired" territory of the drugs trade, at Adam Smith in Baltimore, rather then *Adam Smith in Beijing* (2007)—a book probably composed over the same period as *The Wire*.

In his discussion of Smith's account of the role of commodity exchange and competition in capitalist development, given in the formula C-M-C'—in which commodities are exchanged for money in order to purchase commodities of greater utility (hardly what is going on in the territories *The Wire* maps)—he counterposes to it Marx's general formula of capital, M-C-M', in which "for capitalist investors the purchase of commodities is strictly instrumental to an increase in the monetary value of their assets from M to M'." The formula M-C-M' describes Avon Barksdale's mercantilist street economy of commodity exchange, its accumulative logic (backed up by extreme violence). But if Avon's activities are M-C-M', Stringer's are M-M'. As Arrighi notes, in certain circumstances "the transformation of money into commodities may be skipped altogether (as in Marx's abridged formula of capital, M-M')." In his previous work, *The Long Twentieth Century* (1994), Arrighi fleshes out this point further:

> In phases of material expansion money capital "sets in motion" an increasing mass of commodities [for example, drugs] . . . [I]n phases of financial expansion an increasing mass of money capital "sets itself free" from its commodity form, and accumulation proceeds through financial

deals (as in Marx's abridged formula MM'). Together, the two epochs or phases constitute a full systemic cycle of accumulation (M-C-M').[26]

Stringer's "financial deals" and "abridgement" of the M-C-M' formula to M-M' threatens either to break away from the cycle of the commodity exchange of drugs—and set him free—leaving his friend and partner Avon behind, or to subordinate them both to its logic.

One of the most important contributions *The Wire* makes to crime fiction is the detail with which it dramatizes, on the one hand, the procedures and limits of detection and, on the other, crime as a complex practice that it conceives formally and compositionally, through its narrative loops and cycles of accumulation (which constitutes in turn the TV series' polydiegetic, segmented architecture), not as crime against capitalism, but as crime that is thoroughly capitalized (a neoliberal utopia, in fact). *The Wire* uses the crime and detective fiction genre classically, but creatively, to unpack and unravel Marx's formulas for capital accumulation. The abridged formula M-M' provides the clue to Stringer Bell's tendency toward "freeing" capital from its commodity basis in drugs (and thus to his conflict with Avon), as well as to reading the unreadability of his abstract, apparently contentless existence in his designer apartment—it is, or pretends to be, pure money (the content of the form). Such unreadability constitutes a limit not only for detectives McNulty and Bunk but for *The Wire* too, a limit beyond which it cannot go. So it also returns to the streets, to Avon and Marlo, the corner boys, to M-C-M'.

Repetition and Reproduction

The context of the return to the mercantile accumulation of the corners, as well as to Stringer's story, is told in season 2, which focuses on the plight of the harbor workers' union whose members struggle to survive in a deindustrialized port in the process of being redeveloped for tourism and luxury homes (part of Stringer's investment portfolio). They still refer to themselves as "stevedores." The union turns a blind eye (for money) to the illegal importation of goods, including sex workers, by a "Greek" ("I'm not Greek," says "the Greek"!) Mafia-like outfit. In *The Wire* deindustrialization feeds and drives the criminalization of the economic system. Indeed, it is the dominant form taken by the informal economy.[27] McNulty and the police become involved because a container load of sex workers is murdered.

The main story centers on the trade union leader, Frank Sobotka, his reaction to the murder as he turns against "the Greek," and on his unhinged son Ziggy and his nephew Nick, who, increasingly desperate for work and money, also get involved with "the Greek" and his gang[28]—stealing container trucks of goods to sell on. Its principal object is to reflect on the idea of *workers who have lost their work*, as industry disappears. It also constitutes the dramatic background for the articulation of *The Wire's* own workerist sentiments (which pervade each of its seasons and each of the social institutions it represents) providing it with its critical standpoint throughout. In this respect, the harbor—like the corners, the police, the schools, and the local newspaper—is also subject to the "abridging" effects of the M-M' formula of capital. More specifically, abridgement here means the loss of industry, for the formula M-C-M' refers not only to the buying and selling of retail goods, but to another cycle of accumulation, that of industrial capital—in which money is invested in special kinds of commodities (forces of production, including labor power) that make other commodities, which can be sold for a profit. This is what has been lost, including in the form of its negation: the organizations of the working class. As Sobotka, "Gus" Haynes (the city editor of the *Baltimore Sun*), and McNulty complain, "proper" work—in which, as Sobotka says, "you make something"—has disappeared. This *loss of good work* is melancholically performed, daily, in the local bar at the port, where generations of workers meet to regenerate, and attempt to make good, an increasingly sentimental and nostalgic sense of community. (One question is the degree to which such a "workerism" feeds *The Wire's* own sense of radicalism.) Meanwhile, however, all of their activities are financed by crime. Needless to say, finally, the mysterious "Greek" connection has Sobotka killed.

In "Prologue to Televison" Adorno characteristically sets out the authoritarian and regressive character of telelvison as it plugs "[t]he gap between private existence and the culture industry, which had remained as long as the latter did not dominate all dimensions of the visible." With its new, digitalized, and mobilized delivery platforms, televisuality in a posttelevision age keeps on plugging. *The Wire*, for example, although televisual at the level of production, is almost re-novelized in its consumption in DVD format: episode after episode it may be viewed outside the TV schedules, and almost on demand. Indeed, there is a sense in which it has reflexively incorporated this aspect into its composition. Despite his well-known cultural pessimism, Adorno did evoke future emancipatory possibilities, even for television (without them, critique would be pointless). He concludes his essay as follows:

> In order for television to keep the promise still resonating within the word [i.e., *television*], it must emancipate itself from everything with which it—reckless wish-fulfillment—refutes its own principle and betrays the idea of Good Fortune for the smaller fortunes of the department store.[29]

The "dependent" or "autonomous" character of each artwork cannot be thought of as mutually exclusive, nor be simply read off from their social inscription, but rather need to be established through critical interpretation. *The Wire*'s dependency on HBO's fortune can be conceived as providing one of the material conditions for its freedom—which takes the form of time, the time for Simon and Burns to pursue its realist compositional logic.[30] *The Wire*'s stubborn insistence in this regard eventually leads its narrative loops to *cycles* of accumulation—and their local history.

Returning to the corners and their economy, in season 4 a school is added to *The Wire*'s expanding world, as are the life and times of a number of potential "corner boys." The business in drugs has been taken over by Marlo with extreme violence—and the dead bodies of countless "competitors" hidden in the abandoned houses of the area (now, in the children's minds, an eerie cemetery haunted by ghosts and zombies: typical of zones of continuous "primitive" accumulation in the Americas) by the scary killers Chris and Snoop. At the level of crime, season 4 repeats the conflict between accumulation logics, but refuses to return to the unreadable sphere of finance capital. At one level, seasons 4 and 5 can be experienced as mere repetition. At another, however, the moving story of the corner boys suggests that the addition of another institution has another strategic intention: systematicity. It shows the social *reproduction* of the logic of criminal accumulation and its constitutive violence. Bodie, the head corner boy, is shot as he comes into close contact with McNulty—just as he shot the timid Wallace (another potential informant) in season 1 so as to "step up" (and gain promotion), in Stringer's words. The long but faint thread of his story is one of the main narrative achievements of Simon and Barnes's segmentary composition. Of the schoolboys Michael, Dukie, Randy, and Namond, only the latter escapes the corner—the son of Wee-Bay, one of Avon's imprisoned henchmen, he is taken in by ex-cop "Bunny" Colvin. Randy is lost to the city care system by Sgt. Ellis Carver—a member of the "wire" detail. Despite Prez's efforts, Dukie becomes a street vendor and junkie, exactly like Bubbles. Finally, Michael is groomed by Chris and Snoop and becomes a killer too.[31] In its portrayal of the education system *The Wire* demonstrates the complete failure of hegemony, conceived as the consensual reproductive power of the state. In contrast, however (the dangers of naturalist containment notwithstanding),[32] *The Wire* does show the constitutive, systematic, and reproductive power of M-C-M', in both its abridged and unabridged accumulative forms.

Notes

1. There are few temporal markers of exactly when the action depicted in *The Wire* takes place, but judging from the story of Lester Freamon's marginalization as a detective, which he tells McNulty in a bar, the series begins sometime in 2000 or 2001. This suggest that Simon and Burns are intent on filming and understanding the present, over several years, more or less as it happens.

2. David Simon, *Homicide: A Year on the Killing Streets* (New York: Holt, 2006); David Simon and Edward Burns, *The Corner: A Year in the Life of an Inner-City Neighborhood* (New York: Broadway Books, 1998).

3. In this sense, Bubbles functions like a classical film close-up, that is, as a place of identification.

4. As described by the luckless Gary McCullough in *The Corner*: "There's a corner everywhere . . . The corner dominates . . . I was loyal to the corner . . . it don't care where you come from . . . it's big enough to take us all." Addictions of all kinds are, of course, fundamental to such a culture.

5. Franco Moretti, "The Novel: History and Theory," *New Left Review* 52 (July–August 2008): 115. For Bakhtin, the novel was a city-text of voices, a hierarchical orchestration of ideo- and sociolects. See Mikhail Bakhtin, *The Dialogical Imagination*, ed. Michael Holquist, trans. Caryl Emerson and Michael Holquist (Austin: University of Texas Press, 1981).

6. Michael Connolly's recent series of thrillers starring his LAPD detective

Hieronymous Bosch is another good example of this relaying: from post–Rodney King cultural sensitivity to homeland security.

7. Responding to the question, "Is this how true warriors feel?" the resentful Sergeant Brad "Iceman" Colbert of *Generation Kill* is very specific: "Don't fool yourself. We aren't being warriors down here. They're just using us as machine operators. Semiskilled labor." Both the soldiers in *Generation Kill* and the cops in *The Wire* make do—that is, proceed—with out-of-date technology.

8. Jean Paul Sartre, *L'Imagination* (1936; Paris: PUF, 1981), 162.

9. In contrast, *Generation Kill* has the inverse problem: refusing to "loop" its narrative through other spheres, it remains fixated on the field of military operations.

10. Walter Benjamin, "A Small History of Photography," in *One-Way Street and Other Writings*, trans. Edmund Jephcott and Kingsley Shorter (London: New Left Books, 1979), 256. Benjamin also notes that with such developments "photography turns all life's relationships into literature." He might well have referred to film too. Before working on TV programs, David Simon was a journalist for the *Baltimore Sun*, while Edward Burns was a police officer and subsequently a schoolteacher (like the character Prez in the series).

11. The dead kid had been given the unfortunate nickname of "Snot Boogie." Every Friday he attempts to "snatch and run" with the proceeds from a local craps game. He was regularly caught and beaten up, almost as if in a ritual. This time, however, he was shot dead. Puzzled, McNulty asks the young witness: "Why did you let him play?" "Got to," he answers, "it's America, man!" *The Wire* criticizes and mocks the U.S. state's ideology of "freedom." For another reading of this scene, see Blake D. Ethridge, "Baltimore on *The Wire:* The Tragic Moralism of David Simon," in *Its Not TV: Watching HBO in the Post-television Era*, ed. Marc Leverette, Brian L. Ott, and Cara Louise Buckley (New York: Routledge, 2008), 152–64.

12. Louis Althusser, "Marx in His Limits," in *Philosophy of the Encounter: Late Writings, 1978–1987*, ed. François Matheron and Oliver Corpet, trans. G. M. Goshgarian (London: Verso, 2006), 95–126.

13. John Ellis, *Seeing Things: Television in the Age of Uncertainty* (New York: I.B. Tauris, 2002), 10.

14. See Carlo Ginzburg, "Morelli, Freud and Sherlock Holmes: Clues and Scientific Method," *History Workshop Journal* 9 (1980): 5–36. Ginzburg refers to the emergence of a "medical semiotics."

15. Quoted in Margaret Morse, "An Ontology of Everyday Distraction: The Freeway, the Mall and Television," in *Logics of Television: Essays in Cultural Criticism*, ed. Patricia Mellencamp (Bloomington: Indiana University Press; London: BFI, 1990), 193.

16. In *Seeing Things*, Ellis gives a periodization of televisual eras: a first

"era of scarcity" that lasts until the late 1970s (characterized by few channels broadcasting for part of the day only); a second "era of availability" that lasted approximately until the end of the 1990s (characterized by "managed choice" across a variety of channels—including satellite—twenty-four hours a day); and a contemporary third "era of plenty" (characterized by "television on demand" and interactive platforms). Some also refer to the latter, underlining tendencies toward digital convergence and branding, as "TVIII," in which HBO would be a central player. See Catherine Johnson, "Tele-branding in TVIII: The Network as Brand and the Programme as Brand," *New Review of Film and Television Studies* 5.1 (2007): 5–24.

17. *24*'s impression of speed is further enhanced by the use of the split screen. See Michael Allen, "Divided Interests: Split-Screen Aesthetics in *24*," in *Reading 24: TV against the Clock*, ed. Steven Peacock (New York: I.B. Tauris, 2007). Of course, the split screen in film crime was pioneered in Norman Jewison's *The Thomas Crown Affair* (1968) and Richard Fleischer's *The Boston Strangler* (1968).

18. For a discussion of the relation between "segment" and "flow" in television, a staple of television studies, see in particular Raymond Williams, *Television: Technology and Cultural Form* (London: Fontana/Collins, 1974); John Ellis, *Visible Fictions: Cinema, Television, Video*, rev. ed. (New York: Routledge, 1992); Richard Dienst, *Still Life in Real Time: Theory after Television* (Durham, N.C.: Duke University Press, 1994). For an approach that links the discussion to recent technological developments, see William Uricchio, "Television's Next Generation: Technology/Interface Culture/Flow," in *Television after Television: Essays on a Medium in Transition*, ed. Lynn Spiegel and Jan Olsson (Durham, N.C.: Duke University Press, 2004), 163–82. In "Is Television Studies History?" *Cinema Journal* 47.3 (2008): 127–37, Charlotte Brunsdon notes a masculinizing shift in television discourse, away from feminized melodrama and its inscription into the living room, to masculinized quality cop shows, like *The Wire* and, especially, *The Sopranos*, and their inscription into redesigned living spaces (and TVs) organized around a variety of new delivery systems.

19. McNulty and Lester's partnership is Kantian: without Lester, McNulty's intuition is "blind"; without McNulty, Lester's reason is "empty."

20. This is what makes McNulty a delusional hero who, intent on befriending and helping the corner boys, in fact destroys them: he drags them in rather then helps them out.

21. For example, in season 2 Major Valchek pressurizes Commissioner Burrell to reform the detail that pursued Barksdale in order to investigate Frank Sobotka, the leader of the stevedores union—out of religious jealousy—and thus pave the way for the eventual institutional rise of Daniels. In this context Daniels's own shady past dealings are hinted at. Similarly, McNulty uses (and is used

by) contacts in the local branch of the FBI and the Baltimore judiciary (under his influence, Judge Phelan pushes Burrell into the formation of the special detail in the first place).

22. Such entry into the sphere of the local ruling class is also mediated by lawyers, particularly Maurice "Maury" Levy, who acts for and counsels the crime bosses (Avon and then Marlo), and who remains an important screen presence throughout the series.

23. Omar's death is, however, banal: he is shot dead by a small child robbing a shop, almost by accident—the myth of his invulnerability shattered (at least for the viewers). Omar is a transgressive character in a variety of ways—most annoyingly for the gangsters he robs, in terms of his sexuality (a key theme for many of the back stories in *The Wire*).

24. In this sense, the territory of *The Wire* may be read from the perspective provided by Homi Bhabha's account of racism in his *The Location of Culture* (London: Routledge, 1994).

25. Much to the annoyance of Bunk and Kima, McNulty and Lester transform dead bodies they find into the victims of a serial killer so as to sideline funds happily given them to investigate the "murders" (they generates newspaper sales as well as city office popularity) to pursue their, by now, "private" investigation of Stansfield.

26. See Giovanni Arrighi, *Adam Smith in Beijing: Lineages of the Twenty-first Century* (London: Verso, 2007), 75, and *The Long Twentieth Century: Money, Power and the Origins of Our Times* (London: Verso, 1994), 6.

27. Mike Davis locates this process of informalization in a globalized context in his recent *Planet of Slums* (London: Verso, 2006). For Baltimore, see David Harvey (a critic who has "lived in Baltmore City for most of [his] adult life" and also taught at Johns Hopkins University in Baltimore), "The Spaces of Utopia," in *Spaces of Hope* (Edinburgh: Edinburgh University Press, 2000), 133–81: "Manufacturing jobs accelerated their movement out (mainly southwards and overseas) during the first severe post-war recession in 1973–5 and have not stopped since. . . . Shipbuilding, for example, has all-but disappeared and the industries that stayed have 'downsized'" (148). If season 2 stands out in the series, even geographically, this is because the phases of accumulation foregrounded by Arrighi also have territorial significance. As Harvey makes abundantly clear, the predominance of the abridged formula of finance capital represented by Stringer changes the urban and social geography of Baltimore.

28. In season 2 *The Wire* increasingly presents itself as a drama that is concerned with forms of "white" ethnicity—Irish and Polish, especially—as well as racism. Indeed, as the above discussion of accumulation logics suggests, the series works through and becomes entangled in the social semiotics of "race," including its connotative domains (for example, the economic coding of "race"

and the racist coding of economic logics). This is part of *The Wire*'s realist compositional logic.

29. Theodor W. Adorno, "Prologue to Television," in *Critical Models: Interventions and Catchwords,* trans. Henry W. Pickford (New York: Columbia University Press, 1998), 49–50, 57.

30. Of course, in its autonomy *The Wire* also contributes to "brand" HBO, a subsidiary of Time Warner.

31. Predictably, Michael eventually turns against his teachers. Having killed Snoop, he returns home where his brother invites him to watch a program on TV: it's about "a serial killer that kills serial killers," he says. He is probably watching *Dexter,* but he is unknowingly describing his brother.

32. See my brief reflection on *The Wire* in "*Noir* into History: James Ellroy's *Blood's A Rover,*" *Radical Philosophy* 163 (September–October 2010): 25–33.

PART THREE

Race, Ethnicity, and Class

9

Tracing *The Wire*

Gary Phillips

As rough as that neighborhood could be, we had us a community. Nobody, no victim, who didn't matter. And now all we got is bodies, and predatory motherfuckahs like you. And out where that girl fell, I saw kids acting like Omar, calling you by name, glorifyin' your ass. Makes me sick, motherfuckah, how far we done fell.

—Detective Bunk Moreland to professional thief Omar Little

Neil Brenner and Nik Theodore note that "The linchpin of neoliberal ideology is the belief that open, competitive, and unregulated markets, liberated from all forms of state interference, represent the optimal mechanism for economic development."[1] Their definition provides a framework for examining the pop cultural and real-life roots of *The Wire*. As an example, there is the criminal excess operating among the various tiers of the white-collar realm. More specifically, the financial shenanigans and double- and triple-dipping that went on in the mortgage-lending three-card monte scams led to, among other sleights of hand on Wall Street, the Great Recession. But as there is crime in the suites, there's also crime in the streets. These two realms, which sometimes overlap, are reflected not only in *The Wire* but in other crime and mystery genre books, films, and TV shows—even in comic books and video games such as the True Crime series (*True Crime: Streets of L.A.* used actual street locations and gang names).[2]

David Simon, creator and executive producer (with former Baltimore detective Ed Burns) of *The Wire*, wrote of two competing myths in America in an introduction to *The Wire: Truth be Told*, a book examining the creative and actual arenas that underscored his series that resonated beyond the actual numbers of people who watched the show on HBO.[3] He stated that if you are smarter, shrewder, or frugal or visionary, the first with the best idea, given the process of the free market, you will succeed beyond your wildest imagination. Conversely, if you don't possess those qualities, if you're not slick or cunning, but willing to work hard, be a citizen and devoted to your family, why there was something for you too. Simon went on to note that Baltimore (and by extension other urban areas) with its brown fields, rotting piers, and rusting factories, is testament that the economy shifted, then shifted again, rendering obsolete generations of union-wage workers and workers' families. *The Wire*, then, is a story wedged between these two competing American myths.

In the works of a certain set of African American writers, some known only in black communities and even then not well remembered, cops-and-criminals storylines were produced where the streets and the suites, impacted by racism, collide in the gap between the myths. In fare such as 1970s crime films, "lost novels" such as Clarence Cooper Jr.'s *The Scene*, ghetto lit, TV's *EZ Streets*, *New York Undercover*, and in independent "race films" of the 1930s, these pop cultural antecedents of *The Wire* reflect the conditions Simon wrote about.

This essay, as its name implies, will review and examine various antecedents to *The Wire* in the crime and mystery genres. Whether any of these other works cited herein were known to the show's producers or writers is immaterial. The purpose here is to acknowledge this material that also tackled themes and elements found in *The Wire*—black-on-black crime, black cops chasing black criminals, their relationships to the white power structure, and so on—and how there's always been a readership and an audience for hard-boiled urban crime stories that resonate with and embrace such hardcore fare.

— — —

On the *New York Times* op-ed page on January 4, 2006, contributor Nick Chiles, editor-in-chief of *Odyssey Couleur* magazine, which bills itself as "The nation's first high-end travel magazine for affluent multicultural travelers," published a commentary entitled "Their Eyes Were Reading Smut." Chiles's piece decried the explosion of a subgenre of the book trade alternately called urban lit, street lit, or more usually, ghetto lit. Going into a Borders bookstore in Lithonia, Georgia, in a mall about a half hour drive from his home, Chiles, who is black, wrote about his ghastly encounter in the African American Literature section.

On shelf after shelf, in bookcase after bookcase, all that I could see was lurid book jackets displaying all forms of brown flesh, usually half-naked and in some erotic pose, often accompanied by guns and other symbols of criminal life. I felt as if I was walking into a pornography shop.[4]

Chiles wasn't the first black writer to bemoan the plethora of titles by other black writers with names like *Hood Rat*, *Project Chick*, *The Ski Mask Way*, *Bad Girlz*, and *Oaktown Devil*. Nearly two years before his op-ed ran, there was a segment on NPR by Karen Michel talking about how these stories of bling, flossing, revenge, and getting over were a thriving commodity, be they self-published (Terri Woods, who would go on to be a *New York Times* best-selling author, originally photocopied her typewritten *True to the Game* manuscript and sold copies on the street in front of places like the Mart 125 across from the Apollo Theater in Harlem), published by an indie outfit (which could be the writer and a couple of friends volunteering their labor), or writers who'd sold well being picked up by major mainstream—that is, white—publishing houses.

By the time Chiles noticed ghetto lit, it wasn't just selling to young black folks, though they remained its core audience. There was also an overlap of the readership from this brand of hip-hop-influenced crime fiction to the viewership of *The Wire*, a critically acclaimed program but a perennial ratings lightweight. In its fourth season, *The Wire* averaged 1.6 million viewers on subscription-based HBO. Simon had used the metaphor that *The Wire*, which premiered in 2002, was a novel for the airwaves. Fitting, then, that the show comes on the heels of not only Simon's other riveting cops-and-criminals programmer, *Homicide: Life on the Streets*, which ran on NBC in the 1990s, but the two books that began the new wave of ghetto lit.

True to the Game, by the aforementioned Teri Woods, was initially self-published in 1998. By 1999 (when *Homicide* went off the air), she was on the map after countless hours of hand-selling her book, hustling it, as she would say. Vickie Stringer's *Let That Be the Reason* was also initially self-published in 2002, the same year *The Wire* debuted in the new century. This is from Woods's official biography on her website: "While working as a legal secretary for a law firm and juggling motherhood in Philadelphia, PA, Teri Woods completed her first novel, *True to the Game*. She submitted her story over a period of six years to more than 20 different publishers, all of whom rejected her. When major publishing houses refused to embrace *True to the Game* she wasn't discouraged."[5] Woods's characters and she herself represent the combination of those myths Simon wrote about. She's a hardworking person who, denied access to success, works smarter and shrewder to achieve her goal. Stringer is right out of that in-between place, that land mine territory where the denizens of *The Wire* operate. Stringer began writing her book while doing five years in the federal pen for selling a kilo of cocaine to a snitch, a CI (confidential informant) in police parlance.

Here's an excerpt from an interview Vickie Stringer did in *Inc.* in May 2006 when asked about her background. She was profiled in the business-oriented magazine because the publishing house she'd founded, Triple Crown Publications, had successfully published her and other ghetto lit writers.

> I met a guy one summer who was a big Columbus dealer, fell in love, and dropped out of college after my freshman year. I got my first taste of entrepreneurship in those days, managing both a hair salon and an escort service. I found girls by running a weekly ad in *The Columbus Dispatch* seeking models. When I got pregnant, my boyfriend cut out on me, so when my son, Valen, was born I turned to a familiar business that paid well. I excelled at the drug game; I made $30,000 a week. Even out hustling in the streets everyone does business with people they like and trust.[6]

In *True to the Game,* Philadelphia project girl Gena is an around-the-way girl all about getting men who are "papered up" to buy her things like clothes and jewels. Here's an excerpt from the opening pages of the book when she and her girlfriend take a trip to the Big Apple: "She looked at the girls and could not help staring at them. They had no clothes on. They were sexy and revealing, and Gena wanted to be amongst them, fucking with niggaz, getting her life on. New York was the shit."[7] Gena meets drug lord Quadir and falls for him. He admits to her that he's made so much crack money, become ghetto fabulous if you will, he wants to get out of the life. He has a cornball dream: to become a dentist. But rivals are only a gun barrel away and Quadir is gunned down after paying to get out. What will Gena do to hold onto her material goods? What indeed.

To give the detractors their due, it is the case that a lot of ghetto lit, like its music parallel gangsta rap, is not particularly self-reflective and far too repetitive in plot devices and characterizations. But like gangsta rap, these books speak to an audience of black and brown folk whom white mainstream publishing has ignored. However, like the numbers, the policy racket controlled in 1920s Harlem by black gangsters such as Bumpy Johnson and Queenie St. Clair, (portrayed by Lawrence Fishburn and Cicely Tyson, respectively, in the film *Hoodlum*) an enterprise initially derided by white gangsters as "nigger pool," once it was shown money could be made in this endeavor, suddenly whites were interested.

To be sure, Stringer is not the first convicted felon to turn to crime fiction writing, drawing on past experiences and people she'd met along the way to provide the foundation for stories. Nathan Heard, serving time in Trenton State Penitentiary for armed robbery, wrote the searing *Howard Street* (Dial, 1968), set in his native Newark. It was an unsparing best-selling book about junkies, whores, thieves, and crooked cops. He went on, when he got out, to teach creative writing at the college level and wrote other books, such as the *House of Slammers*. Claude Brown has compared him to Richard Wright and Faulkner. Heard also had a part as Big Pink in *Gordon's War* (1973), about a decorated Vietnam vet and Green Beret, Gordon Hudson, played by Paul Winfield. Hudson returns home to Harlem; his wife OD's, and he and some service buddies use their combat skills to go after the drug dealers.

Decades before Heard and Stringer, there was prisoner number 59623. Chester Himes was incarcerated in the Ohio State Penitentiary at the age of nineteen in 1928, just before the onset of the Great Depression. In *Chester Himes: A Life*,[8] James Sallis (who is also a science fiction and mystery writer, in particular his Lew Griffin series of interlinked novels) recounts how this middle-class kid came to do time. Himes, who'd survived falling down an elevator shaft at the expense of his teeth and back, was a onetime college student at Ohio State University, where black students like him weren't allowed in the dorms or dining hall. One night, in a pattern of self-immolation, as Sallis writes, he took some of his bougie-black fraternity brothers to a whorehouse of his acquaintance in the ghetto. Said Himes of that period in *The Quality of Hurt*, his autobiography: "But by then I was tired of Ohio State University and its policy of discrimination and segregation, fed up with the condescension, which I could never bear, and disgusted with myself for my whoremongering and my inability to play games."⁹ Asked to withdraw after this incident, Himes would go on to be a blackjack dealer and dispense booze with his future wife, Jean Johnson, in a speakeasy behind the gambling place he'd dealt cards called Bunch Boy's. It's in Bunch Boy's he overhears a chauffeur going on about the swag and swank home this elderly white couple possessed in the Cleveland Heights area. Foreshadowing a quasi sociopolitical rhetoric, modern-day dope slangers in films like 1995's *The Belly* (or like Kenyatta, the politicized gang boss in a series of paperback originals ex-con Donald Goines wrote for Holloway House in the mid-1970s, who went after pushers and crooked cops alike) have echoed with observations that racism has left only this one vicious enterprise for a black man to engage in to get over. Himes thus rationalized in the *Quality of Hurt:* "Like many blacks still possessed of a slave mentality, he [the chauffer] boasted of his employer's possessions as though they were his own, or as though he had vested interest in them."¹⁰

Colt .44 in hand, Himes forced entry into the house and robbed the senior citizens of cash and jewelry, escaping in one of their Cadillacs, chased by the cops. In antihero fashion, he managed to elude the law as fresh snow fell but had to abandon the car when it got stuck in mud. He took a train to Chicago to fence his goods with an underworld type called Jew Sam he'd heard mentioned at Bunch Boy's. However, the pawnbroker turned him in. Himes was beaten by the police back at the station house and eventually given twenty to twenty-five years. In the joint, Himes survives running the gambling hustle among the black cons.

Neither Sallis nor Himes points to any specific incident that started him writing. In his autobiography, Himes simply states, "I began writing in prison."¹¹ His first published piece ran in a black-owned magazine called the *Bronzeman*, but what it was about is lost to the ages, as no copy seems to exist. He kept turning out the work, at first for other black-owned publications such as *Abbott's Monthly* and the *Pittsburgh Courier* newspaper. He would "cross over" to the white press with sales to *Esquire* magazine. His first piece for *Esquire*, "Crazy," had only his prisoner number for his byline. Paroled at the age of twenty-six, Himes was turning out short stories like "To What Red Hell," a fictionalized version of a fire at the penitentiary that killed 300 prisoners in 1930, and "Headwaiter," a story based loosely on his uncle.

In 1953, in the wake of his 1940s proletarian novels about race, class, sex, and union organizing, *If He Hollers Let Him Go* and *The Lonely Crusade*, and his prison novel *Cast the First Stone*, bitter at not making much money and divorced from his wife, Himes boarded a ship for France and dedicated the next few years to travel, drinking, and women. He notes, "My main occupation was the search for money."[12] Himes met Marcel Duhamel, who'd published a translated version of *If He Hollers Let Him Go*. Duhamel convinced him to write a detective novel. Duhamel gave Himes an advance of 50,000 francs against a total fee of 400,000 francs. The first of his detective stories, *The Five-Cornered Square* (published in the States by Signet in 1957 as *For Love of Imabelle* but more commonly known as *A Rage in Harlem* [and filmed in 1991]), introduced his two most famous characters, Harlem plainclothes detectives Coffin Ed Johnson and Grave Digger Jones. Sallis notes that these two (like Philip Marlowe in the trial runs Raymond Chandler wrote for *Black Mask*, leading to the realized private eye) were prefigured in a short story Himes had written previously, "He Knew," which featured black detectives John Jones and Henry Walls on a robbery investigation. "I'm putting you two men on this job because it's a Negro neighborhood and I believe that it's Negroes who are pulling these jobs. You fellows are plodders, and it's plodders we need."[13] True to the issues of black-on-black crime and the absurdist nature of crime and crime fighting that Himes suffuses his detective novels with—also evident in *The Wire*—it turns out the robbers are the sons of one of the cops. Matters end tragically. *The Five-Cornered Square* tells the story of a Harlem man who falls for a female con artist; it won France's La Grand Prix du Roman Policier for the best detective novel.

Unlike the hardcore reality of West Baltimore depicted in *The Wire*, Himes's Harlem, a place he only had a passing knowledge of, was one of surrealness and quixotic characters—though arguably those qualities are there in *The Wire* as well. Moving about in their rumpled dark suits, porkpie and snap brim hats, and a dark sedan, Coffin Ed and Grave Digger are truly men in black. And as Himes chronicles their travails, there is always a satiric gallows humor to the plots, as Grave Digger and Coffin Ed chase after fanciful hoodlums in bizarre situations. There's Deke

O'Hara, an ersatz Marcus Garvey, who is looking to bilk the hardworking people of Harlem with his back-to-Africa scam; the country-bred femme fatale Imabelle manipulating men to retrieve stolen gold ore; gold again, hidden in a bail of cotton; and the preacher who falls out of a window, miraculously lands in a bread basket, and then is murdered. These are some of the members of the cast of the absurdist plays that the humorless and at times brutal Coffin Ed and the slightly more idealistic Grave Digger find themselves populating. This from the *All Shot Up* (originally published in the States by Avon, 1960):

> The reason the sergeant couldn't get Grave Digger Jones and Coffin Ed Johnson is that they were in the back room of Mammy Louise's pork store eating hot "chicken feetsy" . . . Their beat-up black hats hung above their overcoats on nails in the outside wall. Sweat beaded on their skulls underneath their short-cropped, kinky hair and streamed down their dark, intent faces. Coffin Ed's hair was peppered with grey.
>
> He had a crescent-shaped scar on the right-side top of his skull, where Grave Digger had hit him with his pistol barrel, the time he had gone berserk after being blinded by acid thrown into his face. That had been more than three years ago, and the acid scars had been covered by skin grafted from his thigh. But the new skin was a shade or so lighter than his natural face skin and it had been grafted on in pieces. The result was that Coffin Ed's face looked as though it had been made up in Hollywood for the role of the Frankenstein monster. Grave Digger's rough lumpy face could have belonged to any number of hard, Harlem characters.[14]

Unlike the creators of *The Wire*, Himes didn't receive any awards from the NAACP for his work, though he published pieces in *Crisis* magazine. Writers such as the aforementioned Donald Goines (who with ex-pimp and writer Robert Beck, aka Iceberg Slim, is the godfather of ghetto lit) Clarence Cooper Jr., Robert Deane Pharr, and Herbert Simmons were also unacceptable to the established civil rights community, or were unnoticed as advancing the race in their writing. But these outsiders are part of a consortium of pop culturists who, like their counterparts in the ranks of today's ghetto lit practitioners, examined the underworld of the neoliberal city, be it generations ago or during the Reagan years or the presidencies of Clinton, George W. Bush, and now Obama.

The critique of those depicting the antihero and romanticized

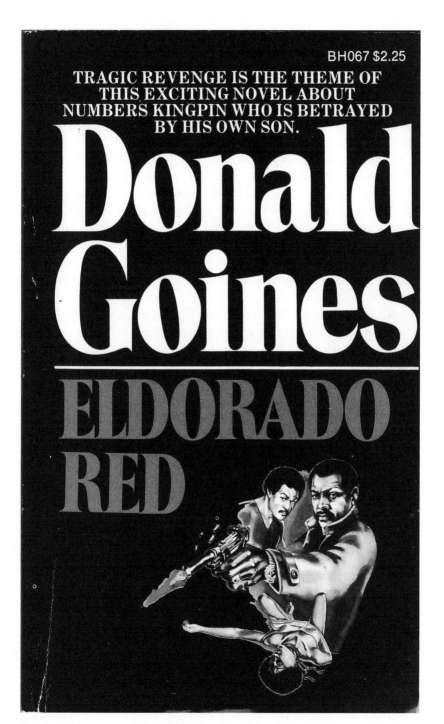

Cover of Donald Goines, *Eldorado Red* (Los Angeles: Holloway House, 1974)

gangster aspects of the black experience didn't begin with Chiles's op-ed. During the Harlem Renaissance of the 1920s, civil rights pioneer W. E. B. DuBois initially argued that black literature could show the complexities of Negro life, as he wrote in his editorial in a 1921 issue of the *Crisis* magazine: "We have criminals and prostitutes, ignorant and debased elements just as all folk have."[15] His position would shift, presaging a tone Chiles would echo decades later. DuBois was responding to other theories about the role of the black creative as advanced by the likes of Alain Locke, a professor of philosophy at Howard University. Locke's 1925 introduction to *The New Negro* anthology called for black artists to smash previous preconceptions about African Americans. In that essay, Locke wrote that "the Negro to-day wishes to be known for what he is, even in his faults and shortcomings, and scorns a craven and precarious survival at the price of seeming to be what he is not."[16] DuBois's rejoinder was to develop his view that art was propaganda, that it should shape public opinion and demonstrate the hard work and fortitude of the black middle class. "In the *Crisis* at least," he wrote in the magazine in January 1926, "you do not have to confine your writings to the portrayals of beggars, scoundrels and prostitutes; you can write about ordinary decent colored people if you want."[17]

The debate about what was and wasn't off-limits went back and forth among many writers in and around the Harlem Renaissance. The publication of *Nigger Heaven*, a novel by white writer Carl Van Vechten in 1926, hardened opinions on both sides of the argument, like the black literati firestorm over ghetto lit. As when *The Wire* was on the air, a white writer was portraying a mostly black underbelly. (As Langston Hughes noted wryly, "More Negroes bought [*Nigger Heaven*] than ever purchased a book by a Negro author.")[18] *Nigger Heaven*, praised by some, such as black writer James Weldon Johnson, was dismissed by DuBois as celebrating pimps and prostitutes and the underclass. In reality, the book was a sprawling look at the jazz clubs, speaks, night life, and intellectual life of Harlem. Just as Zora Neale Hurston's novels garnered recognition and criticism for her portrayal of black southern life and use of heavy black dialect, van Vechten used fiction to tell the tales of scoundrels and strivers. This yin and yang of African American lives is not the sole purview of African Americans to write about. But cut against the context of institutionalized racism in America, these portrayals in our pop culture engender sharper scrutiny. Still there's something to be noted: that as African Americans utilized the art form of film in the 1920s and 1930s, the gangster life of scoundrels and fast women, lifestyles DuBois would decry, were put up on the big screen in glorious black and white.

Ralph Cooper's name is probably only known to a few hardcore cinephiles today, but once upon a time he was called the "Dark Gable." A Harlemite, Cooper was a song-and-dance man who was the originator and emcee of Amateur Night at the Apollo in 1935. The story goes that he was choreographing dance routines in a Shirley Temple movie *Poor Little Rich Girl*, studying the moviemaking process. More likely, given his good looks and stage presence, and given other black entertainers, singers, and musicians he hobnobbed with, like Louis Jordan and Lena Horne, who were making quickie "race movies" (films with African Americans in the lead roles), he was surely aware there was a hunger among black audiences to see themselves in nonsubservient roles. Cooper, like pioneering black filmmakers Spencer Williams and Oscar Micheaux, eschewed trying to break into white Hollywood, though he did travel west to start a brief but groundbreaking career that would include being an actor, cowriter, and producer of several films. Partnering with two white bothers from Canada, Harry and Leo Popkin (the latter would produce the 1950 noir classic, *D.O.A.*), and black director George Randol, they formed Million Dollar Productions to produce films for black moviegoers. But first he and Randol would produce the pioneering *Dark Manhattan* in 1937. Billed as Hollywood's first all-black gangster movie, Cooper stars as Curly Thorpe. In a continuum from Scarface Camonte to Marlo Stanfield, Thorpe is looking to take over the rackets by any means necessary. In this plot, it's the Harlem numbers hustle he's looking to conquer. Along the way in the brisk seventyminute film, shot on sets in Los Angeles, in his ruthless rise he meets and falls for nightclub singer Babe Gray. But she is no gold digger, as rapper Kanye West would warn. Rather, Babe, played by Cleo Hendon, who sings "The Sweetest Moment of my Life" in a scene that included the Cotton Club orchestra, seeks to make Curly a better person, a striver and not a scoundrel. But not unlike the fate of his white underworld counterparts, Paul Muni's *Scarface* and Jimmy Cagney's Tom Powers in *Public Enemy*, Ralph Cooper's Curly Thorpe comes to a violent end. Crime does not pay.

Dark Manhattan premiered at the Apollo, doing gangbusters at the black box office. Million Dollar Productions would go on to make gangster fare like *Bargain With Bullets* (Cooper as Mugsy Moore, a gang lord juggling two women in his life), which was distributed by the white-owned Lowes theater chain; *Gang War*, in which Cooper's Killer Meade seeks to take over the jukebox racket; and *The Duke Is Tops*, a lighthearted effort with a lot of music in which Cooper plays impresario Duke Davis. In *Am I Guilty?* also known as *Racket Doctor*, a film not produced by his company, Cooper pays an idealistic doctor named James Dunbar (echoing Paul Lawrence Dunbar) who gets jammed up by gangsters as he tries to open a free clinic in Harlem.[19] Another film in this first black gangster cycle was called *Gang Smashers*, also called *Gun Moll*. A Toddy Pictures Company release, with a story by Ralph Cooper, it was directed by Leo Popkin. The film featured a black female undercover operative, Laura Jackson. Starring singer Nina Mae McKinney (with famed comedian Mantan Moreland in the cast as a henchman named Gloomy), referred to as the Bronze Garbo, she puts on the guise of nightclub singer cum gun moll to bust up the Harlem Protection Association run by gangster Gat Dalton.

These independently made black gangster films share a low profile with a cadre of writers, around during Himes's time, but who haven't gained his level of postmortem attention. Under the banner of Old School Books, a reprint series of these rediscovered writers was distributed by W. W. Norton in the 1990s. This grouping, like Goines and Beck, rawly portrayed the not so genteel flip side of the black experience. *Corner Boy*, by Herbert Simmons, which won the Houghton Mifflin Literary Fellowship in 1957, is about a young man, Jake Adams, who rises as a drug slanger for the Organization. Robert Deane Pharr's *Giveadamn Brown* is an absurdist tale of a country boy inheriting the Harlem criminal empire of his uncle and the odd characters therein. Pharr, who was a college graduate but who'd worked at a waiter at tony establishments and private clubs, sold his first book, *The Book of Numbers* (Doubleday) in 1969. The novel was about two young African American men cornering the numbers trade in 1930s Richmond, Virginia. The book was made as a film by actor-director Raymond St. Jacques, who'd portrayed Coffin Ed Johnson in two films made from Himes's books. Also in the Old School canon was Clarence Cooper Jr.'s 1960 book, *The Scene* (originally published by Crown). This excerpt from the novel is both current in its description and a cruel precursor to false hope that a federal intervention, the war on drugs, will end the problem of dope in the 'hood:

"Well, sir, I don't mean to sound pessimistic," Stuart began, "but narcotics isn't as easily erased as all that. You see, our biggest problem when we make an arrest is that another peddler or addict is next in line for the empty place. We've got four squads under my swing-shift command, and four under Lieutenant Speer: thirty-two men, working from twelve to fourteen hours. These men can't even begin to cope with the scores of dope violators. Eventually, with Federal help, we will."[20]

Circling back to the novels, or as they would have it, novelizations of their exploits, Terri Woods's and Vicki Stringer's female queenpins aren't pretending to be in the life, as Laura Jackson was in *Gun Moll*. In *The Wire*, embodying the art-imitates-life ethos, is Felicia "Snoop" Pearson, a convicted drug dealer who in a way plays herself—if she'd continued doing what she'd been doing. In the show she is hard; indeed at first glance she's perceived as male. But Snoop the character doesn't have aspirations for taking over the gang and dies a loyal soldier to Marlo Stanfield. As Teresa Wiltz writes of her, Snoop, four years out of prison at twenty-four, was an " undersize woman with an oversize swagger."[21] Cast in the show after a chance meeting with actor Michael K. Williams, who played the killer of kingpin Stringer Bell (with the aid of Fruit of Islam–ish, bowtie-wearing Brother Mouzone) Omar Little, she inhabited her role with experiential gravitas. Taking Michael Lee for a ride in her Nissan SUV, he knows what's up and turns the tables. He asks Snoop to pull over to an alley so he can pee and pulls his gat on her. "Y'all taught me to get there early," he reminds her. Now Snoop knows what time it is and takes her impending demise in stoic fashion—she knew she was never going to see thirty. She leans over, looking at herself in the vehicle's side mirror, a slight tremor in her voice. "How my hair look, Mike?" "You look good, girl." Then he blows the emotionless killer Snoop away.

This scene is reminiscent of the death of King David, the drug lord in Goines's *Never Die Alone* (Holloway House, 1974, filmed with rapper-actor DMX in the title role in 2004). Like Snoop, his demise is a riff on Cab Calloway's request in the song "St. James Infirmary" to be laid out in his coffin with a twenty-dollar gold piece on his watch chain so they'll know he died standin' pat. You want to go out looking good. After making that paper in L.A., King David returns to New York, only to get caught slipping, and is gunned down by a rival. As he lies dying, he says to a passerby, "Help me to my car, mister. Don't want to die layin' in no gutter . . . don't mind payin,' just don't want to die alone in the street."

Despite *The Wire's* arena of heavy-duty masculinity beyond Snoop, there are other strong female characters. Detective Shakima "Kima" Greggs, played by Sonja Sohn, is a tough, smart, single mom who is also a lesbian. Talk about a hard row to hoe in the boys club of the squad room and the corner! In the first season of the show, she's shot and goes through extensive rehab, so defamiliarizing a standard plot device of the police procedural, as it is conventionally the hard-bitten male cop who has to overcome some sort of physical and psychological adversity to get back in the fight. By the last season, Greggs is the one who busts fellow officer Jimmy McNulty, ending his career. It's symbolic that it's Kima Greggs, the upright stalwart cop, who brings McNulty down. She should be the one, because of these characteristics and her lifestyle as the outsider, which has come in for the kind of ribbing you would expect in a mostly male crew of colleagues. McNulty is the maverick cop beloved in cops-and-robbers stories. Further, the womanizing McNulty has no animosity toward Greggs for turning him in, and in fact welcomes her inside the bar as they drink to his departure. Order restored?

Not exactly. Other matters in *The Wire's* last season ended worse for some, and in other ways life went on, the guilty unpunished. Omar Little, a professional thief who with his accomplices robbed the Avon Barksdale and Marlo Stanfield drug houses with a personal code, comes out of retirement on a mission of vengeance. He survives a shootout and a Spider-Man-like escape only to be gunned down by a child psychopath—one of those kids who'd been celebrating Little's dastardly deeds that Bunk Moreland lamented. Scott Templeton, the fabricating *Baltimore Sun* reporter, who McNulty knew was making up stuff in his pieces about the supposed serial killer and is suspected of such by his editor, isn't busted and in fact goes on as the series closes out to more accolades. The world is neither imploding nor set right.

"There ain't no bad guys and there ain't no good guys, just two people who disagree," drug kingpin Stick Henderson (played by Tony King, one of the vigilantes in *Gordon's War*) observes in the 1975 film *Report to the Commissioner*, based on the book of the same title by James Mills. Set in a post-Watergate, post-Vietnam New York City, the book and film offer a jaundiced view to a jaundiced citizenry of the politics of covering your ass when something goes wrong. The question of who gets to point the finger and who has to fall on the sword is raised as a struggle to control perceptions breaks out between the police hierarchy and the politicos in the wake of a cop's accidentally killing an undercover female cop, who has shacked up with Henderson to get the goods on him. These themes are present in *The Wire* in the squad's dealings with the chain of command, the brass's dealings with city hall, as well as the ripple effects of the racialized politics of the mayor's race.[22] Also in *Report* is plainclothes rough-and-tumble detective Crunch Blackstone, played with élan by Yaphet Koto, a character out of the Coffin Ed / Grave Digger / Bunk Moreland mold. It is interesting, too, that a couple of years before this movie, Kotto (who would go on to be the black-Italian head of the squad, Al Giardello, in *Homicide: Life on the Streets*) played the opposite kind of cop, the "Good Negro," the credit to his race by his deeds (à la detective Virgil Tibbs, introduced in the novel *In The Heat of the Night* by John Ball in 1965), Lieutenant Pope in *Across 110th Street*, referring to the physical border of Harlem, and the dividing line between black gangsters and the Mafia.

A latter-day hip-hop-influenced Big Apple was on display in *New York Undercover*, shot on location. It ran for four years on Fox TV from 1994 to 1998. *Miami Vice* in the 1980s ushered in an era of fashionable undercover vice cops—the conceit being that the two high-style leads, the white Sonny Crockett and the black Ricardo Tubbs, would blend in with the high-rolling cocaine dealers they had to get the goods on. *New York Undercover*, with its plainclothesmen, the black J. C. Williams and Puerto Rican Eddie Torres, blended into their undercover environment by wearing unlaced Timberlands, baggy jeans (better to hide your back-up ankle gun), and puffy half-sleeve parkas. Single dad Williams sported a shaved head and trim goatee, Torres a small gold hoop earring. This show was the first crime drama to have two people of color as the leads. The two, along with Afro-Rican detective Nina Moreno, and in season 3 Irish-Italian detective Tommy McNamara, operated out of the Fourth Precinct in Harlem, their boss the white, Brooklyn-accented Lt. Virginia Cooper. While racial matters weren't as deep a current as in *The Wire*, it wasn't just on the edges, as say in *Miami Vice*. When Torres and Williams investigate the alleged gang rape of a Puerto Rican girl by black and white members of a high school football team, the two men have a heated conversation. "Is this a Puerto Rican versus a black thing?" Torres asks, as Williams believes the athletes, who say it was consensual sex, and Torres the young woman. Harkening back to scenes of songs sung in the context of the film, as in *Dark Manhattan* and B crime drama movies like *Black Angel* and *The Strip*, there would invariably be a scene at the detective's hangout, Natalie's (Natalie was played by singer Gladys Knight) where the likes of Aaliyah, The Temptations, Brandy, The Notorious B.I.G., Bone Thugs-N-Harmony, Kirk Franklin, 112, Xscape, or Boyz II Men would perform. Often the camera would cut to the performer, then back to our guys discussing the current case over drinks at the club.

The short-lived *EZ Streets*, created by Paul Haggis (who would go on to make the film *Crash* about the collision of race and racism in Los Angeles) on CBS, used topical music too, but not much in the way of upbeat tunes. There's an opening in the pilot episode where a steel drum is being craned out of the water at the docks. A haunting song, the "Moorlough Shore" sung by Caroline Lavelle, plays on the soundtrack. Among the ones watching the drum as it's placed on the dock is plainclothes detective Cameron Quinn. The drum is opened and we don't see what Quinn sees, but can tell he's upset. As in the noir films *D.O.A.* and *Out of the Past*, the story then unfolds in flashback. We don't learn until we are back on the docks at the end of the story that it's Quinn's murdered father, a crooked cop forced out of the department some time before, who is in the drum.

Only nine episodes were made of *EZ Streets*, with two airing in October 1996; the show was cancelled, then brought back for a brief run in April and March 1997. There was a mobbed-up black mayor, Christian Davidson, a cleaned-up Marion Berry type, it was intimated. Davidson has made a deal with the Irish godfather Fivers Duggan to funnel his dirty money into rebuilding the rusted hulks of the alphabet streets section of the unnamed city just a bridge away from Canada—a clear stand-in for Detroit. Small-time but ambitious homeboy hoodlum Jimmy Murtha, son of a union organizer, is encroaching on Duggan's territory, and Quinn is under orders to bring Murtha down by appearing to be a bent cop too. Setting this up involves him getting an intimate patdown from an unblushing female attorney named Theresa Conners, who is into kinky things. She knows Quinn from high school days (Bunk Moreland and Omar Little also went to the same high school, though years apart), and is sleeping with Murtha. Who is what and what secrets do they hold? Who are the good cops and who aren't? As his old man warned Quinn the last time he'd seen him, angry because he'd had little contact with him for some time, he can only be betrayed by someone he trusts. As Quinn tries to get to the truth, we see him at a police head-quarters full of busted-down furniture against dull browns and beiges, like something from a 1960s Soviet bureaucratic office deep in the bow-els of some nondescript building. There are reel-to-reel tape recorders and manual typewriters clacking, and huge sleds of Detroit iron from another era tooling the rustbelt byways, as when the smoke stacks were belching black and you groused because you had to work overtime at the plant. But now the plant is gone. In a nod to modern times, there's even a softball game in the first episode between Murtha's crew and a Jamaican drug posse. Naturally it ends with nines drawn all around.

The dark, moody *EZ Streets* was a hard sell in the heartland, even though it had whites in the leads as the cops and criminals, unlike *The Wire*. Though it was also a rugged show, *Homicide* had its share of quirky humor and interactions among its black and white characters. Murtha had his wiseguy charm, but it's hard to get to funny when an already angst-riven man finds his father dead in a barrel dumped in the water. Also, one of the subplots in *EZ Streets* was a dark alliance among a clique of cops and gangsters. Even with Democrat Bill Clinton newly minted in office, there was too much shadow of the reproachful Bush the First over the land. What if *EZ Streets* had come out when Clinton was busted for getting a hummer in the Oval Office? A sensationalist president breeds a sensationalist public? Our taste for the unusual and strange, the dangerous and profane, for those who walk the edge we dare not for fear of missing a house or car payment, can't be quenched.

— — —

Is *The Wire* merely as various critics have asserted, à la van Vechten, whites getting a thrill exploring the black exotic? A twenty-first-cen-tury pimping of African American pathologies by hipster whites? There could be some of that, but not in the main. As history has shown, not only is the black audience watching and reading, black storytellers then and now have done their own takes on the outsiders and the underworld too—often being blasted for it as well. Ultimately it's about who gets to tell the story and from what viewpoints. *Bullets or Ballots*, with Depression-era gangster icons Edward G. Robinson and Humphrey Bogart, portrays the Harlem numbers racket. But in this version, a Queenie St. Clair–like character, Nellie LeFleur (played by Louise Beavers) is subservient to Joan Blondell's Lee Morgan. Yet in 1997's *Hoodlum*, Queenie is her own woman and Fishburn's Bumpy Johnson is the tough antihero standing up to kill crazy white gangster Dutch Schultz, who is muscling in on Johnson's numbers empire.[23]

When a black storyteller pitches a so-called black or multicultural project to a mainstream publisher or production company, questions of whether whites in the heartland will pay to read or see this effort—is it relatable as the parlance goes—invariably are part of the discussion. In an equal opportunity world, Clarence Cooper Jr.'s *The Scene* or Nathan Heard's *Howard Street* would have been the basis for hard-hitting filmic or TV interpretations, not unlike the book *The Corner: A Year in the Life of an Inner-City Neighborhood* by Simon and Burns (Broadway Books, 1997), which became a miniseries on HBO, paving the way for *The Wire*.

But as the cops and criminals in the aforementioned examples in this essay might remind us, life ain't fair. You handle your business with the hand you got dealt. Keep telling the stories you want to tell, at the service of neither the literati nor the critics. Push yourself to make the characters and their situations as dimensional and contextual as you can. For one day a group of black and Latino creators just might craft a series about the shenanigans of high-flying white financiers who, as Woody Guthrie warned, can steal more with a pen than a gun.

Let the critics say something about that.

Notes

1. Neil Brenner and Nik Theodore, "Cities and the Geographies of 'Actually Existing Neoliberalism,'" *Antipode* 34 (2002): 356–86.

2. Illustrating this overlap of the streets and suites, Stringer Bell, the thinking man's gangster in *The Wire*, attempts to parlay illicit profits into mainstream investments. In the 2002 film *Empire*, heroin kingpin Vic Ross (the name a possible riff on Rick Ross, a Los Angeles drug kingpin said to have been an inner-city conduit for the CIA-backed contras exporting cocaine to fund their anticommunist insurgency—see Gary Webb, *Dark Alliance: The CIA, the Contras, and the Crack Cocaine Explosion* [New York: Seven Stories Press, 1998])

is ripped off by a con man affecting Wall Street phraseology when he supposedly invests in a legit deal with his ill-gotten gains.

3. Rafael Alvarez, *The Wire: Truth Be Told* (New York: Pocket, 2004).

4. Nick Chiles, "Their Eyes Were Reading Smut," *New York Times*, January 4, 2006, http://www.nytimes.com/2006/01/04/opinion/04chiles.html.

5. http://www.teriwoodspublishing.com/authors.htm.

6. "How I Did It: Vickie Stringer, CEO Triple Crown Productions," *Inc.*, May 1, 2006, http://www.inc.com/magazine/20060501/qa-stringer.html.

7. Teri Woods, *True to the Game* (New York: Grand Central Publishing, 2007), 1

8. James Sallis, *Chester Himes: A Life* (New York: Walker, 2000).

9. Chester Himes, *The Quality of Hurt*, vol. 1 (New York: Thunder's Mouth Press, 1971), 28.

10. Ibid., 47.

11. Ibid., 64.

12. Ibid., 142.

13. Chester Himes, "He Knew," *Abbott's Monthly*, 1933.

14. Chester Himes, *All Shot Up* (New York: Thunder's Mouth Press, 1996), 17–18.

15. W. E. B. DuBois, "Negro Art," *Crisis* 22 (June 1921): 51.

16. Alain Locke, "Enter the New Negro," *Survey Graphic* 6.6 (1925): 631–34.

17. W. E. B. DuBois, "Our Book Shelf," *Crisis* 31 (January 1926): 141, quoted in Abby Arthur Johnson and Ronald Maberry Johnson, *Propaganda & Aesthetics: The Literary Politics of African-American Magazines in the Twentieth Century* (Amherst: University of Massachusetts Press, 1991), 46.

18. Langston Hughes, "The Negro in Art," *Crisis* 31 (April 1926): 278, quoted in Johnson and Johnson, *Propaganda & Aesthetics*, 47.

19. It is a testament to the shoestring budget of these four-wallers that, according to an uncredited post on the Independent Movie Data Base, *The Duke Is Tops* star Lena Horne didn't attend the June 1938 NAACP charity premiere of the movie in Pittsburgh because she hadn't been paid for her work. With these films, just as the black audience for *New York Undercover* and *The Wire* attests to even today, men and women of color want to see themselves represented in pop culture mediums.

20. Clarence Cooper, *The Scene* (New York: W. W. Norton, 1996), 39.

21. Teresa Wiltz, "The Role of Her Life," *Washington Post*, March 16, 2007, http://www.washingtonpost.com/wp-dyn/content/article/2007/03/15/AR 2007031501664.html.

22. A possible conception of the signature gun in your "grill" set piece by director John Woo in his crime films such as *Hard Boiled* and *Face/Off*, there's

a riveting scene of the cop who at that point doesn't know he's shot a fellow officer, Bo Lockley, chasing Stick Henderson on foot and over the rooftops of cars. The two wind up in a department store elevator, sweating, scared, their guns jammed close at each other as they exchange words.

23. In fact the real Bumpy Johnson would survive and in the 1950s operated a string of dry-cleaning stores in the boroughs of New York. Like Omar Little, who eschews cussing, Johnson once had a violent confrontation with an individual, "The Hawk" Hawkins, outside the Vets Club in Harlem for swearing in front of women. See Ron Chepesiuk, *Gangsters of Harlem: The Gritty Underworld of New York's Most Famous Neighborhood* (New York: Barricade Books, 2007).

10

Drinking with McNulty: Irish American Identity and Spaces in *The Wire*

Ruth Barton

I'd like to start this essay with some local background. Dominic West, the actor who plays Jimmy McNulty in *The Wire*, was a student at my university (Trinity College Dublin), graduating with a B.A. in drama studies and English in 1992. As well as appearing in Drama productions, West made his film debut under the direction of another rising talent at TCD, Lenny Abrahamson, who cast West in his short film *3 Joes* in 1991. The comedy chronicles the early morning routines of three young men who share a house together and was shot in the style of a Beckettian silent film. It won the Best Irish Short Film award at the Galway Film Fleadh (Festival) of 1991 and followed this with the Best European Short Film award at the Cork Film Festival of the same year. Abrahamson went on to gain multiple plaudits as the director of *Adam and Paul* (2004) and *Garage* (2007), pared-down dramas that explore issues of alienation in contemporary Irish urban (*Adam and Paul*) and rural (*Garage*) culture. Two of the other Joes, Mikel Murfi and Gary Cooke, have achieved considerable local success, as has the film's scriptwriter, Michael West. Of this group of immensely talented undergraduates, only Dominic West left Ireland permanently and, as he was raised and educated in England, this ought not to have come as a surprise. The fact that West attended Eton, the most elite of British public schools, is often raised in media profiles, and as an isolated piece of information it certainly seems to sit uncomfortably with his antiestablishment McNulty persona. In fact the actor's background is Irish Catholic and he was brought up in a village near Sheffield in northern England. His father owned a plastics factory and decided to send his sixth and youngest child to boarding school. West has spoken in interview of how he had to modify his acquired upper-crust tones on visits home to Sheffield, and the issue of his accent frequently crops up in discussions of his star persona.[1] A further biographical detail is that in the summer of 2010, West married his longtime partner and fellow Trinity student, Catherine Fitzgerald. She is the daughter of Desmond FitzGerald, the Twenty-ninth Knight of Glin, and the reception was held in her family home, Glin Castle, in County Limerick. Thus, West is connected to Ireland by both birth and marriage, but his is a kind of Irishness—public-school educated and at home in a historic castle, that places him considerably at odds with the prevailing stereotypes of Irish identity.

These details are important for my argument for several reasons. In *The Wire*, McNulty's persona as an Irish American defines him to an unusual extent when he is compared with the other central characters. Take, for instance, Councilor (later Mayor) Carcetti, played by Irish actor Aidan Gillen. We know that he is Italian American, but neither his lifestyle nor his looks nor his actions are seen to spring from his ethnic identity. The only group of characters, aside from McNulty, who are defined (and in this case limited) by their ethnic backgrounds are the Polish dockworkers, whose sense of community and family is linked to their emigrant backgrounds. Part of Frank Sobotka's (Chris Bauer) tragedy is that he cannot live up to the role of benevolent patriarch that is expected of a man in his position. The dilution of these inherited values is further exemplified by the failings of his son Ziggy (James Ransone), expressed in part through his rejection of his Polish upbringing in favor of a kind of clownish urban huckster persona. In particular, *The Wire* has been careful to avoid ascribing criminality to ethnic identity so that, although most of the central characters on the street are African American, this is evidently to be explained by social disadvantage rather than the essentialism of skin color. While the African American members of the Baltimore police are familiar to us from other police procedurals, it is hard to argue that they are significantly distinguishable from their white colleagues.[2]

This leaves us with McNulty and the casting of Dominic West. As I wish to explore in the remainder of this essay, the singularity of this character is out of keeping with the rest of the drama and may be explained as being the consequence of a series of tensions that were thrown up in the collision between the actor, the script, and the stereotype. These tensions also mirror the program makers' own unresolved stance toward their creation—specifically the contradictions involved in wishing to make a radically new form of television serial while still finding an audience. It was important for McNulty to be Irish, as I will argue, because of the multiple associations this identity carries in American popular culture, most specifically in relation to an urban, white immigrant identity. Irishness, I will further suggest, comes to stand in for a "structure of feeling" that borrows from and updates Tom Wolfe's *Bonfire of the Vanities*:

> All the cops turned Irish, the Jewish cops . . . but also the Italian cops, the Latin cops, and the black cops. The black cops even; nobody understood the police commissioners, who were usually black, because their skin hid the fact that they had turned Irish. The same was true of assistant district attorneys in the Homicide Bureau. You were supposed to turn Irish. . . . Irish machismo—that was the dour madness that gripped them all.[3]

In other words, Irishness is specifically represented in the figure of McNulty, a character less dour and more engaging than Wolfe's emblematic city cop; but it also comes to stand in for a way of being that distinguishes the characters in the Baltimore police who form one of the groups—alongside the Projects, City Hall, the school, and the newspaper—around which *The Wire* is organized. Finally, Irishness is associated with a particular space, the Irish pub, that is presented to us in a manner that, I will suggest, functions to underline the themes proposed here as well as being part of a long tradition of representation that lends the series a sense of historicity but is also conventional to the point of clichéd.

The Actor

In Rafael Alvarez's book on *The Wire,* David Simon remembers filling the role of McNulty. The audition process had been going smoothly:

> [O]nly the role of McNulty gave us fits, until a bizarre videotape landed in Baltimore, shipped from a London address. On it, an actor was tearing through the orange-sofa scene in which Bunk and McNulty jack up a reluctant D'Angelo, search him, find his pager, then walk him away in handcuffs.[4]

Although the tape was unorthodox, particularly given that no one was reading the remainder of the scene, Simon was drawn to what he saw in the actor: "a square-jawed, Jack-the-Lad sort."[5] The casting process overall was guided by a desire not to showcase star names and to include a share of nonprofessional actors, most of them in minor roles. West fitted the bill by virtue of being almost unknown to American audiences (he had played a number of minor television and film roles, including a photographer in the 1997 Spice Girls' vehicle, *Spice World* [Bob Spiers]). He also looked like the "charming rebel" type that had been created for him, and he was white. Even though Simon always seems to have envisaged McNulty as fatally flawed—he speaks of the character's "intellectual vanity"—the audience is very evidently primed to enjoy McNulty's persona and to experience some of the pleasures of mainstream star identification in terms of his role.[6] It is he who opens the series, and his is the first voice we hear on the precredit sequence: "So your boy's name Snot?" The conversation with the street kid, who explains to McNulty that when they played crap, Snot Boogie always ran away with the cash, concludes with a key exchange:

MCNULTY: I got to ask you. If every time Snot Boogie would grab the money and run away, why did you let him in the game?
KID: What?
MCNULTY: If Snot Boogie always stole the money, why d'you let him play?
KID: Got to. This America, man.

Dressed in his trademark leather jacket, his always immaculate white shirt just visible over his collar, chewing gum, McNulty is not only cool, he is the white audience's link with the Street. Because the black kid is content to chat to him and apparently trusts him, he can explicate the irony of the two worlds. Both are bound to play what is referred to throughout as "the game" by predetermined, inherited social rules.

The Script

The mirroring of these two worlds proceeds via McNulty, whom we will soon see slipping into a courtroom where the trial of D'Angelo Barksdale (Larry Gilliard Jr.) is taking place. A series of edits draws the audience's attention to McNulty's nemesis and street counterpart, the equally cool Stringer Bell, played by British actor Idris Elba. Both men are neatly turned-out, clean-shaven and in suits. Bell has an almost scholarly air with his round gold-rimmed glasses, tapping a legal pad with his pen and carrying a briefcase. Like McNulty, Bell is a renegade within his structure, although unlike McNulty, Bell's defiance is expressed through a desire for social conformity—attending a night class in economics and investing in property. McNulty is a born nonconformist who challenges the system at each turn, has little interest in the trappings of materialism, and has no ambition to become part of the hierarchy of power.

Again, in this first opening episode, this is closely associated with his identity as an Irish American. Furious that McNulty has drawn the attention of Judge Phelan (Peter Gerety) to the gangland structures operating in the Projects, Major Rawls (John Doman) roars at his insubordinate police officer, threatening "his fuckin' Irish ass." In a later episode, he comments that despite McNulty's "negligible Irish ancestry" he is a good worker (season 1, episode 6, "The Wire"). At the conclusion of the opening episode, McNulty withdraws with his mate Bunk Moreland (Wendell Pierce) to drown his sorrows over a pint of Murphy's (stout) in Kavanagh's Irish pub. There they will later wake their dead comrade, Ray Cole, played by the series producer, Robert Colesberry, a sequence to which I will shortly return.

So why insist so repeatedly on McNulty's Irishness as his persona is being established and what effect does this have on how we read his character? Indeed, why should McNulty's Irishness be so clichéd in a television series otherwise widely praised for its refusal to indulge in clichés?[7] In part, the answer is to be found in McNulty's positioning as the show's star. An audience understands a fictional character, as Richard Dyer has argued in his seminal definition of stardom, through familiarity with their type. In particular, audiences work on inference: "The inferences that we make may be outwards, to universals or cultural specificities. They may also be, as it were, inwards, the place of the character in the overall scheme of the film."[8] Faced with the economic necessity of producing one identifiable white hero figure, Simon and his collaborators were forced to fall back on the stock-in-trade of mainstream fiction and create a character to which the audience could relate through their accumulated familiarity with his type. Thus the audience was invited to infer outward by reading McNulty through certain pre-existing stereotypes of the screen Irishman.

The first reference point has to be Errol Flynn, who from his career-making performance as the doctor-turned-pirate in *Captain Blood* (Michael Curtiz, 1935) exemplified the screen image of the dashing Irish rebel. Such a figure played well both to the substantial Irish American film-going audience who easily identified with Flynn's persona and to the wider WASP audience who could take from the figure his romanticism, while explaining away his intrinsic antiestablishment values as Other/Irish. McNulty bears the same semiotic weight. He is the daring white seeker/hero of myth, setting out to right wrongs where lesser individuals would falter, but his many failings (as well as his charm) are all ethnically attributable. He is thus simultaneously an insider and an outsider hero, "us" but, for most of the audience, also "not us."

In another setting, such a description might equally be applied to the Western hero, the singular individual who rides in to save the weakened community, dispatches the gang of villains by virtue of his exceptionality, and rides off into the sunset at the narrative's close. But this is urban America and the star to whom McNulty owes his deepest debt is that archetype of the street-smart, white ethnic American James Cagney. In his essay "Looking for Jimmy," Peter Quinn analyzes the personae of two canonic Jimmies—Jimmy Walker, songwriter and politician, and James Cagney. They had their own way of walking, Quinn argues, "their gait, fast and loose, halfway between a stroll and a dance step, an evanescent strut, an electric edginess, as if they found it difficult to stand still, their ears permanently cocked to the syncopation of the streets." They also interpreted the law idiosyncratically: "Fundamental to Jimmy's style was the presumption that the border between legal and illegal was a question of convenience rather than morality."[9]

Such then is McNulty's heritage, a character who could as easily be a gangster as a cop, at home on America's inner-city streets, bearer of a history as identifiable as that of the other players in *The Wire*'s fictionalized world. He is also, as are his counterparts in the Projects, torn between his loyalties. In particular, McNulty's struggle is between personal ambition and communal values. In his essay "The Fireman on the Stairs," Timothy Meagher remembers how moved he was at the image the Irish American fireman selflessly rescuing white-collar workers in the wake of 9/11.[10] In particular, it was their sense of commitment to their peers in the Fire Department that drove them on to rescue strangers and risk their lives, Meagher writes. Such allegiances must have seemed anachronistic in modern-day America, with its emphasis on individuality:

> If those Irish American values of communalism and "regular guy egalitarianism" seem like an anachronism today, they have not always been so. For a long time nothing seemed to set Irish Americans apart more, nothing seemed more tellingly or indelibly Irish American, than this kind of rough and ready communalism. Moreover, the conflict between such communal loyalties and the values and circumstances of the American environment—values of individualism and circumstances of economic abundance and racial and ethnic diversity—has been the central dynamic of the history of the Irish in America.[11]

Meagher further comments that loyalty to community and the refusal to embrace the ethos of individualism may well account for the relative failure of the Irish to better themselves socially or to move more rapidly into the middle classes and beyond. McNulty is more of an individualist than this, but it is his distrust of, and sense of superiority over, authority, and loyalty to his peers in the force that see him relegated to harbor patrol at the beginning of season 2, and back on foot patrol later in the series again. Yet as his peers remind us over and again, he is one of the most talented investigators on the force. Suspicion of authority is, of course, not uniquely expressed through McNulty but permeates *The Wire*; as Carcetti discovers and others such as Senator Clay Davis (Isiah Whitlock Jr.) remind us, political success inevitably comes at the price of personal probity. McNulty, however, will never achieve career progression. This is, to an extent, admirable, a point reflected in Meagher's assessment of Irish American communalism as "an alternative to a current, free-market individualism in America that seems to encourage indifference, even ridicule, of the poor and working people."[12] These sentiments might equally have been applied to the ethos of *The Wire*, and in becoming the bearer of these values, McNulty thus functions as a reflection of *The Wire*'s ambitions. Yet a tension also runs through the script around its favored detective. He is both a conventional seeker/hero and an advocate for communalism. These tensions, which remain unresolved throughout the series, are evident up until its closing sequences, where, as we will see, McNulty is both punished for his individualism and swiftly rehabilitated.

The Stereotype

The detective is also marked by a fatal flaw that is even more closely associated with his Irish identity and draws from a long history of Irish stereotyping. That is, he is a borderline alcoholic.

In the early sequences of season 1, as I have already mentioned, we soon learn that the character is Irish. By episode 5 ("The Pager"), we know that McNulty is separated from his wife and has been negligent in the parenting of the two sons he adores but can never organize himself to visit according to the agreed-upon schedule. In this episode, during a quiet moment on patrol with Kima (Sonja Sohn), he borrows his colleague's cell phone and we hear one side of a conversation with his wife. A dispute soon erupts over the conditions in his new apartment and its suitability as an overnight stay for the boys. The scene ends with McNulty cursing at the phone and Kima enquiring whether he has just called the mother of his children a "cunt." Soon afterward, McNulty enters his apartment, our first view of his domestic situation. He throws open the door, singing as he goes. The song, "Star of the County Down," is a traditional Irish ballad (that has been covered by the Pogues) and although McNulty is too drunk to remember more than the refrain, in its entirety it is sung from the point of view of a young man who falls in love with the eponymous Star, Rosie McCann, and dreams of marrying her. The rendition of this half-remembered song accompanied by swigs from a bottle of Jameson's (Irish whiskey) leave no stereotype of Irish masculinity unaccounted for. In particular, it is the setting, the domestic space, that recalls an endless succession of alcoholic Irish screen males, of which the best known of many may be Johnny Nolan (James Dunn) in Elia Kazan's *A Tree Grows in Brooklyn* (1945). These men carry in their head an imaginary home-space that they both yearn to reproduce in their own lives and shy away from as inhibiting their freedom. More often than not, they drink away the family money, and their womenfolk must secure social advancement through their own hard work and ambition. As the scene develops, West plays McNulty for the full stage Irishman: he shakes out some new bedding and sets to assembling a bed for the apartment in between refreshing

himself liberally from the bottle. The fractured nature of his family relationships is heightened by the series' style of cutting sharply from
sequence to sequence so that in this episode, for example, numerous
scenes intervene between his initial entry into his apartment and the
moment where he arrives at his former family home to pick up his boys.
In fact, it is not until the following episode ("The Wire") that we see
him playing football with his children, a game he interrupts to respond
to a call from Omar (Michael K. Williams). Outrageously, he brings the
boys with him when he picks up Omar and takes him to the morgue to
view his "boy," who has been tortured and murdered by the Barksdale
gang in a revenge assassination. A cut to the McNulty children playing
ball outside the door sees them flinch as Omar roars in grief on seeing
Brandon's (Michael Kevin Darnall) mutilated body. What passes for parenting on McNulty's part may be little better, the montage editing suggests, than Wallace's (Michael B. Jordan) own domestic arrangements,
which see him and Poot (Tray Chaney) care for a gang of Project kids,
sending them off to school every morning with their schoolbags and a
packed lunch. It beggars belief, then, that McNulty's estranged wife,
Elena (Callie Thorne) should even consider responding to his attempts
at a reconciliation, and only when he sends his two children to tail
Stringer Bell (series 1, episode 8, "Lessons") does she finally call it a day
on their relationship and move to prevent him from seeing their sons.

McNulty's realization that Elena has left him for good is the cue for
a second outburst of drunken behavior that is closely linked by the program makers to the character's Irish heritage. In the precredit sequence
of episode 8 ("Duck and Cover") of season 2, he calls Elena drunk from
a pay phone to plead with her to talk to him but just gets an answer-
ing machine. We cut from McNulty assuring the bartender that he will
take a cab home to his car weaving from side to side of the street in the
dark. In the background the Pogues' "Transmetropolitan" is blaring and
the car swings into the pillars of an overpass. McNulty staggers out to
inspect the damage and the sound diminishes as he slams the car door
closed, indicating that this is diegetic accompaniment—in other words
that McNulty has chosen to play it on his car sound system or it has
happened to come on on the radio. Now muted, the track continues as
the detective aims imaginary shots at imaginary onlookers before returning to his car. Now he aims the battered machine directly at a pillar
only to veer away slightly before impact, so that the side of the car again

hits off the cement. Now slightly sober he next goes to a diner where he picks up the waitress and returns with her for sex in her apartment.

Gerardine Meaney has analyzed the car crash scene in the light of the increasing fracturing of the detective's identity, as well as the series' general exploration of the disintegration of working-class masculinity (the crisis at the docks). McNulty's sense of self is only held together through his commitment to his job: "The drunken self-destruction is linked via the soundtrack to McNulty's Irishness, though the choice of 'Transmetropolitan' hints that it is the migrant condition and not the accident of origin that defines Jimmy's insecure identity"[13]

Just as in the previous "drunken Irishman" sequence, West plays up his stage Irish credentials, not surprising for an actor whose Irish education and actorly training would have thoroughly alerted him to the history and origins of this particular cliché. The sequence is, as was the former drunken sequence in his apartment, a moment of comic relief within a series that seldom makes a play for the audience's sense of humor. We cannot tell to what extent West was guided in these scenes by the show's creators or whether he was deliberately drawing attention through his performance style to this cultural stereotyping. Either way, these moments create a hiatus in the series' otherwise claustrophobic suturing of its audience to a particular time and place. McNulty's invocation of the stage Irishman enables a referencing ("inference") outward to a performative and representational history that reaches back through cinema to the Victorian stage and the melodramas of Dion Boucicault. It is not the occasion here to provide a history of the stage Irishman, but we should just remind ourselves that the figure of the drunken, destructive Irishman is both a colonial stereotype intended to diminish the indigenous Irish and a "writing back" to the colonial center by the colonized who, in the nineteenth century, turned the stereotype back on its creators to provide laughter at their expense. Thus the stage Irishman of the Irish imagination is a crafty subversive whose antiestablishment attitude allowed him and his audience to participate in the pleasures of nonconformity.[14] By enhancing his artificiality and his function as a stereotype, the actor could further point to the constructedness of this dramatic persona. So it is on this tradition, of subversion, "street smarts," charm, and communalism, that I believe both actor and program makers are drawing as they develop McNulty's persona. What distinguishes the performance from the script, however, is the degree of knowingness with which West plays his stereotype.

Behind every such performance, a certain truth also lies and, in this case, we can point to the verifiable history of alcoholism among the poverty-stricken Irish immigrants of the late nineteenth and early twentieth centuries.[15] The Irish imported to America a habit of fighting and drinking to excess and of male socializing in public spaces that evolved into the ritualized brawls of the Irish saloon and later the Irish pub. West's performance of McNulty thus evokes by inference both a representational history and a social history. His is not, however, an archaic stereotype but its reinvigoration. McNulty is a contemporary figure whose domestic entanglements (first with his wife, subsequently with Beadie [Amy Ryan]) speak to present-day anxieties over fatherhood and career. As Meaney (above) notes, his is a classic case of masculine insecurity, here figured as harmful both to himself and to his loved ones. This, of course, doesn't make McNulty Irish, but the invocation of his Irish descent historicizes his actions, while the choice of the Pogues as the soundtrack to his self-destruction adds a contemporary nuance to an old stereotype.

A Structure of Feeling: Irishness and Cultural Identification

Writing on the Pogues, Joe Cleary has noted the following:

> Rowdy binge-drinking, hell-raising subcultures—those of eighteenth-century "rakes," nineteenth-century navvies, mid-twentieth-century poets and novelists, and the pub ballad singers of the 1960s and 1970s—are a recurrent feature of the country's [Ireland's] history. Moreover, variant images of Irish sociability and excess have proven highly marketable, featuring in tourist advertising campaigns from the 1950s through to the present. However we assess traditions of popular bibulousness, festivity or misrule, they have left their mark on contemporary popular culture, most obviously in a vast repertoire of (often highly self-conscious and self-parodying) drinking songs, and also in film where Donnybrook scenes serve not as motifs of social breakdown but as antic expressions of communal harmony and rejuvenation. For the more respectably inclined, these dissolute versions of Irishness—at odds variously with more desirable images of modernizing improvement, religious or cultural purity, industrial discipline or cosmopolitan sophistication—have long been an embarrassment, and contemporary

scholarly discussions of the stereotype do not always escape a similar prissiness.[16]

This description of Irish conviviality will be explored in more detail shortly, when we turn to the place of the Irish pub in *The Wire*. For the moment, Cleary's argument that the Pogues represent a long history of the Irish carnivalesque serves to explain the popularity of the band's music in this series as well as in other film sound tracks.[17] As Cleary further explores, the band's harnessing of punk rock energies to older ballads of loss and cultural dissonance shapes their music in ways that speak to a contemporary need to express alienation from capitalist culture:

> Their music summons up a rowdy world of subaltern excess and mayhem, but this version of carnival is never allowed to become cozily celebratory because it is always shot through with sentiments of anger and aggression, sometimes strident, sometimes more muted. The result is a music that leans heavily on the established aesthetics of folk music and the ballad scene, but which, in combining the tempo of the *céilí* with the belligerence of punk, creates an entirely new structure of feeling all of its own.[18]

This structure of feeling—particularly of anger and loss but also anarchic and celebratory—underpins *The Wire* and defines, as I have been arguing, the figure of McNulty. We might also add that this is a particularly urban sound unlike traditional Irish ballads that often speak to and for a rural culture. By deploying a British-Irish punk-trad band to ventriloquize such sentiments, not just in the car crash sequence, but on other occasions too, the program makers invoke a mood of white male alienation that is both romantic and self-destructive. It also suggests that these sentiments have their roots in the metanarrative of American culture—immigration.

David Simon and the program's creators needed to draw on this set of signifiers, stereotypes and all, in order to create an alternative cultural space that would mirror the largely African American cultural space of the Projects. In this regard, it is no coincidence that Simon drafted in popular novelist Dennis Lehane to work on several of the scripts for the show. Lehane's thriller milieu is the urban Irish ethnic enclave of South Boston, an environment that has sufficiently appealed to filmmakers to ensure the appearance of, to date, two well-regarded adaptations: *Mystic River* (Clint Eastwood, 2003) and *Gone Baby Gone* (Ben Affleck, 2007).[19] Patrick Kenzie, Dennis Lehane's detective, evokes "Southie" in language that is equally reflective of the Baltimore docks of *The Wire*'s season 2 and shares with the television show an ambivalent concern about the destruction of white ethnic working-class cultural and physical spaces:

> The section of Dorchester Avenue that runs through my neighborhood used to have more Irish bars on it than any other street outside Dublin. When I was younger, my father used to participate in a marathon pub crawl to raise money for local charities. Two beers and one shot per bar, and the men would move onto the next one. They'd begin in Fields Corner, the next neighborhood over, and move north up the avenue. The idea was to see which man could remain standing long enough to cross the border into South Boston, less than two miles north.
>
> My father was a hell of a drinker, as were most of the men who signed up for the pub crawl, but in all the years of its existence, not one man ever made it to Southie.
>
> Most of the bars are gone now, replaced by Vietnamese restaurants and corner stores. Now known as the Ho Chi Minh Trail, this four-block section of the avenue is actually a lot more charming than many of my white neighbors seem to find it.[20]

Diane Negra has further analyzed this process of gentrification in relation to "Southie" in terms of anxieties over the erosion of blue-collar traditions and values. Although the old Irish American communities who occupied South Boston were not famed for their liberal values, they were appreciated, particularly in nostalgic retrospect, for their community traditions and loyalties:

> With its history as a proving ground for Irish-inflected efforts to enforce racial and sexual homogeneity (through the vociferous opposition to busing in the 1970s and the 1990s Supreme Court decision upholding local St. Patrick's Day parade organizers' rights to exclude gay and lesbian groups), South Boston sustains an identity that is deeply rooted in concepts of Irish traditionalism. Yet the rising property values, condo-

minium construction, and influx of commuter professionals remaking the area's economy and culture substantiate anthropologist Tim Seiber's contention that "In this post-industrial phase of globalization, there's not much place for the old, ethnic working-class communities."[21]

Patrick Kenzie shares many of Jimmy McNulty's self-destructive tendencies, although, unlike McNulty, he is prone to introspection, and also to musings about the place of Catholicism in his life. This erasure (of Catholicism in *The Wire*) may be in the interests of updating and modernizing the stereotype that drives his character and facilitates a comparison between Irishness as metonymic for white working-class masculinity and Polishness as an anachronistic ethnic identity. It is after all Frank Sobotka's Catholicism and adherence to tradition, namely his decision to donate a stained-glass window to his local church, that, in tandem with the discovery of the dead prostitutes in one of his containers, precipitates the final disenfranchisement of the Polish dockers. By contrast, through the casting of Dominic West as McNulty and the use of the Pogues on the soundtrack, Irishness in the series is expressive of the complex issues of modernity—masculinity, authority, family, professionalism—associated primarily with the members of the police force, who in turn are viewed as representative of "ordinary Joe" America. These converge and are most fully articulated in one specific space, the Irish pub.

Drinking with McNulty

The Irish pub is the locus for the few occasions for self-examination that the series permits its male characters in the police force. In this sense, it stands in for the confessional, and later, as we shall shortly discuss, for the church. In part this is because many of the police officers adhere to the conventional rules of male propriety—whereby emotion may only be publicly expressed through shows of anger. In the pub, men may articulate feelings of failure and vulnerability to each other, most freely when drunk. Most of all, Bunk and McNulty, both of whom suffer from emotional inarticulacy and both of whom struggle to hold down domestic relationships, can communicate with each other in this space. In *The Wire* the pub functions as a kind of time-out from mainstream American life; it can be seen as a "little bit of Ireland" on American soil.

Drinking with "Bunk"

Along with the figure of the stage Irishman, the convivial Irish pub or saloon, peopled by warm-blooded Irish folk always up for the "craic" or a communal brawl, has long been part of the mythology of the Irish in America. Irish pubs, mostly of the sort frequented by the police in *The Wire*, have consistently provided an alternative, often anarchic space, where no one was an outsider and the ordinary limitations of Protestant, temperance culture had no sway (we only need to look at the Irish saloons of John Ford, in films such as *She Wore A Yellow Ribbon* [1949], to see earlier instances of this use of the Irish pub).

In episode 3, season 3 ("Dead Soldiers"), the function of the pub as a surrogate for the church is spelled out. Detective Ray Cole (Robert F. Colesberry) drops dead unexpectedly while working out at the gym. His colleagues gather together in Kavanagh's to hold an Irish wake for their dead friend. Landsman (Delaney Williams) delivers a warm eulogy for Cole, carefully balancing realism—"He wasn't the greatest detective, he wasn't the worst," with praise, recalling cases he solved, to general approval from the gathered policemen. When Landsman pauses, momentarily halted in his recollections by emotion, Lester Freamon calls for music. The barman places a tape in the player and as Landsman resumes, the opening chords of the Pogues' "Body of an American" softly begin to play. Looped to last the duration of Landsman's speech, the lyrics break in to coincide with the end of the eulogy and the listening mourners join in, several of them apparently allocated a line by the script, so that we see McNulty sing and Freamon and Bunk join in. The song, composed by Shane MacGowan, describes the wake of fighter Big Jim Dwyer, whose body has been brought "home" from America to Ireland and expresses the singer's estrangement from this home. In the song, as the party mourns indoors, a group of "tinkers" contemplate hot-wiring the "Yank" Cadillac parked outside. "Fifteen minutes later,"

> *We had our first taste of whiskey (McNulty)*
> *There was uncles giving lectures*
> *On ancient Irish history (Freamon)*
> *. . .*
> *Every bastard there was pisskey. (Bunk)*
>
> *I'm a free born man of the USA." (All join in this chorus)*

The sequence has no narrative function, insofar as it has no effect on the investigation; yet it has strong diegetic and extradiegetic resonances. For one, the writer of the episode (in this case Dennis Lehane) was forced to include the death of Cole since the actor playing him unexpectedly died. Robert Colesberry was also the show's much-loved producer, and the occasion allowed for the cast and production team to memorialize their late colleague. As David Simon said in interview: "I am proud to have sent my man Colesberry off right with the Pogues' 'Body of an American.' We were not just saying goodbye to Ray Cole in that scene, but to one of the show's creators and a true friend and good man. He deserved something evocative."[22] In the commentary to the DVD of the season, Simon elaborates on this, explaining that Landsman is actually invoking in his eulogy some of the best of Colesberry's projects as a producer—*The Corner* (HBO, 2000) *Mississippi Burning* (Alan Parker, 1988), and *After Hours* (Martin Scorsese, 1985), and alluding to

Karen Thorson, Colesberry's widow, who was also one of *The Wire*'s producers.

> [The Pogues] just naturally came into it and "The Body of an American" seems to tell its own story about life and about loss. It just became thematically the perfect thing. . . . The idea that they would lay a guy out on the pool table and do a detective's wake and then sing this song seemed entirely reasonable. They don't have this tradition but they should. . . . The idea that all the detectives, not just the Irish ones, would know the song because they've been to enough wakes is very evocative. Tom Wolfe once wrote that all cops become Irish no matter who they are. I think that's, on some small level, true.[23]

The wake is thus an "invented tradition," something that the Baltimore police "ought" to have done. As it plays out, the occasion is marked by fragmentation and unity. Rather evidently, the laid-out body could not be that of the actual actor (that might have been somewhat overdoing the series' commitment to realism), and so we only see fragments of the corpse—a hand wrapped around a bottle of Jameson's, the other hand, light glinting off the cuff link, laid out on the pool table, the tie, the badge, and so on. Although the edits continue to move us from face to face, the music and singing gives the sequence its unity and sense of communality. It also recalls a long representative history that associates Irishness with what Nina Witoszek and Patrick F. Sheeran have termed a "funerary culture," that is, a culture that openly and vigorously ritualizes death.[24] This places it in sharp to WASP culture with its "stiff upper lip" attitude to mortality.

It is particularly significant that Simon (and presumably Lehane) should have invented this sequence in light of the reference to Wolfe. The concept that in an Irish pub everyone can be Irish is an important selling factor for the Irish tourist industry and is an unspoken promise of the Irish theme pubs that sprang up, literally across the globe, from the early 1990s.[25] The pub in *The Wire*, Kavanagh's, predates theme pubs, but the promise is the same. Everyone can be Irish, this sequence makes clear, regardless of skin color or ethnic background. All you have to be able to do is sing along to the Pogues. This further reinforces my argument that in the schematic structure of *The Wire*, where each side of the Establishment divide has its opposite on the other, Irishness is appropriated as the oppositional identity to the African American culture of the Projects. It isn't the case that all the members of Homicide are Irish (obviously), or that they all behave identically, but that McNulty's exaggerated flaws and charms, his workingman loyalties, and his suspicion of authority, understood to be contingent upon his Irishness, represent a way of being American shared by the members of the Baltimore police force.

Punishing McNulty

It is only in season 5 that the series takes McNulty to task. This is the payback series as far as the detective is concerned, the moment where the program creates a new divide and places McNulty and Freamon on one side, and the remainder of the police department on the other. By faking a story about a serial killer and feeding it to an opportunistic news reporter in order to gain resources for the homicide division, McNulty ups the ante on his seeker/hero identity and abandons communalism, thus forcing the audience to reassess their indulgence of his maverick behavior. As, guided by Lester Freamon, McNulty sinks a set of false teeth into the corpse of a homeless man in order to lend credence to his story, we are forced to look beyond the detective's charm and focus instead on his flaws. This is spelled out in episode 8, "Clarifications," when the department calls in a FBI psychologist to profile the killer. The camera closes in further and further to McNulty's face, as he and Kima listen to the verdict:

> He likely is not a college graduate, but feels nonetheless superior to those with advanced education. And he is likely employed in a bureaucratic entity, possibly civil service or quasi-public service, from which he feels alienated. He has a problem with authority and a deep-seated resentment of those who he feels have impeded his progress professionally. . . . The suspect has trouble with lasting relationships and is possibly a high-functioning alcoholic, with alcohol being used as a trigger in the commission of these crimes. His resentment of the homeless may stem from a personal relationship with someone who is in that cohort, or his victimization of vagrants may merely present an opportunity for him to assert his superiority and intellectual prowess.

As his scheme unravels, and along with it his relationship with his colleagues, most of all Bunk, and the long-suffering Beadie, McNulty is increasingly isolated from the community of officers. No longer is he a charming Irish rogue, or a stage Irish drunk, but he is the inevitable working through of these stereotypes, the ne plus ultra of their worst traits, stripped of redeeming features. He is everything that the psychological profile has listed. This narrative twist functions as a "punishment" for the audience for having willed themselves into believing in a character whose best traits were constructed on a fiction. As McNulty sets out to explain to Beadie (in "Clarifications"), "You start to tell the story and you think you're the hero. Then when you get done talking . . ."

In the same episode, Omar receives his comeuppance, dying at the hand of a young kid with a gun in a convenience store. However, McNulty is "let off," ostensibly in narrative terms because city hall cannot let the details of his and Freamon's actions be made public. Instead both detectives have to choose between desk duty to the end of their working lives or voluntary retirement. Both take the latter. There is a gratifying circularity to this conclusion, mirroring as it does the detectives' own failures, largely because of Establishment corruption, to build a successful court case against the drug criminals. However, it is hard not to feel that Simon and his colleagues were unable to bring themselves to dispose more ruthlessly of their loveable rogue hero. Instead, as they so often did, they resorted to a set of historical clichés about Irishness, dressed up in latter-day clothing, to see off McNulty. In the concluding episode of season 5 ("-30-"), after the detective's fate has been pronounced, we cut to a second wake in the Irish pub. The sequence is introduced with a swift camera pan right over a number of signifiers of Irish Catholicism and culture: a crucifix, a model of hands clasped in prayer, rosary beads, a large golden four-leaf clover beside a statue of the Virgin Mary, and a bottle of Jameson's, before resting on the soles of two somewhat worn shoes. We hear a voice in the background, "What to say about this piece of work?" The camera opens wide to reveal the speaker as Landsman, taking the same position as he did at Cole's wake. "Fuck if I don't find myself without the right words." The mood, is, however, lighter than at the previous wake. The camera pans back to the corpse on the table, and the "mourners" outdo each other in wisecracks at McNulty's expense. Landsman warms to his eulogy:

He was the black sheep, a permanent pariah. He asked no quarter of the bosses and none was given. He learned no lessons; he acknowledged no mistakes; he was as stubborn a Mick as ever stumbled out of the Northeast parish just to take up a patrolman's shield. He brooked no authority. He did what he wanted to do and he said what he wanted to say; in the end he gave me the clearances. He was natural police.

The camera pans from McNulty's feet to his face as he grins and winks at the camera. Soon after, he rises from his table to more laughter and jokes. Echoing Rawls, Landsman refers to the now ex-detective's "negligible Irish ancestry" and as the speech concludes, the strains of the Pogues fade in and the whole room launches into "Body of an American." McNulty passes from cop to cop, dancing a jig with one, embracing another, and a sequence of wide shots allows us to pick out many of the characters that the series has created. Just as the show opened with McNulty, so it closes with him as he pulls off the highway and looks across at Baltimore, allowing for the closing montage of sequences that concludes the various storylines to appear to us as if through his eyes, a final suturing of his perspective to ours.

Conclusion

You could watch *The Wire* from beginning to end without giving much consideration to the series' Irish content. In a sense, Irishness in the United States has become a kind of familiar wallpaper, something that vaguely recalls an era of lower-middle-class respectability, a background to more pressing events in the foreground. The kind of stereotyping that I have explored here has become increasingly distanced from its origins in social disadvantage and from its archetypal figures, and circulates more as a fictional set of identities than a reflection of real lives. I have chosen to draw attention to the many signifiers of Irishness within the series because they seem to me to be crucial in understanding how Simon and his collaborators have constructed one of the polarities, the Baltimore police, on which the series depends for dramatic effect. That Irishness was so meaningful to these individuals is best illustrated by their use of the Pogues, alongside the Irish tradition of the wake, to memorialize one of their colleagues, Robert Colesberry.

As *The Wire* developed, the charisma and despair that increasingly identified the key players in the Projects threatened, in dramatic terms, to encourage the series' audiences to overidentify with this particular grouping. Thus, Simon and his collaborators were forced into reliance on the persona of McNulty to counterbalance these emergent sympathies and to reorient audiences into engaging with the dilemmas of the characters within the police. McNulty's faults had to become both understandable and contemporary to the kind of professional, liberal middle-class viewers who embraced *The Wire* (of which Barack Obama was the most famous). Conveniently and strategically, McNulty's positioning as an urban white ethnic, with a representational history stretching back to that most charismatic of actors, James Cagney, allowed for a greater appeal to that audience than had he been, say, a white WASP figure. It was also important that his own personal dilemmas be both recognizable from his fictional type and consonant with the kind of issues—of career, personal loyalty, and family—that would resonate with that audience.

The problem with McNulty, however, was that the program ended up by creating its own monster. As the series developed, so did Dominic West's offscreen persona. Even before the end of *The Wire*, West had achieved formidable star status (in fact his absence from much of season 4 was to allow for film appearances). By the time season 5 had reached its conclusion, the actor commandeered a substantial and growing fan base, itself facilitated by the social networking potential of the Internet. With his film star looks and his association with a cult television show, he vastly exceeded the public profile of any of his costars, with the possible exception of Idris Elba. This must have been disconcerting to the creators of a show committed to a realist, low-key, alternative identity, and thus, as I have demonstrated, they proceeded to punish us, the viewers, and themselves, the program makers, by deconstructing and punishing the stereotype they had created.

Yet they could only go so far. The final sequences reinstate McNulty as *The Wire*'s star name while also reestablishing his rogue Irish identity, about which the dialogue had been notably silent as he slowly derailed in season 5. Concluding comments by David Simon laud West's performance and particularly his accent, given his Old Etonian background.[26] As I indicated in my introduction to this chapter, in fact West's Irish background is considerably less "negligible" than this discourse around his star persona would have us believe. This, of course, could simply be an oversight. I believe, however, that it was necessary for the show's creators to downplay West's Irishness in order to enhance McNulty's status as a fiction. That West should bring nothing "real" either from his education or his family background to his character was important in the creation of a part that was recognizably inauthentic but also an identification figure for a significant portion of the show's audience. By making McNulty larger than life, yet resonant of a history of performance and stereotype, Simon and his colleagues gifted the series a character that seemed familiar, because of the inferences outward (to other fictional characters), yet was, on closer examination, an obvious fiction. McNulty/West, with his rogue's charm, offsets the otherwise downbeat and deromanticized ambience of the show. At the same time, his Irishness, however negligible, enhances the carnivalesque treatment of authority that is the signature of *The Wire*, both in terms of its storylines and its own positioning within broadcasting history. Overall, his character is expressive of the tension between a need to find an audience and a desire to be different, to refer back to other police procedurals and to fill a new creative space in the televisual landscape. At the same time, he is played with a knowingness that West, with his own immigrant Irish origins and strong Irish connections, brought to the role. That he should emerge as so charismatic certainly speaks to the desires and projections of a considerable proportion of the cult show's audience, and affirms the dramatic requirements of any popular work—that novelty is only palatable when balanced with familiarity. Finally, his persona reminds us of the malleability of Irishness as an identity construct, its chameleon-like ability to service contemporary narrative story-lines, particularly those that revolve around issues of masculinity, and our need to create authority figures while retaining a skepticism about state-endorsed law enforcement. From Errol Flynn, through James Cagney and onward to "Dirty Harry" Callahan, McNulty comes from a long representational tradition that the creators of *The Wire* ultimately found themselves unable to resist.

Notes

I would like to thank members of the Postgraduate Research Seminar in the School of Drama, Film and Music at Trinity College Dublin for their feedback on an earlier draft of this essay.

1. See, for example: Sam Delaney, "I Just Did My Best De Niro Impression," *Guardian*, July 17, 2008, http://www.guardian.co.uk/media/2008/jul/17/televi sion.usa (accessed August 9, 2010). See also "Scene from *The Wire*—McNulty's English Accent," http://www.youtube.com/watch?v=xg_3ZSeHL4g&feature=re lated (accessed August 9, 2010). West's "official" accent is best appreciated by listening to the BBC 4 documentary on the history of the Girl Guides, *100 Year of Girl Guides* (first broadcast August 16, 2009), where he speaks with the un-mistakable voice of the (English upper-class) Establishment.

2. Only the detective, Lester Freamon (Clarke Peters), and Maurice Levy (Michael Kostroff), the criminals' attorney, are typecast. Freamon approximates to the sage African American elder, although this is turned against him in sea-son 5. Levy is more problematically typecast as a Shylock type and his corrup-tion and venality are associated with his Jewishness.

3. Tom Wolfe, *The Bonfire of the Vanities* (London: Cape, 1988), 401–2.

4. In Rafael Alvarez, *"The Wire": Truth Be Told* (Edinburgh: Canongate, 2009), 19; and Delaney, "I Just Did My Best."

5. Alvarez, *The Wire*.

6. Ibid., 61.

7. The only other police officer in the department who is identifiably Irish American is Patrick Mahon, played by Irish American actor Tom Quinn. We meet him briefly in the opening episodes, where he is laid up in hospital and looking forward to taking early retirement based on poor health. He urges his friend and colleague Augustus Polk (Nat Benchley) to guarantee himself the same easy layoff by falling down the stairs at the precinct. Both are clearly la-beled as drunks and wastrels, and boast none of the charm or work ethic of the younger-generation Irish American, McNulty. It has been suggested that the duo are meant to be read as a wordplay—Polk/Mahon invoke the Irish expression *póg mo thóin*. See http://en.wikipedia.org/wiki/Police_of_The_Wire#Patrick_ Mahon (accessed August 16, 2010).

8. Richard Dyer, *Stars* (London: BFI, 1990), 132.

9. Peter Quinn, "Looking for Jimmy," in *Making the Irish American*, ed. J. J. Lee and Marion Casey (New York: NYU Press, 2006), 672.

10. Timothy Meagher, "The Fireman on the Stairs," in Lee and Casey, *Mak-ing the Irish American*.

11. Ibid., 610.

12. Ibid., 639.

13. Gerardine Meaney, "Not Irish Enough? Masculinity and Ethnicity in *The Wire* and *Rescue Me*," in *Irish Postmodernisms and Popular Culture*, ed. Anne Mulhall, Moynagh Sullivan, and Wanda Balzano (London: Palgrave Macmillan, 2007), 12.

14. The reading on the history and politics of the stage Irishman is extensive.

A good summary and application of the stereotype to the American context can be found in W. H. A. Williams, *'Twas Only an Irishman's Dream: The Image of Ireland and the Irish in American Popular Song Lyrics, 1800–1920* (Urbana: University of Illinois Press, 1996). See also Richard Cave, "Staging the Irishman," in J. S. Bratton, Richard Allen Cave, Breandon Gregory, Heidi J. Holder, and Michael Pickering, *Acts of Supremacy: The British Empire and the Stage, 1790–1930* (Manchester: Manchester University Press, 1991), 62–128.

15. See, for instance, Daniel Patrick Moynihan, "The Irish," in Lee and Casey, *Making the Irish American,* 475–525.

16. Joe Cleary, *Outrageous Fortune: Capital and Culture in Modern Ireland* (Dublin: Field Day Publications in association with the Keough-Naughton Institute for Irish Studies at the University of Notre Dame, 2006), 264.

17. Including the Pogues or Shane MacGowan in a soundtrack that explores Irish immigrant identities and the link to Ireland is close to being a cliché already. We can include here, among many examples, *P.S. I Love You* (Richard LaGravenese, 2007); *Ladder 49* (Jay Russell, 2004); *The Matchmaker* (Mark Joffe, 1997).

18. Cleary, *Outrageous Fortune,* 277.

19. *Shutter Island* (Martin Scorsese, 2010) is also a Lehane adaptation but not of one of the author's South Boston thrillers.

20. Dennis Lehane, *Gone Baby Gone* (London: Bantam, 1999), 61.

21. Diane Negra, "Irishness, Anger and Masculinity in Recent Film and Television," in *Screening Irish-America,* ed. Ruth Barton (Dublin: Irish Academic Press, 2009), 288–89.

22. http://hollywoodjesus.com/wire_about.htm (accessed August 19, 2010).

23. David Simon, "Dead Soldiers," *The Wire,* season 3, DVD (HBO, 2004). The reference is to *Bonfire of the Vanities.* For the reference to Wolfe, see note 3 above.

24. Nina Witoszek and Patrick F. Sheeran, *Talking to the Dead: A Study of Irish Funerary Traditions* (Amsterdam: Rodopi, 1998).

25. For an analysis of the cultural significance of the Irish pub, see Mark McGovern, "'The Cracked Pint Glass of the Servant': The Irish Pub, Irish Identity and the Tourist Eye," in *Irish Tourism: Image, Culture and Identity,* ed. Michael Cronin and Barbara O'Connor (Clevedon: Channel View, 2003), 83–103.

26. In Alvarez, *The Wire,* 490–91.

11

Contested Memories: Representing Work in *The Wire*

Sherry Linkon, Alexander Russo, and John Russo

Economic decline often generates powerful artistic representations. Some of America's most memorable art, literature, and film emerged during and commented on the Great Depression. Similarly, novelists, filmmakers, songwriters, and visual artists have found inspiration in the social disruptions of the economic restructuring of the last four decades.[1] At their best, as in David Simon's *The Wire*, these works not only provide insight into the experience of deindustrialization. They also reveal the nature and limitations of individual and social responses to the effects of economic restructuring and the capitalist system that underlies it. Given the series' sociological structure and attention to how individuals and communities are affected by and respond to economic change, we should not be surprised that Simon drew on William Julius Wilson's studies of race, class, and economic and social struggles in American cities.[2] *The Wire* offers a critical commentary on the effects of economic restructuring on American cities, work-based communities, and the meaning of work itself.

The Wire announces deindustrialization as a central theme from the beginning, through its use of the Baltimore landscape. Throughout the series, events play out in crumbling, often abandoned buildings or on streets that show the wear and tear of a city without the resources for significant maintenance. Along with scenes of urban decay, Simon uses long-abandoned Bethlehem Steel shipyards and empty grain elevators as visual synecdoches for the widespread patterns of disinvestment and deindustrialization of the last four decades. Economic restructuring undermines long-standing social structures and practices, as well as the identities of workers and their communities. That disruption contributes to an ongoing legitimation crisis as individuals struggle to pursue the ideal of good work, often by resisting the standard practices of the social institutions within which they operate, even as those institutions maintain power despite their ineffectiveness. *The Wire* draws attention to how work-based communities use narratives to transmit the values that define good work, but it also highlights how economic restructuring changes the nature of work and undermines shared narratives about it. The series shows that some forms of work are disappearing, while others are persistently challenged by emerging ideas about efficiency and accountability. In the process, workers' identities and the narratives that serve to define them, their communities of memory, are at risk. At the same time, *The Wire* reveals that these communities of memory, which can serve as the basis for collective and individual agency, may themselves limit the ability of workers to resist or critique the interests or power of capital.

Deindustrialization and Communities of Memory

Throughout *The Wire,* the story line traces the impact of economic restructuring on urban neighborhoods, then on the decline of traditional blue-collar work on the docks, and finally on professional work in schools and the newspaper. We follow workers as they struggle to preserve not only jobs but also the identity and value associated with their work. Whether facing the literal loss of jobs, like the dockworkers featured in season 2, or more qualitative changes in work practices, like the police officers, journalists, and even some of the drug dealers, workers and their struggles to pursue good work amid structural and economic changes take center stage across the series. Longshoremen's union president Frank Sobotka breaks the law to protect jobs because he believes in the value of blue-collar work, even as he sees it declining in the face of technological and economic change. Likewise, throughout the series, the quality of "natural police" is shown to be a value worth defending against institutional changes that seem to support those who have not developed it and undermine those who do. McNulty and Daniels pursue "natural policing" in distinct ways, but both resist institutional changes, in contrast to Herc, Valchek, and police commissioner

Burrell, who lack both an understanding of and investment in good police work. In season 5, veteran journalist and city editor Gus Haynes, like Sobotka, wants to preserve not just jobs but also high-quality work, even as he recognizes that the work he values is being undermined by competing economic interests and managers who do not share his commitment to serious journalism. Haynes also shares with Daniels the belief that good work, in journalism as in policing, involves both talent and training. Both serve as mentors to younger workers, though their efforts illustrate the limits of mentoring in the face of economic restructuring.

While highlighting changes in work, *The Wire* makes clear that deindustrialization and economic restructuring affect not only those who are displaced or whose work is challenged but also the effectiveness of social institutions. In this way *The Wire* testifies to the social costs of deindustrialization. Deindustrialization is often misunderstood as a specific event, with factory closings affecting primarily those who lose their jobs and their communities at the time. Yet, as Jefferson Cowie and Joseph Heathcott have argued, "What was labeled deindustrialization in the intense political heat of the late 1970s and early 1980s turned out to be a more socially complicated, historically deep, geographically diverse, and politically perplexing phenomenon than previously thought."[3] As we have written elsewhere, deindustrialization creates both immediate and long-term effects, not only for displaced workers and their families but for whole communities.[4] For individuals, widespread job loss correlates with increased incidents of domestic violence, homelessness, and heart disease, while municipalities are left with insufficient tax bases to protect residents from crime and fire, creating physical decline in the public and private built environment. But deindustrialization generates social and psychological effects as well. Rates of depression, drug and alcohol abuse, and suicide increase, people lose their social networks, and communities may internalize what has happened, blaming themselves for the loss of jobs rather than understanding the economic violence that has been done to them.

Deindustrialization also undermines identity and agency. As we discovered in studying the closing of steel mills in Youngstown, Ohio, the first question raised by many when they heard that the local steel company was closing its largest plant was "Who are we now? What is Youngstown if we no longer make steel?"[5] Studies of deindustrialized cities show that loss of identity creates additional problems, because communities without a clear sense of identity have difficulty planning for the future or advocating for their interests.[6] Both individuals and communities rely in part on memory to define their identities and social positions. As Robert Bellah and colleagues have argued, communities function best when they have a shared sense of their past.[7] This collective narrative about what has happened, how people responded, and the essential character or values serves as a *community of memory*. Communities of memory often form around geographical or ethnic communities, but they may also exist in communities based on shared work. Communities of memory develop out of shared experience and subtle, usually indirect and ongoing negotiations among participants about how to define the community's key qualities, core values, and essential elements. Communities of memory are constructed and reproduced through shared experience as well as storytelling, images, and the process of socializing younger members of the group. Thus, as Tim Strangleman has written about railway workers in Britain, older workers teach newcomers not only the technicalities of how to do a job but also the stories, ideas, and values that give the work meaning.[8] Artistic and media representations can contribute to communities of memory by providing images and narratives that reinforce or challenge a group's existing story. *The Wire* is thus at once a representation of communities of memory and a representation that makes its own contributions to the national community of memory about economic restructuring.

Among the most significant social costs of deindustrialization is the undermining of communities of memory. When workplaces close or are reorganized, the social networks around which communities of memory have been formed may disintegrate, and even those that survive must adapt to changing conditions. What once seemed the defining quality of a work-based community—such as the detective's focus on getting a big conviction rather than accumulating statistics or the dedication to thorough reporting at the newspaper—may be redefined, even as some members of the group resist change.

Because communities of memory are maintained and evolve through representations as well as social interaction, deindustrialization creates additional challenges. The landscape contributes to communities of memory, through landmarks that represent key events or shaped social interactions, and when landscapes change, as when old industrial buildings are torn down or transformed into condominiums, the narratives and meanings associated with a place can change. *The Wire* addresses this directly in season 3, episode 1, when the housing project that has been the center of the drug operation is torn down. New narratives, whether produced by participants or by outsiders, such as news media, songwriters, or television producers, may also suggest new ways of understanding a community's experiences and identity.

Communities of memory form the basis for collective agency by providing a set of ideas and a shared identity that allow groups to defend challenges, respond to change, and advocate for their own interests. Thus, unions often use labor history as the basis for organizing, encouraging workers to connect today's struggle to protect benefits or work rules with historical battles for the eight-hour day or workplace safety. This use of the past also occurs less intentionally, as we see among the members of the longshoremen's union in *The Wire*, who maintain their commitment to the job and to each other in part by reminiscing about the quality of their lives in the "good old days" when they had steady work. At their most effective, when groups understand their past struggles, including the history of divisions and conflicts, communities of memory can provide the insight, social networks, and shared values necessary to address difficulties.

At the same time, just as communities of memory can enable groups to respond effectively to changes, they can also make change difficult. When communities of memory reinforce long-standing practices and structures or comfortable but incomplete understandings of the group's history or values, they can become obstacles to change. Those who challenge or resist the narratives and practices embedded in communities of memory may be sanctioned or simply ignored. Communities of memory may also, as we will discuss later, frame people's understanding of problems in ways that keep them from recognizing or challenging the larger social changes that affect them. Thus, communities of memory are important for the effective operation of organizations or cities even as they create obstacles. *The Wire* highlights the communities of memory surrounding several workplaces, with an emphasis on the drug operation, the police detectives, the longshoremen, and the newspaper. Along with showing how these work-based communities of memory work, even as they are being challenged by economic restructuring, the series also reveals the complex role that communities of memory play in defining and enforcing ideas about good work as well as how workers navigate their individual paths within those communities of memory. Yet at the same time, the series reveals the limitations of communities of memory, especially as resources for challenging large-scale economic structures.

Within *The Wire*, most characters are part of a broad Baltimore community of memory, one shaped by economic struggle, urban problems, and repeated patterns of failure to solve those problems. At various moments, city officials invoke this community of memory in their public statements, but we also see how individual characters draw on their knowledge of the city and its past. For example, we can understand Brooklyn native Herc's blunders in navigating the racial, ethnic, and class landscape of Baltimore as a matter not only of race but also place. McNulty is also white, but he is a Baltimore native and as a member of the broader community of memory associated with the city is better prepared to navigate its complexities. At the same time, as the series makes clear, the city is too large and contested to function well as a single community of memory, and the structure of the series emphasizes the salience of a number of more narrow, work-based clusters.

The Wire illustrates how communities of memory are formed and operate. The drug operation and the police department, especially the detectives, reveal how shared experience, social networks, and representations help to construct and preserve communities of memory. The Barksdale-Bell drug operation functions well, in part, because its members come from the same neighborhood, and they have a clear sense of connection with their side of town and even with the specific structures—the housing projects and corners—that form their workplace. That provides shared experience. Departments provide a parallel element of position among the police. In both organizations, social networks involve not only workplace relationships but also highly visible and protected hierarchical structures. For both, as well, relationships and ideas are reinforced through narratives, so that experience, relationships, and representations work together to construct and reproduce communities of memories. At various moments in the series, members of the drug operation refer to previous experiences and draw on family ties to evoke loyalty. Within the police department, community of memory is similarly rooted in shared experience and relationships, though few are based in blood ties. In season 2, episode 4, for example, as Daniels assembles the team to investigate Sobotka and the deaths of the women in the shipping crate, he and others draw on their shared history and working relationships to persuade Carver to join the team and even to pressure Rawls to allow McNulty to work on the investigation. As the team begins working, past relationships and roles fall back into place, as the community of memory is reconstructed through, at the same time it enables, shared work. In both cases, as in several other work-based communities represented in the series, memory establishes a basis for collective effort.

Representations take on added importance when work disappears, social networks crumble, and new experiences threaten shared values and understandings, in part because they do not simply preserve shared memory. They also comment on and revise it. Representations recount but also interpret the past, and representations created after major changes such as deindustrialization also offer (though sometimes only implicitly) explanations of the relationship between the past and the present. *The Wire* both demonstrates the uses of representations within the series, through stories and, in some scenes, music, and is itself a representation of work and place. The role of representations is highlighted, in season 2, episode 1, when the dockworkers, gathered at their regular bar, collectively tell a story about a former coworker, passing the narrative from speaker to speaker, with some parts told almost in unison. Later in that episode, music reinforces the social network, when, as the band belts out "Sixteen Tons," the workers sing along. The song invokes a long-defunct version of their work; longshoremen may once have "loaded sixteen tons" (of cargo, not coal), but today their job is more likely to involve driving crates around the dockyard or tracking them on a computer screen. Yet the workers still identify with the image of themselves as men who perform hard physical labor, an image that is all the more important because it does not fit the contemporary reality.

Of course, representations do not always establish or enact collective identities. In the first episode of season 2, part of the action of the season is set off by a conflict between Sobotka and Valchek over two stained glass windows, one representing dockworkers and another representing police officers. Both men belong to the same parish, and they presumably share a neighborhood community of memory. They also share a sense of pride in the hard work of Polish-American men, and

Sobotka and Valchek in front of the church window

the (relative) prosperity and dignity it has provided. Yet their different images define work differently, and their battle over whose image will represent their shared identity reveals divisions within the Polish community. Representations thus serve as a means of contesting meaning and identity within and across communities of memory.

The Wire also comments on the nature and influence of representations themselves, which becomes especially clear in season 5. The newspaper plotline is built primarily around a set of news stories, written by Scott Templeton, based on limited reporting and quite a bit of fabrication. His stories succeed—that is, he is able to write them without doing serious reporting, his editors believe them to be true and good, they increase readership, and they win awards—because the draw on comfortable, existing narratives. Even more significantly, this plot line highlights the inadequacy of contemporary representations and standard narratives to make visible and explain the complex real world. Given the realities of economic restructuring and the news media's ever-increasing focus on marketing rather than reporting, this season seems to suggest that the very nature of contemporary media, as well as the power of dominant narratives, makes it almost impossible to uncover the full effects of the economic and social changes of the past thirty years. While *The Wire* is a representation of work and the deindustrialized city from the very beginning, and every season offers commentary on and interpretation of the communities of memory it examines, in season 5 the series overtly addresses the problem of representation itself.

Along with making clear how communities of memory are constituted, *The Wire* emphasizes relationships among communities of memory, as the battle over the nave window suggests. While the communities of memory in the series have distinct identities and boundaries, they are interconnected and in many ways similar. Actions and language echo across different communities, highlighting the similarities across these apparently separate, different groups. Short, seemingly insignificant phrases pop up in multiple scenes, in different settings, within a single episode, for example. In season 2, episode 3, when Beadie Russell bids goodnight to Bunk and McNulty after an evening at the bar, she says, "Excuse me, gents." The line is repeated later in that episode as a prisoner excuses himself to let Avon speak privately with D'Angelo in the prison library. The situations are different, but the repeated phrase creates a linguistic tie. More significant echoes suggest that similarities run deeper than mere words. Over the course of the first episode of season 2, shipping containers get misplaced on the docks a scene or two after evidence is misplaced at police headquarters. The theme of misplacement is further developed as the drug dealers dismantle a car looking for a lost package a few minutes before we see the evidence room being dismantled in search of a very different lost package. In all four scenes, issues of trust and surveillance, opportunities for on-the-job theft, and the enforcement and breakdown of internal discipline are played out. At the same time, the misplacement of physical objects echoes the season's thematic focus on the displacement of workers. That theme is also indirectly present in another parallel, the use of communication technologies as tools for locating the missing items—the same technologies that are, in part, responsible for the decline in jobs on the docks. Such parallels and echoes occur throughout the series, and along with interactions among characters across the various communities of memory and structural links that characters may not be aware of but that are clear to the audience (such as The Greek interacting with both the drug operation and the longshoreman's union), they emphasize that all of these communities are responding to the same external economic and social pressures.

The Wire makes clear that communities of memory are contested. While they may involve some nostalgia, they are not simply idealizations of a better past. Rather, communities of memory form the backdrop for negotiations over the relationship between the past and the present. How each community adapts to economic restructuring is based, to a great extent, on how it negotiates this relationship. By structuring the series around separate, interconnected, and often similar work-based communities, Simon highlights the underlying function and nature of communities of memory. Those communities matter because they play important roles in defining "good work," negotiating challenges to good work (from within and outside of workplaces), and responding to economic restructuring and challenging the broader system. As *The Wire* shows, communities of memory are, on the one hand, challenged by economic and social change and, on the other, made resistant to change (in productive and problematic ways) through the power of shared memory.

Developing and Defending Good Work

Work-based communities of memory provide not only group and individual identity, but also a basis for efforts to find dignity and a sense of accomplishment at work as well as responses to changes in work. The show posits a distinction between "real" and "unreal" work. The former provides intrinsic, internal rewards, and the latter is constructed as a means of pursuing some sort of political or personal agenda. Without romanticizing the therapeutic value of work in creating and maintaining social identity, *The Wire* advocates for the social and psychological value of meaningful, sustained work. While the series reveals the challenges to good work posed by economic restructuring, it also shows how workers persist in understanding their work as meaningful even in the face of institutional obstacles. As Jacob Weisberg has noted, writing about season 3, *The Wire* "is filled with characters who should quit but don't."[9] That persistence is grounded in communities of memory, especially for the police officers, the dockworkers, and the journalists.

Perhaps the most clearly articulated discussion of good work appears in *The Wire*'s use of the ideal of "real police" work, as defined through internalized values and the inherent satisfaction in pursuing "quality" cases. This definition is contrasted with the kind of public-relations, statistics-driven casework that produces splashy headlines and evening news shots—"drugs on the table"—but little in the way of long-term impact on crime or criminal organizations. Still, *The Wire* is ambivalent about the impetus for this attitude toward work. On one hand, there are repeated references to individuals being "natural police," implying an innate drive. Bunk, McNulty, Freamon, and Greggs all share this trait. Yet this talent is most effective for those who most fully embrace the community of memory of the detective unit, a set of values and a professional identity developed through mentoring. Moreover, the series asks us to consider the costs and limits of acting on this talent. The multiple-season arcs paralleling McNulty and Greggs with Daniels and Carver demonstrate this possibility and ambivalence. Individual characters lose significant personal relationships when they invest too deeply in their abilities as "natural police," and in McNulty's case, his sometimes extreme methods, which reflect both ability and commitment, may yield results but also come at some professional cost.

We see the role of community of memory in constructing good work most clearly in situations where younger workers are mentored by their more experienced colleagues. While mentoring does not always "take"—consider Prop Joe's failed effort to mentor Marlo, for example—the theme of mentoring provides opportunities for characters to articulate the values and narratives that shape their communities of memory. Mentorship involves a pedagogical practice of valuing "good work" rather than gaming the system. In season 1, episode 13, Daniels gives Carver advice on how to lead and mentor officers following the latter's promotion, earned in exchange for providing Burrell information on the unit: "You show them it's about the work, it'll be about the work. You show them some other kinda game, then that's the game they'll play." Daniels draws on past experience, telling a story as a way of conveying the difference between real police work and playing the game: "I came on in the Eastern, and there was a piece-of-shit lieutenant hoping to be a captain, piece-of-shit sergeants hoping to be lieutenants. Pretty soon we had piece-of-shit patrolmen trying to figure the job for themselves. And some of what happens then is hard as hell to live down. Comes a day you're gonna have to decide whether it's about you or about the work." Carver develops into an officer who values police work slowly and through critical interventions from Daniels and Colvin. In the first episode of season 3, when a low-level runner from the drug gang evades Carver's unit, he unleashes a stunning array of police forces, including marked and unmarked units, K-9 units, and helicopter searches in an ineffective effort to capture the kid. Frustrated by the failure of all this firepower, he climbs on top of the squad car to yell after them. By season 4, episode 1, he has begun to value informants and gain extensive knowledge of his district, forsaking the flashier display of force for a more subtle and effective approach. This time, when his targets escape, Carver can let them go because he knows who they are and where they will be later in the day. Similarly, in season 5, Gus mentors both Alma Gutierrez and Mike Fletcher in practices of "good journalism," schooling them (and viewers) in the subtleties of getting quotes, developing sources, and meeting deadlines. As a result, Gutierrez is both able and committed to assist when, in episode 10, Gus confronts Templeton about his fabrication of a quote. Templeton throws his notebook at him, declaring that the notes in it prove his case. Gutierrez "fact checks" this claim and discovers that the notebook is empty.

Mentoring does not just teach younger workers the skills to do their jobs; when done well, it also gives them a sense of ownership of the idea of good work, making them full members of the community of memory. Thus, Gutierrez not only shows Gus that Templeton's notebook is empty, she also takes it to managing editor Thomas Klebanow. These actions parallel Greggs's decision to inform Daniels that McNulty invented the serial killer earlier in season 5, episode 9, and, to some extent, Carver's decision to write up Colicchio for excessive force.[10] Perhaps ironically, some of those who are successfully mentored find themselves promoted, though it isn't clear that their promotions will be good either for them or for the perpetuation of good work. Following Gus's demotion, Fletcher is promoted to editor of the City Desk, though it's unclear whether he will have any more luck that Gus did in resisting the changes developing at the paper. Carver, too, ends the series with a promotion and the responsibility of educating a new generation of policemen, but he, too, will have to work within the problematic culture of the department.

If we read mentorship as a means of socializing younger workers into the community of memory, then the failure of mentorship may signal Simon's doubts about how effectively communities of memory can be invoked in institutional settings. Three examples suggest the implications for absent or failed mentoring: Templeton, Marlo, and Herc. While all three value the history of the work they do on some level, none has sufficient understanding of or respect for its traditions to follow them. They willingly break work rules and treat those who would enforce them with disdain. Gus explains the values of good reporting to Templeton, but the latter largely ignores them. Like Templeton, Marlo has the opportunity to learn from a mentor who is deeply invested in the community of memory, Prop Joe, and like Templeton, he ignores what he has been taught. Marlo's approach to managing the drug operation regularly violates the established rules that have previously kept relative peace, at least among the dealers, on the Baltimore streets. Prop Joe and others lament his lack of respect for the right way of doing things just as Haynes complains about Templeton's fake reporting. In both cases, the problem lies not with the mentor—both Gus and Prop Joe have successfully guided other younger workers—or with the values promoted by the communities of memory, but in the rejection of those values in favor of strategies that align with the economic and structural changes occurring in the surrounding context. By showing that both Marlo and Templeton succeed despite violating the standard practices of their work, Simon makes clear the consequences posed by the more individualistic, immediate-result-oriented values of the new economy.

This is made even more clear in the case of Herc, who as C. W. Marshall and Tiffany Potter write, embodies the failure of institutional systems of policing but also the consequences of poor mentoring.[11] His lack of understanding of compassion causes him to exacerbate and perpetuate the structural conditions that he justifiably chafes against. Marshall and Potter link this to Herc's whiteness, but other white police officers understand their situation much better. The difference may be that Herc has not received appropriate mentoring. Herc's mentor, after all, is Valchek, whose definition of good police work exemplifies the problems Daniels outlined in mentoring Carver. Valchek's attitude is most clearly stated in season 2, episode 1, when he tries to persuade Pryzbylewski to follow a safe path to promotion, explaining that Pryzbylewski will work a day shift and move his way up through the ranks, in part because he is Valchek's son-in-law. While Valchek, like Daniels, draws on experience, social networks, and narratives in navigating his own career and advising others, his understanding of work is shaped more by his personal interests than by an investment in the community of memory that values "real police." That Herc has not been mentored earlier, and that he finally receives advice from someone who cares more about personal position than police work, helps explain his failures and frustrations. While talented workers may be developed into good workers through mentorship and investment in the community of memory, *The Wire* also shows that communities of memory in themselves may not be sufficient to perpetuate good work.

Simon further explores the limits of community of memory as a basis for good work through McNulty. McNulty clearly has a deep investment in the shared idea of good police work, and he is seen (and sees himself) as almost the embodiment of the idea of "natural police,"[12] but despite his sometimes extreme and often creative efforts, his pursuit of good work is clearly limited. McNulty embodies the complex relationship among the ability of "natural police," the limits of individual pursuit of good work, and the costs of investing too much in the job. In season 4, while working as a beat cop, he takes on the role of mentor. In episode 10, McNulty sees a young uniformed officer, Baker, writing "quality of life" tickets for open containers and parking in a bus stop. Baker explains, "I go where they tell me," and this is a dictate from downtown to improve crime statistics for the new Carcetti administration. In response, McNulty explains that the officer on patrol is the "one true dictatorship" in America: "We can lock a guy up on a humble, lock him up for real, or say fuck it, pull ourselves under the expressway and drink ourselves to death . . . and our side partners will cover it. So no one, I mean no one, tells us how to waste our shift."[13] Here the idea of police work as craft is paramount, as is the tension between the institutional powers and workers. McNulty's comments make clear that he understands that, because the institution serves its own needs, it cannot be trusted to recognize and develop potential within its workforce. This must come from peers. In McNulty's preindustrial and communitarian vision of work, the officer has the freedom to control the quality of his work, good or bad, with assistance from his peers. Later McNulty enlists Baker to help run down some leads in response to a pattern he has noticed in a series of church robberies, and in the process he shows Baker the value of tracking information in incident reports.

McNulty recounts the story to Bunk later in that episode, telling him they brought in two felony robberies in the midst of all the drunken disorderlies, squeegee boys, and public urinators. Bunk remarks, "Kid got the point." McNulty replies, "He might turn out to be decent police," to which Bunk affirms, "Gotta come from somewhere, the younger generation." Without proper mentorship, this scene suggests, officers will follow the dictates of their superiors but will not develop the ability to recognize crime patterns that is necessary to good police work.[14] The story also serves to reinforce McNulty's "natural police" instincts and his participation in the community of memory.

Yet McNulty is also seen as investing too much in the police force community of memory. Ignoring Freamon's warning that "the job will not save you,"[15] McNulty sacrifices all other elements of his personal life for the cases he pursues. This is by no means an uncommon trope within television procedurals. However, *The Wire* contrasts McNulty with the heroes of other televised police dramas. While other series feature charismatic, repressed loners who always succeed with their investigations, McNulty often finds his abilities and hard work stymied. Moreover, *The Wire* makes clear that this is not due solely to McNulty's personal failures, though his ego certainly contributes to his problems, but also to the limitations of the institution—rules, hierarchies, budget limitations, as well as the relative lack of power of detectives in the larger economic structure. Neither talent nor a commitment to the values and practices of good police work can overcome the power of the institution, which is defined within the police force community of memory oppositionally. The detectives, especially, regard the institution of the police department as an impediment, as the source of "unreal" work, while they represent "real police." The tension between the hierarchy and those on the ground is highlighted in season 3, when McNulty figures out that he has been lured into a brief affair by Carcetti advisor Theresa D'Agostino simply because she wants information. The experience reminds him that he is a pawn within larger political struggles.

McNulty also illustrates the problems associated with excessive identification with one's work. His inability to maintain any relationship with a woman and his uneven presence in his sons' lives suggest a personal cost, and the ups and downs of his career across the series make clear that his extreme actions have professional costs as well.

While *The Wire* clearly suggests the social and psychological importance of good work, it also argues for balance. Throughout the series,
certain characters represent a middle path with a healthy, but not
obsessive, valuing of work. Greggs, like McNulty, had become alien-
ated from her partner and child because of her excessive commitment
to the job, combined with alcohol and promiscuous sex. In season 5,
however, she takes steps to reintegrate herself into their lives. She also
reports McNulty's fabrications to Daniels. Significantly, at the end of
the series, Greggs is partnered with Bunk, both "natural police" who
pursue a somewhat more contained model of police investigation than
McNulty's creative excesses, the sprawling investigative work of the
narcotics unit, or the numbers-driven facade of ComStat. In this way,
her story line illustrates how the boundaries a work-based community
of memory can be productive.

Communities of Memory and the Limits of Resistance

Simon has called *The Wire* "a meditation on the death of work and
the American working class."[16] Throughout the series, characters reminisce about their work and how it has changed, displaying and explaining the bitterness many people feel in postindustrial America. Frank
Sobotka speaks for the working class when he says, "We used to make
shit in this country. Build shit. Now we just put our hand in the next
guy's pocket."[17] While housing and the finance industry boomed during
the years when the series first ran, economic stability continued to decline for American workers, and *The Wire* captures their alienation and
frustration. Feeling used and ignored by a range of political, economic,
and religious organizations, working people have become increasingly
cynical about the role of social institutions. In the first scene of season
2, McNulty, assigned to the marine unit as punishment for flouting authority and threatening to uncover corruption in season 1, responds to
a call of a disabled craft, the *Capitol Gains*, a party boat out of Washington, D.C., filled with lobbyists and politicians. The head lobbyist
offers a bribe to McNulty to "tow us out of the way so the band can
play on a little longer." The next scene shows the *Capitol Gains* from
the perspective of the police boat, under tow but moored as the party
continues into the night, as an obviously discomfited McNulty looks
on. Later in that season, when confronted by an FBI agent offering to

help his union if he "rolls over" on The Greek and others, Sobotka responds resentfully: "Twenty-five years we been dyin' slow down there. Drydocks rustin', piers standin' empty. My friends and their kids like we got the cancer. No lifeline got throwed, all that time. Nuthin' from nobody. . . . And now you wanna help us. Help me?" These scenes suggest that even those who are most committed to good work recognize that larger forces are reshaping their work, and they have few options for responding.

The Wire highlights the common economic and social position of those who have been abandoned by economic restructuring. On the one hand, we see similarities among the dockworkers and the drug operation, which intersect mostly indirectly in their dealings with The Greek. All have found that the only way to survive in the new economy of Baltimore is to violate both legal and traditional moral codes. Participants have developed their own moral codes along with structures and practices that echo those in public institutions. At the same time, the series shows how economic struggle creates common ground among workers and communities that might otherwise not connect. As Sobotka explains in a conversation with a rival leader in his local, "Black, white. What's the difference, Nat? Until we get that fuckin' canal dredged, we're all niggers, pardon my French." His comment might well apply beyond the union hall: dockworkers, drug dealers, police detectives—what's the difference? It also suggests the ways that the older modes of politics—here the union practice of alternating the position of treasurer between white and black members—fails in the face of new challenges created by advanced capitalism and deindustrialization.

While the series humanizes and individualizes its diverse characters, its theme is always the power of institutions over the individual, and more broadly the way those institutions are shaped by the interests of capitalism. Across the series, Simon uses the highly effective but also violent drug operation as a framework for looking at institutional failure in government, unions, education, and journalism. All of the other institutions aim, at least in part, to undermine the drug operation, and none succeeds. In his own comments on the series, Simon suggests that institutional failure is, at heart, economic:

The fact that these [characters] really are the excess people in America, we—our economy doesn't need them. We don't need ten or 15 percent of our population. And certainly the ones that are undereducated, that have been ill served by the inner city school system that have been unprepared for the technocracy of the modern economy. We pretend to need them. We pretend to educate the kids. We pretend that we're actually including them in the American ideal, but we're not. And they're not foolish. They get it.[18]

From Simon's perspective, when institutions fail and people do not have access to "good" work, they turn to the corner, or buying votes, or inventing news stories. Moreover, Simon sees capitalism as the source of institutional failure, as he explained in a 2009 interview in *Vice*: "We've given ourselves over to the Olympian god that is capitalism and now we're reaping the whirlwind. This is the America that unencumbered capitalism has built. . . . *The Wire* was trying take the scales from people's eyes and say, 'This is what you've built.'"[19]

Simon's critique of capitalism plays out indirectly in his representation of power structures. Helena Sheehan and Seamus Sweeney have described *The Wire* as "a powerfully polemical discourse," though they note that capitalism is "largely invisible" in the series.[20] The capitalists who control most of the institutions in the series play little or no role in the associated communities of memory. The focus remains on the effects of capitalism, not its primary actors. Meagan O'Rourke observes that The Greek functions as a symbol for capitalism as he "sits in the foreground, silent and unacknowledged, at a café counter while underlings conduct business on his behalf." According to O'Rourke, it is in part because he is not the focus of the scene that The Greek "represented capitalism in its purest form."[21] As Sheehan and Sweeney point out, we notice his presence only when "his interests are directly threatened."[22] In most of the series, the agents of capitalism are even less visible than The Greek. While Barksdale, Stringer, Prop Joe, and eventually Marlo manage drug operations, all depend on suppliers who exist outside the frame of the series, suppliers who are in turn part of larger, international operations serving even more powerful, though entirely invisible, bosses. The interests that have contributed to the decline of shipping in Baltimore harbor are similarly distant, though their presence is reflected in scenes with developers and signs announcing new condos in former industrial sites. At the newspaper, power is represented by the managing editor, not the chairman of the board or stockholders.[23]

At the same time, the series is as concerned with the working class's inability to resist economic restructuring as it is with the loss of jobs. Equally important, *The Wire* shows that older solutions that provided agency under capitalism may offer only limited effectiveness in the twenty-first century. First, we see characters whose commitment to good work leads them to immoral extremes. McNulty fabricates a serial killer in his passion for pursuing the drug gang. Sobotka continues to work for The Greek, even after he understands the illegal and immoral nature of the work, because he cares more about protecting the longshoremen's way of life. For both, pursuing good work in dysfunctional ways seems like the only option. They lack the economic and social capital to challenge the changes occurring around them, but they are also so invested in their vision of good work that they refuse to acknowledge that the old ways can no longer be preserved. Rather than casting blame on those whose only means of survival is operating outside of the traditional moral code, *The Wire* provides a complex analysis of why such violations are rational and perhaps even necessary responses, positioning them not only within work-based communities of memory but also within the broader economic and political hierarchy. In so doing, the series humanizes and in many cases evokes sympathy for those who break the law, not only by representing them as complex characters but also by drawing attention to how work and communities are being challenges by institutional failures based in economic restructuring.

In so doing, Simon doesn't let his characters off the hook. Rather, he takes a more Gramscian approach, recognizing that part of the power of capitalism is that it persuades those with limited power that their interests lie in pursuing a better position within the system rather than overthrowing it. As he explained in an interview with Bill Moyers, "As long as they [the capitalists] placate enough people, as long as they throw enough scraps from the table that enough people get a little bit to eat, I just don't see a change coming."[24] This idea is illustrated in a famous scene in season 1, episode 3, when D'Angelo explains the workplace hierarchy using the game of chess. Along with noting that "the King stay the king," he explains that "the pawns get capped quick," to which Bodie provides an important rejoinder: "Unless they some smartass pawns." This exchange encapsulates *The Wire's* view that workers' acceptance of the systems within which they work, and their pursuit of individual position within those systems, may undermine both individual opportunity and any possibility of challenging the system. Bodie illustrates this pattern well. For much of the series, he tries to play the game, seeking to advance in the Barksdale operation through being a "smart-ass pawn." By season 4, his hard work has gone unrewarded, and his success in establishing a thriving quarter is negated by Marlo's appropriation of it. Bodie may recognize that "this game is rigged . . . we like the little bitches on the chessboard," but that self-knowledge is rewarded only with a quick and brutal death. Similarly, Gus's commitment to the community of memory of good journalism ultimately earns him a demotion. Their efforts to defend good work within the system of capitalism cannot overcome the interests of profit in the new economy, but nor can they imagine a more radical, structural means of resistance, in part because of their investment in their respective communities of memory.

The Wire thus suggests that communities of memory can also encourage people to embrace the failed (some would say false) promises of capitalism and inhibit people's ability to stand up for their own interests within it, much less fight for broader change. We see how communities of memory reinforce investment in capitalism when workers reminisce about how the system once valued them. After all, what Sobotka desires in his lobbying efforts is not to overthrow the existing system of power. He seeks to exert influence on that system to return it to old ways of operating. At the same time, Simon makes clear through scenes that highlight new building and gentrification and abandoned factories that the old ways will not come back. Dredging the canal would not be enough to revitalize the docks, nor would more jobs restore the old way of life. The contrast between the memory of dock work and the contemporary reality is highlighted in a conversation between Sobotka and his son. Ziggy describes his vision of the good old days: "I remember you, Uncle Walt, Uncle Jerry, Peepop, always talking shit. . . . I remember when youse all went down to picket them scabs down at the piers." Frank's response—"So tell me Mr. Back-in-the-day, what the fuck are we doing down here with the wharf rats in the middle of the night?"—refers not only to the present moment but to the larger economic shifts that have shaped it.[25] Both men know that the past will not come back, and on some level both recognize that their investment in it is part of what is holding them back. Similar scenes appear in relation to every institution and its work over the course of the series as characters discuss what good work could be, based almost entirely on what it once was or what they wanted it to be. Through such scenes, Simon gives a human face to the loss of work so common to the working class over the last few decades.

At the same time communities of memory provide codes of living that can empower individuals to make specific individual interventions. The series provides its own "utopian moments" (Fletcher's promotion to City Desk Editor, Pryz coming into his own as a teacher, the Greggs and Bunk partnership, Daniels's promotion of Carver) that point to the possibility of future social change, at least on an individual, if not structural, level. Simon may not have faith in institutions, but he presents workers' communities of memory as sources of a budding humanism that is linked to craft mentorship and common humanity. As Richard Sennett has argued, craftsmanship has not waned in industrial society; rather it is a "technique for conducting a particular way of life. . . . the desire to do a job well for its own sake" remains a fundamental human impulse.[26] All the "good work" in *The Wire* is, in a sense, craft work—limited in scope, linking head and hand, and ruled by the exercising of "skill, commitment, and judgment." Even in the face of deindustrialization and institutional failures, this desire manifests itself as the will to make a place for oneself in the world, a limited pragmatic goal, to be sure, and one for which capitalism has no inherent need. For all the contradictions *The Wire* reveals in communities of memory, they remain a potential, albeit limited resource, for pursuing good work and maintaining dignity in the face of a dehumanizing system.

Notes

1. Examples of artistic works representing deindustrialization range from several Bruce Springsteen songs, including "Youngstown" and "Born in the USA," novels such as Richard Russo's *Empire Falls*, the 1983 film *All the Right Moves*, and photography projects like Bill Bamberger's study of the closing of a furniture factory, *Closing: The Life and Death of an American Factory* (New York: DoubleTake / W. W. Norton, 1998).

2. Jolie du Pre, "My Interview with William Julius Wilson of *When Work Disappears*, the Influence of Season 2 of HBOs *The Wire*," November 19, 2009, http://www.associatedcontent.com/article/2398110/my_interview_with_william_julius_wilson.html?cat=38.

3. Jefferson Cowie and Joseph Heathcott, "The Meanings of Deindustrializa-

tion," in *Beyond the Ruins: The Meanings of Deindustrialization*, ed. Jefferson Cowie and Joseph Heathcott (Ithaca, N.Y.: Cornell University Press, 2003), 2.

4. John Russo and Sherry Linkon, "The Social Costs of Deindustrialization," in *Manufacturing a Better Future for America*, ed. Richard McCormack (Washington, D.C.: Alliance for American Manufacturing, 2009), 183–215.

5. Sherry Lee Linkon and John Russo, *Steeltown USA: Work and Memory in Youngstown* (Lawrence: University of Kansas Press, 2002).

6. Several articles in Cowie and Heathcott, *Beyond the Ruins*, including our piece, "Collateral Damage: Deindustrialization and the Uses of Youngstown," examine this theme.

7. Robert Bellah, Richard Madsen, William M. Sullivan, Ann Swidler, and Steven M. Tipton, *Habits of the Heart: Individualism and Commitment in American Life* (Berkeley: University of California Press, 1985).

8. Tim Strangleman, *Work Identity at the End of the Line? Privatisation and Culture Change in the UK Rail Industry* (Basingstoke: Palgrave MacMillan, 2004).

9. Jacob Weisberg, "The Wire on Fire," *Slate*, September 13, 2006, http://www.slate.com/id/2149566.

10. Season 5, episode 4.

11. C. W. Marshall and Tiffany Potter, "The Life and Times of Fuzzy Dunlop: Herc and the Modern Urban Crime Environment," *darkmatter*, May 29, 2009, http://www.darkmatter101.org/site/2009/05/29/the-life-and-times-of-fuzzy-dunlop-herc-and-the-modern-urban-crime-environment.

12. In a DVD extra prequel, McNulty's origins as a homicide cop are explained. Cole messed up a case and arrested the wrong guy, and McNulty, while on the recapture squad, figures this out and saves the department embarrassment. This demonstrates natural ability and drive but also helps explain how he becomes a homicide police without being "properly" socialized.

13. Season 4, episode 10.

14. For an example of this see the character of Oscar Requer in season 5, episode 4. Here the show provides another example of a talented homicide officer benched by a hierarchy more interested in power than proper procedure. Freamon and McNulty can rely on him to help them because of his alienation from the bosses.

15. Season 3, episode 9.

16. "Totally Wired," Guardian Unlimited guideblog, January 13, 2005, http://blogs.guardian.co.uk/theguide/archives/tv_and_radio/2005/01/totally_wired.html.

17. Season 2, episode 11.

18. *Bill Moyers Journal*, April 21, 2009.

19. "David Simon," *Vice*, December 2009, http://www.viceland.com/int/v16n12/htdocs/david-simon-280.php.

20. Helena Sheehan and Sheamus Sweeney, "*The Wire* and the World: Narrative and Metanarrative," *Jump Cut*, 2009, http://www.ejumpcut.org/archive/jc51.2009/Wire/index.html.

21. Quoted in Sheehan and Sweeney, "*Wire* and the World."

22. Ibid.

23. While Simon critiques the power of capitalism, he does not see overthrowing capitalism as a likely or necessary solution. Rather, as he explained in a conversation with Bill Moyers, the problem lies in how capitalism is managed: "if you don't manage it in some way that you incorporate all of society, maybe not to the same degree, but if everybody's not benefiting on some level and if you don't have a sense of shared purpose, national purpose, then all it is is a pyramid scheme."

24. *Bill Moyers Journal.*

25. Season 2, episode 6.

26. Richard Sennett, *The Craftsman* (New Haven: Yale University Press, 2008), 8–9.

12

Policing the Borders of White Masculinity: Labor, Whiteness, and the Neoliberal City in *The Wire*

Hamilton Carroll

It's all about self-preservation, Jimmy.
　—Sergeant Jay Landsman, *The Wire*

In the cold open of the first episode of season 2 of *The Wire* (2003), the season's primary focus on the transformations of the postindustrial city and their effects on working-class white men is immediately addressed. Relegated to the marine unit after the wrap-up of the criminal investigation into an organization of African American drug dealers that concluded season 1, Irish American homicide detective Jimmy McNulty (Dominic West) is seen patrolling Baltimore Harbor in a police launch with his new partner. The subject of labor comes up immediately. Looking out over the moribund port that serves as the backdrop to the city's recently regenerated Inner Harbor, McNulty comments that his father used to work in one of the city's shipyards but was laid off in 1973. His partner, in turn, tells McNulty that his own uncle had suffered a similar fate in 1978. Following this conversation, the two men come to the aid of a stricken party boat that, suffering from engine trouble, has been stranded in the middle of a primary shipping lane. The camera zooms in on the back of the boat and the viewer sees that it is registered in Washington, D.C., and named *Capitol Gains* (with an o). The pun on *capital gains* in the ship's name, its out-of-town registration, and the associated symbolism of a D.C.-based pleasure boat blocking a primary shipping lane in the Baltimore Harbor clearly foreground the show's intention to focus on the transformations contemporary forms of capital accumulation have wrought on the regional American cities of which Baltimore stands as a representative.[1] Industry has given way to finance; ships and ports have given way to the stock market and global capitalism. It is these transformations that preoccupy season 2 of *The Wire* and from which its central thesis—and the creators of the show certainly have an argument to make—can be derived: the shift from manufacturing to neoliberal forms of capital accumulation has radically altered the social, political, and cultural fabric of the city in profound and negative ways. Baltimore has been transformed in this view from a working city of solid American values into a speculative site of consumer culture, urban gentrification, and blighted working-class neighborhoods. As the season's opening scene suggests, the show takes the white ethnic, working-class men who made up the majority of the blue-collar labor force to be those most affected by the transformations it charts, and, in its second season at least, it is these men that are its central focus.

In this way *The Wire* turns its attention from the black drug dealers on which the first season focused to an examination of Baltimore's white ethnic working classes. Constructed around two interlinked criminal investigations centered on the city's moribund port—one into the deaths of thirteen illegal immigrants smuggled into the country to work in the sex trade and one into the criminal activities of a group of Baltimore longshoremen—*The Wire* developed a season-long exploration of the corrosive effects of globalization on traditional forms of labor and on the second-tier U.S. cities for which Baltimore stands as a representational example. The show's depictions of white blue-collar labor— the police, the criminal organizations, and the dockworkers alike— highlight its attention to the transformations of the regional city under neoliberalism. *The Wire* contrasts the highly mythologized worlds of working-class masculine labor—the police station and the union office—with the spaces of criminality that arise as the inhabitants of those worlds lose their franchise on the putative rewards of possessive individualism. As they attempt to understand their places in the altered social, political, and cultural landscapes of the postindustrial city, the show's principal characters are required, sometimes quite literally, to construct new cartographies of urban space. As such, the representation of spaces (both real and symbolic) and the ways in which characters are able to move in, through, and between various locations of power and privilege is a central aspect of the show's discursive strategies.

While much critical and popular attention has focused on *The Wire*'s multifaceted representations of explicitly raced subjects as they navigate the city of Baltimore and its primary institutions, the show's representations of white masculinity, and in particular its second season, frequently have been overlooked by commentators whose primary attention is on its depictions of contemporary African American experience.[2] In this essay I use an examination of the show's second season to analyze its representations of white masculinity. I argue that, in spite of—or perhaps because of—its focus on contemporary U.S. institutional racism (understood to primarily affect people of color), *The Wire* stages a prolonged examination of the transformations of white masculinist privilege in twentieth-century America that is as significant as its focus on African American urban life. I analyze the show's representations of the white male laboring subject alongside its concomitant representations of the spatial and technological transformations of the failing city under neoliberalism. I conclude with a related analysis of the show's status as a piece of regional culture produced by regional authors and writers, arguing that it constitutes an exemplary postindustrial object of neoliberal culture made possible, in part, by the very transformations it charts.

The Wire's second-season dissertation on the effects of globalization and neoliberalism on the working classes of urban America focuses primarily on a group of Baltimore longshoremen and on their various attempts to cope with the altered landscape of labor with which they find themselves confronted. Central to the second season are the stories of union boss Frank Sobotka (Chris Bauer), on the one hand, and of his son, Ziggy (James Ransone) and nephew, Nick (Pablo Schreiber), on the other, as they attempt to negotiate the altered landscape of labor, opportunity, and sociocultural expectations wrought by neoliberalism. As such, the show's focus is bigenerational, with Frank trying to return the port to a former glory that he himself remembers, while Nick and Ziggy struggle to break free from the shackles of the expectations passed down to them by the previous generation (embodied in Frank and the character of Nick's father, a retired union worker) and its collective memory of a time of plenitude that they themselves have never experienced. Through this generational dynamic, the show posits two central questions: How do you maintain your dignity when the world you were raised in and the values you were brought up by have been transformed? How do you acquire dignity when the standards by which you are being measured no longer pertain and you have been offered no alternatives? The show's response to these questions is one of profound pessimism, and, at season's end, one of this trio of central characters is dead, one in jail awaiting trial for murder, and one in jail in connection with drug-smuggling charges.

Season 2 of *The Wire*, then, constitutes an example of the discourse of white male injury that has become a pervasive feature of contemporary U.S. culture. Such discourses, David Savran argues, are "an attempt by white men to respond to and regroup in the face of particular social and economic challenges [such as] the end of the post–World War II economic boom."[3] As dockworker Little Big Roy (Richard Pelzman) opines in an early scene (in a line that is used as the tag for the first episode), the port "ain't never gonna be what it was," and over the course of the season each of these characters is forced to come to terms with that fact. Thus the trials confronting them represent the sociocultural conditions described by Susan Faludi in *Stiffed: The Betrayal of the American Man*, her best-selling study of the decline of opportunity for men in the contemporary United States. Drawing a series of links between the transformation of labor from manufacturing to service work and the concomitant rise of male insecurity, Faludi argues that men have been let down by a society in which the values by which they were raised and the skills they have been taught to be proud of are no longer relevant. Traditional forms of masculine labor, Faludi claims, "generated a pride founded in the certainty that what you did bespoke a know-how not acquired overnight."[4] Denied the traditional outlets for masculinist self-expression grounded in hard work and the tenets of possessive individualism, men (and white men in particular) have been left behind in contemporary society. Such also are the views on labor, masculinity, and self-worth represented in *The Wire*. Manual labor is valorized, as are the cultures that arise from it. The racial and class dynamics that stand at the center of working-class labor culture are intensified in the contemporary conditions under which white masculinity perceives itself to have been disenfranchised in direct proportion to the gains of women and people of color under affirmative action.[5] Over the course of the second season the attempts of the three central characters to deal with the altered reality of contemporary labor are represented, and if the trio of Frank, Ziggy, and Nick Sobotka suggests a triangulation of patriarchal responsibility and respectability based on generational difference, *The Wire* provides each character with a different relationship to power and its putative benefits. Working through these relationships exposes the now common discourse of injury on which the show relies.

"The Future Is Now": Globalization and the Nostalgia of Blue-Collar Labor

A rumpled and overweight bear of a man, who nevertheless comes across as small, Frank Sobotka is understood to be a good man forced by altered circumstances to break the law. The automation and computerization of the cargo-shipping process has rendered the sort of work that Frank and his union members do, and the values by which they live, all but obsolete. Frank's tenure as the head of a local union office (the fictional International Brotherhood of Stevedores [IBS]) has seen rapidly declining employment opportunities for his members, coupled to shrinking union membership and a concomitant reduction in union power. Jobs have been lost and, with them, a sense of continuity and security. As he laments in one episode: "For twenty-five years we've been dying slowly down there. Drydocks rusting, piers standing empty. My friends and their kids like we've got the cancer. No lifeline got throwed all that time. Nothing from nobody." What Frank is confronted with is not only the loss of job prospects for himself and his men, but also a radical transformation in his sociocultural expectations. As he tells a lobbyist he has hired, following a presentation to the union hierarchy about the successful automation of the Rotterdam port (offered as a vision of a glorious technologically enabled future):

> Down here [at the port] it's still "Who's your old man?" until you got kids of your own, then it's "Who's your son?" But after that horror show I seen today. Robots! Piers full of robots. My kid'll be lucky if he's still punching numbers five years from now.

The transformations Frank decries are merely the endgame of a process that has been going on for two decades or more. As the scene with which this essay began makes clear, Frank is witnessing the end—and not the beginning—of a process of disinvestment in manual labor and working-class communities that has transformed the landscape of Baltimore and, by extension, many other midtier American cities.

Writing in 1992, David Harvey outlined the changes Baltimore has been undergoing since the 1970s:

> Over the last twenty-five years, Baltimore has lost a fifth of its population, more than half of its white population, and a hard to enumerate but very large proportion of its middle class, white and black. It has lost more than ten per cent of its jobs since 1970, and those that remain are increasingly held by commuters. By 1985, the city's median household income was just over half that of surrounding counties and the needs of its poor for services were far more than the city's eroded tax base could support.[6]

As manufacturing jobs became increasingly hard to come by and the United States shifts from a manufacturing to a service economy, the demographics of the city were radically transformed.[7] Like many American cities, Baltimore was hollowed out by white flight and other demographic shifts. The city that remains, moreover, is radically altered by the subsequent shift in the demographics of the inner city and harbor area in which, following a period of decay and dereliction, the urban regeneration of the 1980s and 1990s (illustrated most clearly by the reclamation and rebuilding of Baltimore's Inner Harbor as a tourist destination) takes hold.[8] Having hired a lobbyist and handed out thousands of dollars in bribes, Frank Sobotka wishes to see the port regain some of its former glory by persuading the city council to support two projects: one to dredge a shipping canal so that it can be used by modern supercargo ships and one to reopen a derelict grain pier. Frank's wishes are nothing more than a pipe dream, as he faces overwhelming competition from a development consortium that wishes to have the grain pier rezoned as a residential area so that the buildings can be transformed into high-priced condominiums (a process that, in the last episode of the season, is shown to have come about). Defeated by global transformations in transportation and shipping practices, on the one hand, and the local transformation of the city's postindustrial ruins into a consumer playground for a gentrified population, on the other, Frank sees not only his job, but his way of life disappearing.[9] What *The Wire* represents as the inevitable result of neoliberal economic practices is the destruction of American working-class culture and society; not only these men's livelihoods, but also their ways of life.

"Piers full of robots," therefore, threaten not only the characters' possibilities for work, but also an entire working community of men held together by common experience and the generational pull of secure employment. As the men's world collapses around them, the extended social and communal structures of the white working classes are also destroyed. The security Frank sees vanishing before his eyes is not only that of work, but also that of stable and clearly delineated kinship structures. What Frank is afraid of is the loss of patriarchal authority encoded in the questions "Who's your old man?" and "Who's your son?" As the authority vested in him through his role as union boss and his seniority in the port diminishes, his control over home and family is also undercut. This, as I shall discuss later, is further symbolized in the failure of his son, Ziggy, to live up to his—and the community's—expectations. Since it is constituted through secure and stable domestic relationships as much as through the world of work and spaces of homosociality outside the home, patriarchal authority has been eroded across all aspects of male life. Mike Hill argues that the "conditions of [contemporary] labor now impinge on the traditional domestic arrangements that it once required, with the consequence of diminishing the real numbers of traditional male-headed heterosexual families."[10] Likewise, explaining how transformations in labor have "worked to detach individuals from the traditional authority of work, community, and family," George Lipsitz suggests the corrosive effects industrial downsizing have had on not only white masculinity but all lower- and middle-income communities.[11] In *The Wire*, Frank Sobotka represents the apotheosis of such transformations. Over the course of the season, Frank is transformed from the focus of the criminal investigation into a minor player whose death seemingly changes nothing. At season's end, he is murdered after crime boss The Greek (Bill Raymond) discovers that he has agreed to turn state's witness against the organization in a misguided attempt to save Ziggy from prison. Literally gone at season's end, Frank stands as a symbol of the evisceration of patriarchal power and responsibility that subtends the forms of possessive individualism on which traditional working-class culture is grounded.

To overly romanticize the heyday of U.S. labor that characters such as Frank Sobotka long for, however, means to ignore or obfuscate the attendant costs to women and people of color upon which that plenitude partially relied. As David Harvey cautions, the "what it was" for which the dockworkers mourn must also be understood in its full complexity. "We should be careful not to romanticize the lost era of powerful industry and commerce and the strong traditions and labor culture it nurtured," he argues:

> Many of the traditional industries (including the [Baltimore] port before containerization) were onerous and dangerous. The division in the labor force between relatively affluent white male workers and the less-skilled, less-powerful women and African Americans was always a barrier to efforts to improve the lot of working people.[12]

Such divisions were grounded, in part, on ideologies of identity in which race and class were understood to be coterminous. As David Roediger points out, "working class formation and the systematic development of a sense of whiteness [historically] went hand in hand for the US white working class."[13] And in this system different racial groups often perceive themselves to be in competition—rather than alliance—in the face of economic strife. As David Wellman suggests, "Political-economic troubles are experienced as racial and gendered, rather than class, grievances."[14] As such, the history of class-based socially progressive movements in the United States is littered with failures forged from the inability of workers to see beyond racial lines or to locate common cause with other working groups.[15] In *The Wire*, this inability is represented not only in the trials of Frank Sobotka, but also in the navigations of his nephew, Nick, as he attempts to find his own way in the new world. In the character of Nick the show develops its exploration of white working-class plight in relation to not only the collapse of blue-collar labor but also the concomitant gentrification of working-class neighborhoods that quickly followed in its wake.

Like Frank, Nick Sobotka is a well-meaning and dutiful man struggling to find a place for himself in a world that no longer values the types of masculine endeavor that he was raised to believe in. Unlike Frank, Nick has never been given the opportunity. The father of a young child, Nick wishes to provide for his girlfriend, Aimee (Kristin Proctor), and daughter, but can see no way of doing so. He lives in his parents' basement and, because he and Aimee are unmarried, is forced to sneak her out of the house in the morning before his mother wakes up. Constrained by circumstances seemingly beyond his control, Nick—like Frank—turns to crime as a means of attaining a standard of living that he has been encouraged to expect. While Frank turns to crime ostensibly to help his community, Nick is motivated more by the desire for personal gain. As he tells Aimee in an early episode, "I can't keep getting up in the morning not knowing if I'm gonna get paid." In an attempt to remove such uncertainty from his life, Nick joins with his cousin Ziggy and makes a side agreement with The Greek to provide contraband stolen from the port, starts to deal heroin purchased from "White" Mike McArdle (Brook Yeaton)—a high school contemporary of Nick's—and eventually starts distributing heroin in large quantities. At the denouement of the season, Nick has turned himself in and is facing charges for heroin distribution.

As the story of Frank Sobotka charts the transformations brought about by the burgeoning service economy and the automation of the shipping industry, the story of Nick Sobotka highlights the erosion of stable working-class communities and the phenomenon of urban gentrification. Not only does gentrification take the form of the transformation of the derelict sites of industrial labor, such as the grain peer, into high-priced condominiums, but also of the transformation of working-class neighborhoods into yuppie havens. With the money he makes dealing drugs, Nick dreams of buying a house and thereby making his family respectable, but his expectations are soon dashed as he comes up against the financial realities of urban gentrification and realizes that petty theft and small-time heroin dealing are not enough to move him up the socioeconomic ladder. This is depicted most clearly in a scene in which, looking for a house to buy, Nick and Aimee are shocked to discover that a small row house they are viewing is expected to sell for around $350,000. Nick is particularly chagrined by this discovery not only because of the high asking price, but also because the house used to belong to his aunt who had died the previous year. Having been refurbished in a style more appealing to the young urban professionals that are the estate agent's target clientele, the small row house signifies a broken link in the bonds of working-class community. Not only are the houses being taken away from working-class families, but the whole

neighborhood has also been reclaimed by the city in the name of gentrification and the related increase in tax income. In a conversation with a
real estate agent about the house, Nick and Aimee discover that, in an
effort to attract upscale home-buyers, part of the Locust Point neighborhood in which they grew up has been rezoned as part of Federal Hill, an
upscale Baltimore neighborhood.

In these ways the show is merely charting the actual transformations of Baltimore's white working-class neighborhoods. David Harvey
notes that in the first wave of urban gentrification, between the early
1970s and the late 1980s, housing prices in South Baltimore rose from
$10,000 to over $100,000. This astronomic increase in the cost of housing priced the working classes out of their traditional neighborhoods.
The subsequent increase in property taxes completed the transformation of the area.[16] What is ironic about the process of gentrification that
The Wire depicts is that it relies, in a variety of ways, on nostalgia for
the ways of life it is partially responsible for destroying. As the derelict
grain peer becomes "The Grainery," sites of labor become signifiers of
the city's working-class heritage transformed into a consumable local
heritage.[17] As such, derelict factories, warehouses, and other sites of
manufacture become the most sought-after locations for urban transformation. Their shells cored out and their interior spaces transformed
from sites of labor to sites of consumption, such as shops and restaurants, and dwelling spaces, these buildings substitute consumption for
production. What *The Wire* depicts in the character of Nick, then, is
an allegory of sociocultural disenfranchisement in which, at the very
moment when working-class communities begin to vanish, their loss is
encoded in the city sites (and sights) that replace them. It is after these
scenes that Nick finally admits defeat and contacts the Greek organization independently of his uncle and starts supplying heroin to the local
(white) dealers in large quantities. It is clear to the viewer that Nick
would rather be working, that while his turn to a life of crime is motivated by self-interest, it is also seemingly unavoidable. Unable to con-
form to the social expectations of either his own community or society
at large, Nick is a sign of the ways in which the local and the federal
governments' disinvestment in the working classes produces criminality. If Nick, like Frank, is understood to turn to crime out of a sense of
necessity and of frustration at the limited opportunities available to

the white working classes in contemporary Baltimore, Ziggy Sobotka suffers from a more acute form of sociocultural distress and attempts to overcome the limitations on his life in profoundly different ways.

The White Man's Penis: Racial Cross-Dressing and the Embodiment of Class

Inasmuch as the transformations of masculinity depicted in *The Wire* are seen to be a result of the altered landscapes of labor and opportunity in postindustrial America, they also suggest much about contemporary U.S. racial imaginaries. While the world in which Frank Sobotka lives has been transformed by the shifting demographics of the postindustrial city, the world for which he pines hewed to strict ethnic and racial demarcations. In the world in which he currently finds himself racial boundaries have been blurred as multiculturalism and affirmative action have each transformed contemporary society. Thus the rigidly demarcated ethnic boundaries of Frank Sobotka's Locust Point neighborhood have been broken down, and the show's depictions of the neoliberal, postindustrial city also evidence a commensurate focus on the cultural transformations of neoliberalism, most particularly in its representations of white racial cross-dressing. Season 2 of *The Wire* is replete with numerous examples of young white men "acting" black by adopting African-American vernacular language, styles of dress, moral codes, and recreational habits. The street-level drug dealer, Frog (Gary "D. Reign" Senkus), and "White" Mike, Nick's supplier, are two such examples. Each of these men performs blackness through the adoption of African American modes of expression that, if they were not familiar to the show's audience before, would certainly have been recognizable to anyone familiar with its first season. In fact, season 2 derives much humor from the juxtaposition of the white drug dealers that populate white working-class neighborhoods with their better-trained, "professional," and putatively "authentic" African American contemporaries. As white narcotics detective Herc (Domenick Lombardozzi) complains to fellow officer Kima (Sonja Song) in the opening episode of the second season, Baltimore's white drug dealers are so inept they should create a different set of laws for them to "even things out." "Affirmative action," Keema replies ironically. In this way the show encourages its viewers to see the white characters' adoption of African American styles—and lifestyles—as a misguided attempt to maintain cultural and social relevance. Nowhere is this more apparent than in the character of Ziggy.

Frank Sobotka's son, Ziggy, is burdened by a weight of parental expectation that he cannot bear. As a way of rejecting his father's blue-collar values of masculine responsibility and self-reliance, he also engages in the act of racial cross-dressing. Unlike Frog or "White" Mike, however, Ziggy mimics an obsolete style of African American masculine embodiment drawn from the era of blaxploitation cinema and 1970s funk. Ziggy plays the goof and refuses to take his father's values seriously. He is uncommitted to work, unable to hold down gainful employment, careless with money, and a conspicuous consumer of a sort that his father abhors. He relies on various strategies of embodiment to transform himself from Frank Sobotka's fuckup of a son into a man in his own right. Slight and somewhat goofy in appearance, Ziggy does not look like he belongs in a place of manual labor such as the port authority. Lacking the physical presence of his cousin or of his father, Ziggy is often teased and baited by his fellow longshoremen. Frustrated by his inability to fight back, he frequently resorts to one of the only means of masculine expression available to him: flashing his large penis at his coworkers in the local bar. At other times, he dresses in a 1970s-style Italian leather coat that, while he thinks it makes him look like a pimp, African American drug dealer Cheese Wagstaff (Method Man) believes "not even a black man could style." Such self-conscious displays mark Ziggy inasmuch as they suggest that his attempts at embodiment are, like his father's attempts to resuscitate the port, the last resort of someone who has failed to come to terms with altered expectations for masculinity. Unable to live up to his father's ideals, Ziggy has railed against them by inhabiting other forms of race-based self-expression. Ziggy's dick and his eccentric sartorial decisions do not mark him as impressive or virile, however; they do not endow him with a masculinity borrowed from black culture, but make him a laughingstock and the butt of many of his coworkers' jokes. In spite of his symbolically large phallus, Ziggy fails completely to inhabit a position of virile or dominant masculine authority.

Ziggy's overidentification with the embodiment of black hypermasculinity grounded in the physicality of the penis and the sartorial style of the 1970s pusher draws on a long history of racial cross-identification. Working through the contradictory identifications apparent in the

Trying to hustle, Ziggy is ripped off by Frog

white working-class consumption of blackface minstrelsy, Eric Lott famously describes the "ideologies of working-class manhood, which shaped white men's contradictory feelings about black men."[18] Producing a profound overidentification grounded in various forms of white racial disavowal, white fantasies of black masculinity—then as now—often focus on the embodied locus of black sexuality. As a disavowal of the actual power of white masculinity (routed through the fantasy power of a threatening black masculinity), such fantasies typically frame white investments in black sexuality negatively. "Because of the power of the black man's penis in white American psychic life," Lott points out, "the pleasure minstrelsy's largely white and male audiences derived from their investment in 'blackness' always carried a threat of castration—a threat obsessively reversed in white lynching rituals."[19] Reading Ziggy's racial cross-dressing alongside his juvenile identification with his own hyperembodied phallic overinvestment reveals the full extent of his failure. In spite of his big dick, Ziggy still needs the masculinizing sheath of an adopted black masculinity as a prophylactic against his own lack of patriarchal authority; in spite of this adoption, he still fails to signify as a man. Suffering a dialectical over- and under-embodiment, Ziggy symbolizes a profound form of self-abnegation. In a discussion of lynching, racial identification, and sexual power, Robyn Wiegman suggests that "in [the] destruction of the phallic black beast, the white masculine reclaims the hypermasculinity that his own mythology of black sexual excess has denied him, finding in sexual violence the sexual pleasure necessary to uphold both his tenuous masculine and white racial identities."[20] Wiegman further suggests that "in the image of white men embracing—with hate, fear, and a chilling form of empowered delight—the same penis they were so over-determinedly driven to destroy, one encounters a sadistic enactment of the homoerotic at the very moment of its most extreme disavowal" (99). That the penis "embraced" in *The Wire* is the white man's penis only serves to suggest (as the same embrace does in *Boogie Nights* [1997]) the abject failure of white male embodiment through which contemporary forms of white masculinity's black racial cross-identification become necessary. Having, in the example of Ziggy, precisely what the white man is always afraid the black man actually has, here makes no difference. In the case of Ziggy, this cross-identification becomes doubly fraught as he also attempts to inhabit a no less inauthentic masculine subjectivity derived from an offshoot of the very period of U.S. labor history his father pines for: a 1970s white working-class masculine identity. If Ziggy wishes to inhabit the ontological space of an empowering black masculine subject, he also wishes to ennoble himself by adopting the signifiers of white working-class masculine identity.

Ziggy is not only the owner of an expensive Italian leather coat and a large penis, but he is also the owner of a vintage (if somewhat rundown) Chevrolet Camaro. In his choice of car Ziggy has chosen to pin his hopes on a prior moment in the history of U.S. labor. If Frank wants to see the docks returned to their former glory, Ziggy wants his car—itself an emblem of that glory—to ennoble him by providing him, if only as a fantasy, with some of the power his father does not believe he will ever have. One of a variety of cars introduced in the 1960s by rival dealers in the aftermath of the Ford Mustang, the Camaro is often referred to as a "pony car." The Camaro is one of the symbolic "muscle cars" that relied, for their very existence, on U.S. modes of consumption (of gas and other resources) that bespoke a belief in plenitude and limitless access to resources and the things they made possible. A fantasy of both virile American masculinity and working-class American pride, cars like the Camaro were (and are) symbols of the mythic masculinity of the middle decades of the American Century. With a popularity that peaked in the early 1980s, the Camaro and other cars like it were designed to appeal to an exploding population of young consumers who, not yet tied to the responsibilities of home and family, had money to spend. These vehicles they spoke to both the American belief in the virility of youth and the values of labor. In contemporary culture, however, the forms of white masculinity embodied in the Camaro and other muscle cars are reactionary and outmoded. A step out of touch, Ziggy's car is a symbol of a prior era, one that—as the evidence around him clearly shows—is over. Overidentifying with a plethora of outmoded forms of masculinist self-expression, Ziggy ends up empowered by none of them. That Ziggy dotes on his car—he calls it "Princess"—only highlights his inability to differentiate between sign and signifier. Ziggy's Chevy both confirms his desire to shore up his own waning masculinity with the icons of a prior age and highlights his repeated inability to do so.[21]

Seeking the authority of both black and white symbols of patriarchal power (both equally reactionary), Ziggy becomes, as he himself complains, "the punch line to every joke." His phallic power has been eroded to such an extent that his procreative abilities also become suspect. After Ziggy posts photographs of his penis on a coworker's computer, that coworker, Maui (Lance Irwin), creates an elaborate practical joke involving a faked paternity suit. As he sits in the bar agonizing over the paternity suit he believes he has just been served, Ziggy complains to Nick (who has just handed him a large roll of bills offered in payment for the car Cheese had destroyed) that "[heroin] packages were my thing. Fuck if you don't handle that business better, too." As Ziggy bemoans his fate, the Diana Ross and the Supremes hit "Love Child" blares out over the jukebox with the off-key accompaniment of Maui and the other stevedores. The joke, of course, is that it is hard to believe Ziggy capable of getting anyone pregnant and doubly hard to imagine him being able to deal with the responsibility if he did. Ziggy's failure not to get someone pregnant is juxtaposed with his inability to successfully resolve a conflict with Cheese that is the only result of his solo attempt at drug dealing. Suitable neither for fatherhood nor for the gritty realities of drug dealing, Ziggy is left with nothing and at the close of the season is awaiting trial for a senseless murder he committed in frustration at his inability to signify anything, for anybody, but a joke. As he rejects his father by "acting black," Ziggy also tries to emulate him by "acting white." That both forms of identification are forms of cross-dressing highlights the degree to which identity—as a performance—relies on the illusion of authenticity. White masculinity, for Ziggy (and by extension anyone), is an act; it is, however, an act that fails Ziggy because he fails at it. The modes of authority that should adhere to him "naturally," because of his status on the dock as "Frank Sobotka's son," do not. As his attempts to signify as a man through the dual cross-identification with black masculinity, on the one hand, and a prior form of working-class masculinity, on the other, attests, Ziggy is himself bereft of authority. In this doubled process of identification and rejection, the forms of white working-class masculinity for which the characters in *The Wire* pine are shown to be themselves obsolete.

Conclusion: The Other America and Neoliberalism's Cultural Front

David Simon and Ed Burns have each made much of *The Wire*'s attention (particularly in its second season) to the white working classes, masculinity, and the decline of blue-collar labor in the United States. For Burns, the economic bubble of the Reagan years transformed the nation's expectations about work and responsibility. "We've forgotten what it's like to be a working man," he told a reporter for the *New York Times* in an interview published in advance of the duo's 2008 HBO show, *Generation Kill*. "There was a flush of money," he continued, "and we've forgotten our roots. These stories have a power because it's when men stood up."[22] For Simon, the show's attention to such transformations is essential. He argues that in the show a "simulated Baltimore would stand in for urban America, and the fundamental problems of urbanity would be fully addressed." In the show's second season, those problems would be "the death of work and the destruction of the American working class in the post-industrial era."[23] Simon has called the second season "an elegy for America's working-class."[24] As an elegy, *The Wire* is a work of nostalgia. That *The Wire*'s second season speaks to a series of socioeconomic transformations that were already, in many ways, history at the time of the show's creation suggests the point. Like Frank, like Nick, like Ziggy, the creators of *The Wire* themselves hark back to a previous era, one in which the transformations the show charts have not yet taken place and are not, therefore, already history. This provides the show with a sense of political investment that, in some ways, obfuscates its nostalgia. The show, moreover, is nostalgic not only for a prior moment in U.S. labor history, but also for a particular sense of place.

The Wire, Simon argues, is "about the American city: How it works, or doesn't, and ultimately, what is at stake for all of us in these times." In that way, he explains, the show is "very much about place." Simon, moreover, believes that *The Wire* is unique among television shows not only because of what it focuses on, but because of who is doing that focusing. Speaking of the show's unique feel, he suggests that its writers contribute a seldom-seen perspective on American society because of their own lived experiences and their individual literary foci:

> The chumps making it live in Baltimore, or, in the case of guys like [Richard] Price, [George] Pelecanos, and [Dennis] Lehane, they are at least writing in their literary work about second-tier East Coast rust-belt places like Jersey City, northeast Washington, or Dorchester, rather than Manhattan, Georgetown, or Back Bay Boston. We are of the other America or the America that has been left behind in the postindustrial age.[25]

Of himself, Simon has stated, "I don't live in Westwood, L.A., or on the Upper West Side of New York. I live in Baltimore."[26] There is, then, for Simon a regional specificity that safeguards the show by preventing it from becoming "just another" TV cop show while also accounting for its central themes and its putative authenticity. The show's broad focus on the death of U.S. labor, on the destruction of community, and on the failure of U.S. political culture is grounded in its regional specificity: *The Wire* is not just an "American" show, but a "Baltimore" show. As such, the show serves as an example of the very forms of regional culture that have arisen under the cultural globalization to which it attends. Therefore, while the show is set in Baltimore and much has been made—by Simon and others—of the show's verisimilitude born in part out of its regional specificities, the city comes to stand for the more widespread disappearance of traditional modes of urban life grounded in hard work, community, and social responsibility.[27] Baltimore, Simon claims, is the "deconstruction of the American Dream."[28] The American Dream, though, is a dream with a particular dreamer in mind. As the analysis of the preceding pages shows, that that dream has, for some, become a nightmare is predicated on the assumption that it should have been theirs to have in the first place. If the world of contemporary urban blight in *The Wire* is all but exclusively African American, the world of working-class disenfranchisement it maps in its second season is almost entirely white. As such, the show's black characters are locked into a contemporary present in which there is no workable past; it's white working-class characters, on the other hand, are given a past, even if—as is so clearly the case—its use-value becomes more attenuated every day and provokes the sorts of psychosis that I have described in these pages.

Moreover, *The Wire*'s indictment of neoliberal models of capital accumulation is complicated by the fact that the show appeared on a channel, HBO, that was itself at the forefront of the transformations of the culture industries under neoliberalism. As Toby Miller has argued, while HBO is an example of the "organized, centralized, inflexible post-Fordism of contemporary cultural capitalism," it also represents the "disorganized, decentralized, flexible post-Fordism of contemporary cultural capitalism." The network, Miller points out, "relies on a wide variety of workers, many of whom do not have tenure and benefits, who are employed by small companies even when they sell their labor to the giant corporation of Time Warner that is the network's parent organization."[29] If, as Simon has suggested, the show would not have been possible on any other network, it is itself, then, an exemplar of the global economic transformations that, in the culture industries, HBO helped bring into being. A regionally specific show produced for a transnational media conglomerate and airing on a premium cable channel; popular with a global audience; and disseminated on cable television, through "on demand" access, via scheduled repeats, on DVD, and through electronic downloads (both legal and illegal), *The Wire* is itself exemplary of the global transformations it wishes to critique. In both its content and its own modes of production, then, *The Wire* provides an object lesson in the transformations of U.S. labor that subtend global economic restructuring. This essay has charted some of those transformations and the representations of working-class culture that they produce.

Notes

1. "Capital gain" is the type of profit realized from investment in stocks, bonds, and real estate. In the United States, as in many other countries, capital gain is subject to income tax, although often at a more favorable rate. The pun on capitol/capital in the pleasure boat's name symbolizes the main point of the entire scene: that smaller cities such as Baltimore have been squeezed dry by their bigger neighbors (in this case Washington, D.C.) and by the shift from industry to an economy based on service and financial speculation.

2. In this regard, it is interesting that scholarly attention to the show typically excludes discussion of its second season. In his much-discussed sociology course on *The Wire* taught at Harvard, William Julius Wilson omits the second season entirely "for brevity" (see Amanda M. Fairbanks, "Deconstructing 'The Wire,'" *New York Times*, December 29, 2009, http://www.nytimes.com/2010/01/03/education/03wire-t.html). University of California film scholar Linda Williams also foregoes season 2 in her own undergraduate course dedicated to the show (see http://filmstudies.berkeley.edu/undergrad%20courses%20Sp2009.html#105.) Thus, while the show's co-creator, David Simon, has suggested that one reason for *The Wire*'s relative lack of success (it famously never won an Emmy) is because it is too black, it is also the case that the show has been perceived to be such at the expense of its other concerns. If reasons of brevity are not sufficient to justify the omission of a whole season of a show that only ran for five twelve-episode-long seasons, what else might account for this phenomenon? As I suggest in these pages, the omission of season 2 from scholarly attention to the show "allows" *The Wire* to be about black urban experience.

3. David Savran, *Taking It Like a Man: White Masculinity, Masochism, and Contemporary American Culture* (Princeton, N.J.: Princeton University Press, 1998), 5.

4. Susan Faludi, *Stiffed: The Betrayal of the American Man* (New York: Perennial, 1999), 86.

5. For more on this phenomenon and the forms of contemporary cultural production it has produced, see my *Affirmative Reaction: New Formations of White Masculinity* (Durham, N.C.: Duke University Press, 2010).

6. David Harvey, *Spaces of Capital: Towards a Critical Geography* (New York: Routledge, 2001), 140.

7. Statistics that appeared in the *Baltimore Sun* in 1988 and that are reproduced by Harvey show an almost relational shift from laboring to clerical work. In 1966, 43 percent of employed adults worked as laborers (compared to 8 percent in 1988); correspondingly, 1 percent were employed in clerical work (compared to 30 percent in 1988). Harvey, *Spaces of Capital*, 141.

8. The status of Baltimore's Inner Harbor as a tourist hotspot that stands out-

side of the realities of the city proper is highlighted to good effect in a scene from the third season of the show in which inner-city rivals Stringer Bell (Idris Elba) and Omar Little (Michael K. Williams) attend a meeting organized by East Side drug boss Proposition Joe (Robert F. Chew). Surrounded by crowds of unwitting tourists, the two men negotiate the end of a violent vendetta that has seen them both lose friends and allies. The colorful, crowded plaza in which the men meet stands in stark contrast to the gray and barren streets that are their usual terrains.

9. It is not only legitimate business, but also crime that has become globalized. As The Greek himself points out to Frank, "The world is a smaller place now" than it was in Frank's heyday; or, as Nick explains to Ziggy, "They're global like." Frank's failure to understand the transformations of labor and capital under globalization, as much as Nick's growing realization that local players such as they are have been rendered inconsequential, highlights the socioeconomic realities the show seeks to represent.

10. Mike Hill, *After Whiteness: Unmaking an American Majority* (New York: New York University Press, 2004), 93.

11. George Lipsitz, "Listening to Learn and Learning to Listen: Popular Culture, Cultural Theory, and American Studies," *American Quarterly* 42.4 (1990): 630.

12. Harvey, *Spaces of Capital*, 145.

13. David R. Roediger, *The Wages of Whiteness: Race and the Making of the American Working Class*, rev. ed. (London: Verso, 1999), 8.

14. David Wellman, "Minstrel Shows, Affirmative Action Talk, and Angry White Men," in *Displacing Whiteness: Essays in Social and Cultural Criticism*, ed. Ruth Frankenberg (Durham, N.C.: Duke University Press, 1997), 321.

15. Such is shown to be the case in *The Wire* when the union members are shown to be more concerned with the election of an African American as the next union boss than with the broader labor transformations that affect them all.

16. Harvey, *Spaces of Capital*, 153.

17. Harvey's essay on Baltimore's gentrification closes with a photograph of a row of houses, each replete with the faux-antique coach lamps that Harvey sees as a signifier of gentrification and which clearly constitute a nostalgia for prior forms of social and cultural life. See Harvey, *Spaces of Capital*, 157.

18. Eric Lott, *Love and Theft: Blackface Minstrelsy and the American Working Class* (Oxford: Oxford University Press, 1995), 9.

19. Ibid.

20. Robyn Wiegman, *American Anatomies: Theorizing Race and Gender* (Durham, N.C.: Duke University Press, 1995), 98.

21. The car becomes a source of narrative tension in the show when it is

taken by Cheese in forced part-payment for a heroin "package" Ziggy has taken to sell but which, having been ripped off by Frog, he is unable to pay for. Perhaps seeing the car for what it is, Cheese and his corner boys set fire to it and Nick is required to intervene and seek restitution for his cousin.

22. Michael Wilson, "After 'The Wire,' Moving On to Battles Beyond the Streets," *New York Times*, July 6, 2008, http://www.nytimes.com/2008/07/06/arts/television/06wils.html.

23. Nick Hornby, interview with David Simon, *The Believer*, August 2007, http://www.believermag.com/issues/200708/?read=interview_simon.   Simon makes the same point in an interview published in the *Guardian*. See "Totally Wired," January 13, 2005, http://blogs.guardian.co.uk/theguide/archives/tv_and_radio/2005/01/totally_wired.html.

24. David Simon, "Finale Letter," http://www.hbo.com/thewire/finaleletter/.

24. Simon, interview.

26. Meghan O'Rourke, "Behind the Wire," *Slate*, December 1, 2006, http://www.slate.com/id/2154694/pagenum/all/.

27. The show is also well known for using local actors, such as James Ransone, and locals as both extras and also major characters. The character Snoop, for example was played by a local woman, Felicia Pearson.

28. Oliver Burkeman, "Arrogant? Moi?" *Guardian*, March 28, 2009, http://www.guardian.co.uk/media/2009/mar/28/david-simon-the-wire-interview.

29. Toby Miller, foreword to *It's Not TV: Watching HBO in the Post-television Era*, ed. Marc Leverette, Brian L. Ott, and Cara Louise Buckley (New York: Routledge, 2008), x.

Appendix: Plot Summaries

Each season of *The Wire* uses a particular focus on Baltimore while continuing the drama of the characters' webs of association and conflict. The first season looks at the drug trade in the African American public housing projects. The second treats the white ethnic laborers at the docks. The third involves local politics. The fourth handles the public educational system, while the fifth looks at daily newspaper journalism.

Season 1 introduces us to the world of the Baltimore homicide division and the drug trade milieu of the West Baltimore "corner boys," the pawns in narcotics dealing, and their superiors. Detective James "Jimmy" McNulty goes behind the backs of his superiors (in ascending order, Sargent Jay Landsman, Major William A. Rawls, and Deputy Commissioner Ervin H. Burrell) to get Judge Daniel Phelan to instigate a team to investigate the rise of a new druglord, Avon Barksdale. Other homicide detectives are Detectives William "Bunk" Moreland and Ray Cole. After having watched Barksdale's nephew D'Angelo Barksdale escape a murder conviction, McNulty manages to get a special detail instituted, run by Lieutenant Cedric Daniels and staffed by police castoffs, including Detective Lester Freamon, Detective Roland "Prez" Pryzbylewski, Detectives Leandor Sydor, Shakima "Kima" Greggs, Thomas "Herk" Hauk, and Ellis Carver. Their liaison with the prosecutors' office is Assistant District Attorney Rhonda Pearlman. Their target is Avon Barksdale's organization, which Barksdale has built up with his main lieutenant Stringer Bell and muscle from men like Wee-Bey and Stinkum, and also Wendell "Orlando" Blocker, who represents the legitimate face to an adult dance bar. D'Angelo is given leadership of a gang in the Pit of the housing projects, and helped by corner boys,

Preston "Bodie" Broadus, Wallace, and Poot. Within this world, we also meet Bubbles, a junkie and confidential informant to Kima; Omar, a gay thief who specializes in robbing from the drug dealers, often to sell their goods back at a discount, but will aid the police as an act of revenge against the Barksdale organization for their murder of his lover; and Proposition Joe Stewart, the leader of the East Baltimore drug trade.

Despite the police superiors' desire not to pursue the investigation, McNulty aggressively wonders about Daniels's own legitimacy, especially as he pushes for a wiretap of the telephones in the project. In this he gains respect for Freamon. In the pit, young Wallace becomes depressed and, in turn, suspect to Stringer Bell as an informant. Bell later orders Bodie and Poot to murder Wallace. Freamon becomes both the sleuth of information and mentor to Prez in deciphering the trail of the wiretaps, as well as helping Shardene, a dancer at Orlando's club, which doubles as Avon's headquarters, to give information on Barksdale. Omar fails in an attempted street attack on Avon. A police-staged "buy" with an undercover Kima goes wrong and she is seriously wounded. A raid on the Barksdale headquarters leaves Stringer Bell untouched, and with a new office in a funeral parlor, but D'Angelo and Avon imprisoned. D'Angelo's mother, Brianna, talks him out of turning state's evidence and taking a jail sentence instead. The unit is broken up, with Freamon placed in Homicide, McNulty and Daniels disciplined with dead-end placements, the harbor patrol for the former, the evidence room for the latter.

Season 2 turns to examine the "death of work" and the effects of a deindustrialized Baltimore harbor. The new set of characters centers around union boss Frank Sobotaka, his son Ziggy, his nephew Nick, and other stevedores, like Horseface Pakusa and Johnny Fifty. New players in the drug trade are the drug connection "The Greek," his lieutenant Spiros "Vondas" Vondoupoulos, muscle Sergei "Serge" Malatov, and associate George "Double-G" Glekas. We also meet Prez's father-in-law, Major Stanislaus Valchek, and the single mother and Harbor beat officer Beatrice "Beadie" Russell. The tensions in this season focus around Sobotka's deals with The Greek's drug organization to help land illegal shipments in return for money that Sobotka uses for graft to influence politicians to help rebuild the harbor's infrastructure and ensure the continuation of a stable working-class life for the next generation. These plans start to unravel as one of the containers is found to include

East European women who died from asphyxiation while being shipped to serve in the sex trade, while Sobotka is also undergoing surveillance from Valchek, due to a feud over who has the rights to ornament their church. In the background of this season, we also witness Stringer Bell's attempts to keep the Barksdale organization afloat as their drug connections are disrupted by a DEA operation.

Bunk and Freamon are assigned to the case of the murdered women, and joined by Beadie Russell. Sobotka's inept son, Ziggy, and capable nephew, Nick, themselves get more involved in links with The Greek's illegality. In prison, Avon attempts to look after a reluctant D'Angelo by cautioning him against taking heroin. Unbeknownst to D'Angelo, Avon has set up a scheme where a drug-dealing prison guard, who is giving the Barksdale gang trouble, will first be given poisoned heroin and then be accused by Avon, whose information his lawyer Maurice Levy manages to leverage into a reduced sentence. When D'Angelo's hostility to Avon does not abate, Stringer Bell arranges for D'Angelo to be murdered in such a way that it looks like a suicide, so that Avon remains unaware of the assassination. Bell meanwhile also works to get Avon to accept a deal where the Westside gang distributes the drugs they receive from Eastside Proposition Joe. Avon, unaware of Bell's machinations, arranges for a Nation of Islam hit man Brother Mouzone to remove the Eastsiders from the projects. Bell attempts to trick Omar into believing that Mouzone killed Omar's lover. Although Omar ambushes Mouzone, he later realizes that he has been set up. Ziggy, in an act of passion from the abused, murders Glekas, causing the gangsters to clean out Glekas's office before the detectives arrive on their own case. After Ziggy's arrest, Frank decides to turn evidence, but this is found out and the Greek kills him. Nick then turns evidence in return for witness protection. The case is solved, but without anyone brought to trial. With Frank gone, his plan for the revitalized harbor is dead as well, and the region is advertised as being sold for luxury apartments.

Season 3 focuses explicitly on politics, policing, and social policy initiatives and implicitly on the blockages to reform. The season begins with the image of the Franklin Terrace housing projects' demolition, which visualizes the collapse of a central location for West Baltimore's Barksdale organization. Throughout the season Stringer Bell attempts to move the trade from a "gangster" to a "business" model and expand into property speculation while accepting that Proposition

Joe will secure heroin and distribute it to the other gangs for a percentage, a cooperative deal that decreases gang warfare and the concomitant police surveillance. While Stringer looks to insert the drug trade within Baltimore's crony capitalism, white city councilman Tommy Carcetti decides to use crime as his platform for political advancement. Carcetti challenges the status quo of Commissioner Burrell and Mayor Royce. Another upstart is Marlo Stanfield, who makes an aggressive challenge to Barksdale. Marlo, with his lieutenants Chris Partlow and the female Snoop, represent a ruthless empire-building. The other structural challenger will be Major Howard "Bunny" Colvin's efforts to provide the lower crime statistics that the new qualitative policing of Burrell and Rawls demands by surreptitiously setting up a protected zone for trade to junkies, a cordon sanitaire known as Hamsterdam. One more challenge appears with Omar's vendetta against the Barksdale gang run by Stringer Bell while Avon is in prison. The reconstituted Major Crimes Unit goes after an Eastside lieutenant, Cheese Wagstaff, while a released Barksdale muscle enforcer, Denis "Cutty" Wise, gives up on returning to the gang and instead sets up a boxing ring for the neighborhood youth. Bell's vision comes to an end when Mouzone and Omar collude to assassinate him, but not before Avon and Bell have mutually sought to incriminate each other to the police. Colvin's plans are made public and he is demoted and forced to resign.

With Stringer gone, season 4 focuses on the school system and the varied pathways of four young friends, two sons of drug gangsters, Randy Wagstaff and Namond Brice (Wee-Bey's son), and two sons of drug addicts, Duquan "Dukie" Weems and Michael Lee. With the involvement of newly retired Bunny Colvin in a school program that tries to understand the psychology of disruptive students, Colvin ultimately rescues Namond from a life as a corner boy, which he was temperamentally unsuited for, and informally adopts him. Randy's entrepreneurship in the school leads him to being caught by school authorities, and after he gives information on a murder associated with Marlo's gang, he suffers from the lack of police protection and ends up in the dangerous environment of child homes. Along with Bell and Bubbles, Randy's failure indicates the limits to aspirational African American small business. Duquan's effective homelessness seems to be helped by his tutelage under Prez, who has now become a schoolteacher after retiring from the force. But having done well enough to advance to higher grades, and

without the oversight of caring teachers, he slips back into homelessness and the drug use that destroyed his family in the first instance.
Michael was the most fiercely independent of the four, and at first he
resists subordination as a corner boy. But when his sexually abusive
stepfather returns, he asks Marlo for help and Chris Partlow murders
the man, implicitly because Chris has also been abused and silently
understands Michael's anger. Unlike the clinical murders by Chris and
Snoop, where they dispose of the corpses in abandoned row houses,
Chris's murder of Michael's stepfather will provide the DNA evidence
that allows Bunk to indict him.

In addition to the story of the four boys' varied trajectory through
the school system, the season charts the rise of Marlo Stanfield and
Freamon's search for the location of the bodies he knows must exist
in the trail of Marlo's takeover of the Barksdale organization. Proposition Joe tries to incorporate Marlo within the co-op and to convince the
latter of the need for protection; he tells Omar the details of a poker
game where Marlo plays. Joe knows that Omar will rob the game, and
he hopes that this will bring Marlo into the co-op's arms. Herc, now
attached to Mayor Royce's security detail, discovers the mayor in com-
promising actions and ends up promoted and back in the Major Crimes
Unit, where he loses an expensive camera to a wilier Marlo. Meanwhile
Carcetti charts his strategy for what becomes a successful election to
mayor. Marlo's crew kills Bodie when he is spotted talking to McNulty,
and Bubbles is in despair after having accidentally caused the death of
his protégé Sherrod and failed in his own suicide attempt.

The final season focuses mainly on the failure of news reporting and
the reluctance to do probing inquiries into the social conditions framing
Baltimore in favor of more superficial and sensational pieces that might
win Pulitzer Prizes. A *Baltimore Sun* journalist, Scott Templeton, resorts to fabricating sources, and becomes intertwined with McNulty's
(and then Freamon's) fabrication of a serial murderer as a means to gain
resources (not least for the investigation into the bodies found in the
vacant buildings) for a Carcetti-run Baltimore that is defunding municipal services due to budget cuts. Bubbles, with some help by his Narcotics Anonymous friend Walon, goes straight and ultimately seems
to have achieved redemption and guarded acceptance back into his
sister's home. Marlo successfully bypasses Proposition Joe and makes
his connection directly with The Greek and he dissolves the co-op. He

also sets the stage for hunting Omar, who has returned to Baltimore to avenge the Marlo-ordered death of his friends. In what is the most fan-disappointing moment, Omar is gunned down. The season ends with McNulty and Freamon caught in their lies and taking retirement, thus ending Freamon's chasing of the money up to the level of politicians and lawyers. Levy realizes that the wiretap that catches Marlo must be of questionable legality, and a deal is stuck between Levy and Pearlman that gives Chris up for the murders and leaves Marlo free so long as he abandons the drug trade. The show ends, though, with the viewers being shown that while names might change, the social structure remains, as Michael becomes the new Omar and the drug trade leaders regenerate links with The Greek. In the end, those with the tragic flaw of pride, staged as the belief that an individual can overcome the larger social structure, are brought down.

Contributors

John Atlas is president of the National Housing Institute, a think tank based in Montclair, N.J. He is a former Charles Revson Fellow at Columbia University, and author of *Seeds of Change* (Vanderbilt University Press, 2010). For twenty-two years he was the legal director for Passaic County Legal Aid Society, located in the inner city of Paterson, N.J.

Paul Allen Anderson is Associate Professor in the Program in American Culture and Center for Afroamerican and African Studies at the University of Michigan. His publications include *Deep River: Music and Memory in Harlem Renaissance Thought* (Duke University Press, 2001).

Ruth Barton is Head of Film Studies at Trinity College Dublin. She has published widely on Irish cinema and on stardom. Her publications include *Irish National Cinema* (Routledge, 2004) and *Acting Irish in Hollywood: From Fitzgerald to Farrell* (Irish Academic Press, 2006). She edited the collection *Screening Irish-America* (Irish Academic Press, 2009). Her most recent publications are *Hedy Lamarr: The Most Beautiful Woman in Film* (University of Kentucky Press, 2010) and (as editor) "Screening the Irish in Britain," a special issue of *Irish Studies Review* 19.1 (2011).

Hamilton Carroll is a lecturer in American Literature and Culture at the University of Leeds. He is the author of *Affirmative Reaction: New Formations of White Masculinity* (Duke University Press, 2011). He has published various articles on whiteness, masculinity, American literature, film, and literary and cultural responses to the events of September 11, 2001.

Peter Dreier is E.P. Clapp Distinguished Professor of Politics, director of the Urban and Environmental Policy program at Occidental College in Los Angeles, and chair of the Horizon Institute, a Los Angeles–based think tank. He is the author of *The Next Los Angeles: The Struggle for a Livable City* (University of California Press, 2006), *Place Matters: Metropolitics for the 21st Century* (University of Kansas Press, 2nd ed., 2004), and *Regions That Work: How Cities and Suburbs Can Grow Together* (University of Minnesota Press, 2000).

Frank Kelleter is chair of American Studies at University of Göttingen. His main fields of interest include the American colonial and Enlightenment periods, theories of American modernity, and American media and popular culture since the nineteenth century. He is the author of three monographs, among them the volume *Amerikanische Aufklärung*. Currently, he is the director of the six-project Research Unit "Popular Seriality—Aesthetics and Practice," funded by the German Research Foundation.

Liam Kennedy is Professor of American Studies and Director of the Clinton Institute for American Studies at University College Dublin. He is the author of *Susan Sontag* (University of Manchester Press, 1995) and *Race and Urban Space in American Culture* (Edinburgh University Press, 2000), and editor, with Maria Balshaw, of *Urban Space and Representation* (Pluto, 2000) and of *Visual Culture and Urban Regeneration* (Routledge, 2004).

Marsha Kinder is University Professor and Professor of Critical Studies in the School of Cinema-Television, University of Southern California. She is the author of *Blood Cinema: The Reconstruction of National Cinema in Spain* (University of California Press, 1993) and *Playing with Power in Movies, Television and Video Games* (University of California Press, 1991), and editor of *Refiguring Spain* (Duke University Press, 1997) and *Luis Bunuel's "The Discreet Charm of the Bourgeoi-*

sie" (Cambridge University Press, 1999). She is director of the Labyrinth Project, an art collective and research initiative on interactive cinema and database narrative at USC's Annenberg Center for Communication.

John Kraniauskas is a Reader in Latin American Studies at Birkbeck, University of London. He edited, introduced, and translated Carlos Monsiváis, *Mexican Postcards* (Verso, 1997) and is a founding editor of the *Journal of Latin American Cultural Studies.* He has written and published on Latin American literature and film, as well as on the novels of James Ellroy and on topics in cultural theory and political philosophy. He is preparing two books: one on Eva-Peronism and state form and another to be titled *Transculturation, Subalternity, Accumulation: Reflections from Latin America.*

Sherry Linkon is Professor of English and American Studies and codirector of the Center for Working-Class Studies at Youngstown State University. Along with writing about issues of class and deindustrialization in American culture, she has published two books and numerous articles on teaching. She is the coauthor, with John Russo, of *Steeltown USA: Work and Memory in Youngstown* (University Press of Kansas, 2002).

Jason Mittell is Associate Professor of American Studies and Film & Media Culture at Middlebury College. He is the author of *Genre and Television: From Cop Shows to Cartoons in American Culture* (Routledge, 2004), and *Television and American Culture* (Oxford University Press, 2009). He is currently writing a book on narrative complexity in contemporary American television.

Gary Phillips is a Himes Award winner and twice Shamus short-listed for his crime fiction. He is most recently the editor and a contributor to the anthologies *Politics Noir* (Verso, 2008) and the best-selling *Orange County Noir* (Akashic, 2010). He also wrote *High Rollers* (Boom! Studios, 2008), a graphic novel about a striving gangster, and his mystery novella, *The Underbelly*, with an aging semihomeless, flashback-prone black Vietnam vet as the protagonist, is on shelves now, part of PM Press's Outspoken Authors series.

Carlo Rotella, Director of American Studies and Professor of English at Boston College, is the author of *October Cities* (University of California Press, 1998), *Good with Their Hands* (University of California Press, 2002), and *Cut Time: An Education at the Fights* (Houghton Mifflin, 2003). He contributes regularly to the *New York Times Magazine* and the *Washington Post Magazine* and writes an op-ed column for the *Boston Globe*, and his work has appeared in the *New Yorker, Harper's, Slate, American Scholar, American Quarterly, Critical Inquiry*, and *The Best American Essays.*

Alexander Russo is an Associate Professor of Media Studies at Catholic University of America. His research interests include culture industries, the history of media technologies, sound studies, and media geographies. He is the author of *Points on the Dial: Golden Age Radio beyond the Networks* (Duke University Press, 2010) as well as essays in *Historical Journal of Film, Radio, and Television, Velvet Light Trap, Down to Earth: Geopolitics, Systems, Domains, and Cultures of Satellites*, and *The Radio Reader: Essays in the Cultural History of Radio.*

John Russo is the Coordinator of the Labor Studies Program and is the founder and codirector of the Center for Working-Class Studies at Youngstown State University. He has written widely on labor and social issues and is recognized as a national expert on labor unions and working-class issues.

Stephen Shapiro is Professor in the Department of English & Comparative Literary Studies at the University of Warwick. His recent work includes *The Culture and Commerce of the Early American Novel: Reading the Atlantic World-System* (Penn State University Press, 2009), *How to Read Marx's Capital* (Pluto, 2008), and, with Anne Schwan, *How to Read Foucault's Discipline and Punish* (Pluto, 2011).

Index